6

Sexual Divisions and Society: Process and Change

EXPLORATIONS IN SOCIOLOGY

A series under the auspices of
The British Sociological Association

Sexual Divisions and Society: Process and Change

---

edited by
DIANA LEONARD BARKER AND SHEILA ALLEN

TAVISTOCK PUBLICATIONS

First published in 1976
by Tavistock Publications Limited
11 New Fetter Lane, London EC4P 4EE
Set by Red Lion Setters, Holborn, London
Printed in Great Britain by
Cambridge University Press

ISBN 0 422 74820 X(hardbound)
ISBN 0 422 74830 7(paperback)

Contents

Contributors

Philip Abrams. Studied History at Cambridge University. Lecturer in Sociology at the London School of Economics, at Cambridge University, and at the University of Chicago; now Professor of Sociology at the University of Durham.

Currently interested in Political Sociology and the Sociology of Social Policy.

Sheila Allen. Studied Sociology at LSE; postgraduate Anthropology, LSE. Research Assistant at LSE; Lecturer in Sociology at the University of Birmingham, and at the University of Leicester; Senior Lecturer, Reader, and now Professor of Sociology at the University of Bradford.

Author of *New Minorities, Old Conflicts* (1971) and articles on race relations, migrant labour, sociology of youth and occupational entry.

Currently completing study of Youth and Work; Differential Ethnic Experience.

Diana Leonard Barker, born in St Augustine (Trinidad). Studied Natural Sciences and then Archaeology and Anthropology at Cambridge University. Trained as a teacher and taught science for several years. Research student at University College, Swansea; Research Assistant and then teaching at the University of Essex.

Author of various articles on young people and wedding rituals.

Currently completing *The Process and Ritual of Courtship and Marriage in a South Wales Town* and working with Christine Delphy on a book on the socio-economic position of women in the family.

Mike Brake. Was formerly a ballet dancer, an occupational therapist, and a probation officer. Graduated in Psychology and Sociology, University of Leeds; MSc at LSE. Has taught in various polytechnics and universities, including three visits as Visiting Associate Professor at the California State University.

Author of various articles on drug abuse, youth culture, and striptease and at present editing two books, one on radical social work and the other on sexuality.

Currently interested in deviance and sexual politics.

Delia Davin. Taught English in Peking; 1963:5, BA in Chinese Studies, University of Leeds; Postgraduate study in Tokyo, Hongkong, and Paris; Ph.D. 1974; now Lecturer in Social and Economic History, University of York.

Author of a forthcoming book on Women in China as well as several articles on the subject.

Currently on leave in Peking, working at the Foreign Languages Press.

Christine Delphy, born in Paris. Graduated in Sociology at the Sorbonne; Studied at the Universities of Chicago and California at Berkeley.

Author of various articles on inheritance, social stratification, and the family.

Currently Attaché de Recherche at the Centre Nationale de Recherche Scientifique, Paris, working on the domestic mode of production and exploitation.

Yves Dezalay, born Le Mans (France). Studied Sociology at the Sorbonne, at the Institut d'Etudes Politiques, and at the Ecole Nationale de la Statistique Economique. Worked with Bourdieu at the Centre de Sociologie Europénne; since 1968 has worked at the Service de Coordination de la Recherche du Ministère de la Justice, Paris, where he is currently a Chargé de Recherche.

Author of various articles on divorce.

Currently interested in the evolution of the internal functioning of the judicial system as a means of social control.

Ronald Frankenberg. Studied at the Universities of Cambridge and Manchester, BA (Hons), MA(Econ) and PhD. Educational Officer, South Wales Area of the National Union of Mineworkers; Lecturer, Senior Lecturer, and Reader in Sociology at University of Manchester; Seconded Professor of Sociology and Dean of the School of Humanities and Social Science, University of Zambia, one time Joint Editor, *African Social Research*; Acting Director of the Institute for Social Research; now Joint Managing Editor *Sociological Review* and Professor and Head of Department of Sociology, University of Keele.

Jalna Hanmer. Lecturer in Community Work, London School of Economics. Current research includes the sociology of sexual divisions and community action.

Hilary Land. Graduated in Mathematics and Psychology, University of Bristol; Diploma in Social Administration, LSE. Worked for four years as a research assistant to Professors Abel-Smith and Townsend on a national survey of poverty, and then as a research assistant to Professor Parker on a study of the development of social policy; Now a lecturer in the Department of Social Administration at the University of Bristol.

Author of *Large Families in London*, 1970 and co-author with P. Hall, R.A. Parker, and A. Webb of *Change, Choice and Conflict in Social Policy* 1975.

Andrew McCulloch. Studied at the University of Newcastle upon Tyne, BA(Fine Art) and at the University of Essex, MA(Sociology). Research Assistant, University of Durham, and at the University of Essex; Currently Senior Research Officer, University of Bath, investigating housing.

Sally Macintyre. Studied at Durham University, BA(Social Theory and Administration) and at London University, MSc(Sociology as applied to Medicine). Now a Research Fellow at Aberdeen University in the Medical Research Council's Medical Sociology Unit.

Vanessa Maher, born Kitale (Kenya). Studied at Cambridge University, BA(Archaeology and Anthropology), PhD(Social Anthropology). Did fieldwork in the Middle Atlas of Morocco, 1969-71, with grants from the Department of Education and Science and the Wenner-Gren Foundation for Anthropological Research; Currently engaged on preliminary research into the impact of industrialization on family roles in Italy at the Institute of Sociology, University of Milan, financed by a Leverhulme European Scholarship.

Hilary Rose. Professor of Applied Social Studies, University of Bradford. Current interests include the sociology of scientific knowledge and community action.

Jenny Shaw. Studied Sociology at LSE. Taught at North East London Polytechnic; Currently Lecturer in Sociology, University of Sussex and working on school attendance.

Preface

With the exception of the editors' contribution, all papers brought together in this volume were originally presented at the British Sociological Association's Conference on Sexual Divisions and Society, held at Aberdeen University in April 1974.

A second volume of papers arising from that conference will be published by Longman in 1976.

SHEILA ALLEN AND DIANA LEONARD BARKER

Sexual Divisions and Society

Tom Bottomore began his foreword to the first volume in this series by commenting that recently, 'not only has there been a remarkable expansion of sociological teaching and research, but the subject has come alive in a way that was scarcely conceivable ten or fifteen years ago' (Zubaida 1970:xi). We could justly reword this and apply it to the study of sexuality, gender divisions, and the position of women in society. While only a decade ago J.A. and Olive Banks could remark that, 'the organised feminist movements, if they continue at all today, can only be counted alongside vegetarianism and nudism as bordering on the cult (Banks and Banks 1964:547); today, with the advent of the Women's Liberation Movement and the related Gay Liberation Front, there has been a revival, and feminism and interest in gender constitute an enthusiasm.

Some sociologists have become personally involved or sympathetic to these movements and used their professional skills to analyse and relate sociological material on relevant problems. They have recognized that there were serious lacumae and biases in current sociological accounts and looked to the movements for impetus and reanalysis; and the movements have given encouragement and an audience to those who have long been interested in the area. The cumulative effect of these developments has been to produce a significant, creative spurt, of which the papers presented in this volume are a part. But unlike the earlier expansion of sociology to which Bottomore referred, much of the current exchange of information, research, and interest in sexual divisions and society has occurred outside and thus without the supports and advantages of the formal academic structure.

Many of the arguments put forward by Sami Zubaida in his introduction to *Race and Racialism* (1970) apply equally well to the present collection; and while we should like to believe that it is unnecessary to repeat them here, our experience in organizing the 1974 BSA conference leads us to think that as far as gender is concerned, the lessons are still to be learned.[1] He argued that mainstream sociology had neglected to incorporate the notion of race or ethnicity as an integral part of its theoretical underpinnings and that explanations of racialism were *ad hoc*. The same can be said of mainstream sociology and sexual divisions and the phenomenon of sexism.[2] But while Zubaida could point to large bodies of existing work on race relations, which claimed to be sociological but which were social problem and social psychological in orientation and explanation, we are not able to do the same. Some work, of course, exists that takes women, or some sub-groups of women, as a problem and attempts to explain their behaviour in terms of their being women, but for the most part sociology has included women completely within the term 'men' (or as part of their husbands), rather than asking how and when the relationship between the sexes (*or* between men and men, or women and women, for it is not only heterosexual relationships that are problematic) is pertinent to the explanation of social structure and behaviour.

The sociology of the family is a case in point. In this area it might be expected that work on gender relationships would be the most advanced and the theory most critical. However, it suffers from a marked lack of status in British sociology, deriving from its lack of 'theory' — except for Parsonian functionalism, its concern with the so-called non-work/non-market area of social activity, and its attention to women and children. In consequence it is frequently not taught at all, or given to the woman in the department, and rarely specified as a preferred specialism in job advertisements. It has certainly not shown the expansion in research or teaching experienced in many areas of sociology.[3]

There is an even more marked lack of sociological interest in sexuality (human sexual conduct). Ken Plummer reports that from a journal search over ten years, articles 'dealing with sexual conduct (even broadly defined) could be counted on two hands' (Plummer 1974). The sociology of social movements has similarly ignored the feminist movements of the nineteenth and early twentieth century (Banks and Banks 1964: McGregor 1955), and the contemporary liberation movements (Freeman 1973).

The papers in this volume thus deal with aspects of social relationships consistently neglected by sociologists, and ridiculed or denigrated by some. But in so far as sexism constitutes unproblematic, commonsense behaviour in contemporary British culture, it should not surprise us that it appears thus in sociology. In organizing the conference, one of our main objectives was to examine the nature of mainstream sociological assumptions in terms of the emphasis given, or in most cases not given, to the salience of gender. We also aimed to bring to the attention of sociologists work that has recently been undertaken outside institutionalized sociology and for the most part by those who would not regard themselves as professional sociologists, since it is relevant to some of the central questions of sociological explanation. It is, of course, not as yet respectable for most sociologists to concern themselves with the far-reaching questions that have been raised in what might be broadly termed as women's liberation or gay liberation literature; but this means that the sociology taught on many courses lags behind the level of consciousness of these issues already reached by the students themselves. Those who write here owe a heavy debt to sources outside accepted sociological circles.

Many of the papers start by pointing out the problematic nature of 'taken for granted' assumptions about the relations of men and women, and to do this they often use the perspectives of interactionism or Marxism. They also show the blindness to behaviour patterns and informal social structures that follow from taking the viewpoint of middle-aged or elderly males of high status.

'Only after a substantial, polemical, and varied experience of the society in question is it possible to discover that statements gravely and precisely articulated are statements of ideology, reflecting either the behaviour of the dominant social group, which may be the minority, or the ideological tendency to confuse the substance of an act with its legal enactment, thus attributing the agency of all significant social processes to men.' (Maher, page 72)

For example, in the first paper, Ronald Frankenberg looks critically at the work of those who have described the organization and dynamics of communities in Britain and at those who have made secondary analyses of the studies, and he points to the invisibility of women in the reports or to their treatment in terms of descriptive 'trivia'.[4]

His earlier perceptive remark that community studies are the industrial sociology of the housewife (1966:232) is developed in his present paper, which criticizes the common statement that the modern family has lost its productive functions and is now primarily a unit of consumption (Fletcher 1966; Young and Willmott 1973). The neglect of productive relations within the family is a theme that is echoed in other contributions (Delphy, Rose and Hanmer) and has been remarked on in many articles from the women's movement over the past few years.[5] But sociologists have continued to see work and therefore work relations as something that takes place outside the home (eg. Wedderburn and Craig 1974) and as involving only some members of the family, primarily the husband-father. This must have ignored their experience of everyday life, even those with 'non working' spouses, mothers, and sisters. More than this, however, it points to the failure of sociological theory to come to terms with the facts of the reproduction of labour power within a particular form of the division of labour and to integrate these into a theory of societal organization. The association between industrialization and the changing form of the family, familiar to all first year sociology students, stops short of incorporating at a theoretical level the link between domestic production and social production. Consequently the social relations of production within the family are ignored in all their manifestations in social interaction both inside and outside the family.

Frankenberg proposes instead that we look at the family as a unit producing labour power — concerned, that is, with reproduction, socialization, and servicing — and at community studies as accounts of 'conflicts between interest groups (classes, sexes and generations) in interlocking processes of production'. By asking what is produced, how, and for whose benefit, his reanalysis prompts further questions concerning the ideological supports for, and the social controls exercised by, those who profit. He also notes the extent to which fieldworkers, usually male, have been 'captured' by one group of their informants, usually the men: viz. Rees's view of the Welsh parish, and Dennis and his colleages' 'miner's eye view'. And he suggests that whereas we are used to assuming that commodities are generally becoming more and more mass produced, the production of labour power by women has become more individuated. There has been a move from the 'factory situation' of Bethnal Green and St. Ebbes, to 'cottage child production' in Greenleigh and Barton.

Vanessa Maher is also concerned with the relationships formed by women in their work as wives, and she contests the idea that these are primarily 'expressive' and relatively unimportant in the total social structure. Using fieldwork data from Morocco, she argues that in a situation where women lack economic autonomy, are segregated from men, and thus lack, *inter alia*, direct access to markets and most wage labour, they create a 'women's network' of instrumental relationships. Marriage is insecure in the area where she lived, due to migration, divorce, and early widowhood, and so women cannot depend for support on husbands, and only to a limited extent on fathers and brothers. The women's network is an important mechanism affording women some security, distributing resources, and creating status through the local communities.

Further, Maher is able to make interesting comparisons with the instrumental aspects of the relationships that women forge *within* their families — especially with their sons — in the familistic cultures of Greece, Italy, and Portugal.

Her paper includes a valuable note on methodology. British community studies have been noticeably reticent on this score, which makes it very difficult for us now to reassess their accounts. Maher discusses the extent to which particular social areas are accessible to male fieldworkers and to female fieldworkers in the societies she has worked in, and she criticizes the past tendency of anthropologists and sociologists to see informal structures as unimportant and to favour coherent, unambiguous accounts of value-systems given by dominant groups and to dismiss those given by women and other powerless groups as 'confused' and 'personal'.

The next five papers deal with the ways in which different agencies serve to reinforce sexual differentiation by processes that mediate the dominant ideological presuppositions of a society differentiated along sex lines. Each of the papers is concerned with an area of research of traditional interest to sociologists — marriage and divorce, medicine, social security, and education — but the approach adopted is far from the traditional one.

Using material from a study of divorce in a provincial town in France on which they were both engaged, two authors examine the social processes involved in divorce proceedings. First, Christine Delphy attempts to disentangle the meaning and function of marriage as a socio-economic institution, using the light thrown on marriage by divorce; and then Yves Dezalay looks at the legal system in relation to working-class divorces.

Delphy first considers whether marriage should be viewed as a form of work contract whereby the husband appropriates all the work performed by his wife — in housework, childbearing and, when he is an entrepreneur, self-employed artisan, or farmer or professional, in his money earning activities as well. This appropriation might be seen as an exchange for up-keep, were it not for the fact that when married women have jobs, and thereby earn their own upkeep, they are still required to do the domestic work or pay from their wage or salary to have it done. We anticipate that some will argue that husbands also contribute unpaid domestic labour, painting the house, mending the car, or helping with children, but men's domestic work is voluntary and usually occasional, often applied to things that are the husband's property. Domestic work and child care are the wife's primary, continuous responsibilities, and their value is appropriated by her husband and possibly also by the husband's employer (see Gardiner 1976).

As Delphy and Dezalay point out, during marriage this exploitation of the woman may not be visible or recognized, for the stress on 'sharing' and the words of the marriage contract suggest that an equal contribution from each spouse is involved. It is at divorce that the disparity is made clear, for the woman's obligation to carry out domestic, childbearing and child rearing duties carries sanctions. One is reminded that, until recently in Britain, awards for damages to a husband against an adulterer included compensation not only for loss of conjugal rights, but also for the services of the woman as housewife (and mother)(Puxon 1967:108, Eekelaar 1971:251).

That the work performed by a wife has value of an exchange kind becomes apparent if the services she usually provides are bought in the market. This point is developed by Cynthia Epstein in her account of *Woman's Place*, when she quotes an earlier study showing that almost half the full-time professional and business women interviewed had *two or more* full-time servants to maintain their homes and look after their children during the day (Epstein 1971:138). The elite position of middle-class couples where both spouses are earning and are able to buy the services that the marriage contract places on the wife, necessarily involves them in the exploitation of others, predominantly women, by the normal working of the market and/or the use of kinship obligations of mothers, aunts, or unmarried daughters. The sexist and class consequences of the childcare proposals which Rhona and Robert Rapoport (1971), for example, find themselves compelled to recommend need to be emphasized.

Delphy pursues her argument further, saying that it is arguable that the ex-husband continues to appropriate his ex-wife's labour after divorce, since she is almost always the one who continues to care for their young children, on a relatively small allowance, which is often not paid (a point made also by Land). But she suggests it may in fact be more useful to see as a fundamental social principle the attribution to women of the responsibility for young children, from which men are collectively exempted (see also Maher's and Abrams and McCulloch's papers). Marriage, from this perspective, appears as the wife providing domestic services for her husband in exchange for his contribution towards the upkeep of the children: women's responsibility for childcare is what makes the husband's appropriation of his wife's labour possible.

Thus Delphy's final suggestion is that the family has two juxtaposed economic functions — it is the place where women rear children and it is an economic production unit headed by the *paterfamilias*.

In this latter development of her argument, that women are accorded collective responsibility for childcare, Delphy may seem to be approaching the position of some anthropologists and ethnologists who argue that the 'fundamental dyad' is that of mother and child, not husband and wife. But her ideas do not imply the biological reductionism of, for example, Fox (1967:27), which has so bedevilled cross-cultural accounts of 'marriage' and 'the family' (see eg. Mair 1971). There is, rather, a social attribution justified by 'biological' ideology (see Ortner 1974) comparable with the use that Sally McIntyre describes the medical profession as making of 'maternal instincts'.

Dezalay's paper concentrates on the ways in which judicial proceedings surrounding divorce serve to reinforce the different obligations of men as husbands and women as wives. He argues that while legal agencies give the appearance of being disinterested helpers, coming to the aid of couples in difficulties — difficulties presented as deriving from the couple's personal failures — and as looking after 'the child's interest', they are in fact authoritarian, coercing their 'clients' into 'correct' gender behaviour. Where dissuasive actions aimed at 're-education' fail, and a couple do separate, they are made scapegoats. The process of divorce is made so traumatic, expensive, long drawn out, fraught, and public, that other couples are dissuaded from following the same route.

He argues that what we are in fact witnessing in divorce and in marriage, is the juxtaposition of two systems of social control: one, which defines and sanctions the woman in relation to her performance in the family, and the other, which concerns itself with the man as breadwinner and therefore as worker. The legal sanctions are used in his case to ensure his continued participation within the work-force and by thus performing he will be defined as a 'good' or 'bad' husband. The relationship of marriage, he argues, is inherently conflictual because it involves the exploitation of the woman. But this exploitation is dissembled, and the conflict compounded, by making women appear responsible for the exploitation of men in the labour market — a point illustrated by Frankenberg in his comments on *Coal is our Life* in relation to husbands who see their wives as 'passive object(s) for the support of which (a man) is driven to unpleasant underground work'.

The duality of judicial intervention, which gives an appearance of helping while it is being coercive in divorce proceedings, thus contributes to the division of workers, turning men and women against each other, and helps to establish a docile work-force.

There are as yet no studies of British divorce proceedings comparable to these two papers, though the perspective used would enable us to understand more fully the class and sex differentiation involved in recent legislation. The consequences of the use of 'the child's interest' as a focal point when the decisions are in the hands of upper middle-class male judges or magistrates, advised by social workers trained in social control that is in the interests of the dominant sex and class values, are likely to distort the interests of the child, the mother, and the working-class father.

The paper by Hilary Land brings together in a systematic way material on the historical development and current operation of British social security provision. She analyses it in terms of its ideological presuppositions which serve to legitimize and maintain the power that dominant groups exercise over the weaker sections of society and she brings out the extent to which those who are female, married, poor, and old are institutionally subjected to unequal treatment (see Syson and Young 1974). She shows how the British social security system, by perpetuating inegalitarian family relationships, is a means of reinforcing, rather than compensating for the economic inequalities between men and women in the labour market. The assumptions made about the place of married women derive, she argues, from the particular economic and demographic concerns of the 1930s; but they still survive in the restructured social security system of 1973.

The whole gamut of national insurance pensions, sickness and unemployment benefit, taxation, family income supplement, and supplementary benefit all encourage conventional gender divisions. There is a studied ignoring of the fact that most women now work outside the home for most of their lives and that for very many (one in six of all non-pensioner households) this paid work by the wife/mother is vitally necessary. There is no provision for the situation in which a man chooses to stay at home while his wife goes out to work, or where they share domestic responsibility, and cohabitation clauses assume that if a woman lives with a man, he supports her. Conventional divisions are supported by a further series of 'statutory provisions, administrative procedures and business practices' which all assume women's financial dependence on their husbands, or the men they live with, and which do not allow women financial independence nor allow them to have adult male dependents.[6]

In discussing a recently adopted demand of the Women's Liberation Movement, Mary McIntosh argues,

'This demand (for the abolition of the legal definition of women as dependent on man) is one that not only expresses the indignity and servitude implied in women's dependence on men, it also highlights the role of the State in creating and recreating this dependence. It shatters the image of the family as part of organic civil society which the State merely recognises and respects. It uncovers the fact that the 'welfare' state has systematically underpinned the family whenever it was crumbling, rather than substituting for it. It invites thoughts about why the State — not just the 'Society' beloved of bourgeois sociologists — needs the family'. (McIntosh 1974:5)

Land supports Dezalay's argument when she suggests that the arguments raised against family allowances and tax-credits reflect the need of the State for men to be kept at work by having dependent children and a wife to support and that this applies particularly to the working class, 'the poor man needs the greater incentive of totally dependent children to keep him at his unrewarding work; the professional man apparently does not.'[7]

While Beveridge saw motherhood as an important social function, times have changed and maternity grants have declined. In the latest tax-credit scheme, married women are seen as either workers or dependents, not as mothers or carers for the sick or disabled. As workers, no distinction is made between women without children who work, and the working mother (who can claim no housekeeper or child minder allowance against tax); nor between the wife who stays at home because she has children or sick relatives, and the wife who stays at home from choice. The last category comprises mainly the wives of men with middle or high incomes, and tax allowances for such wives are worth double the value of the present national spending on family allowances. Thus the state continues to advantage the better off and to subsidize marriage *per se*, while contributing relatively little to the cost of raising the future generation.

Not only is minimal help given with the costs of raising children or caring for the sick or elderly within the home, but such 'activity' is not regarded as *work* — it is not credited with national insurance stamps, and if the woman falls sick, there is no 'benefit' forthcoming to pay for her replacement, nor does it give her a pension.[8]

An awareness of the issues that Land raises is of relevance to

those who are endeavouring to develop theoretical understandings
of the operation of social welfare provisions, as well as to those
concerned with social policy provisions. The recent White Paper
published by the 1974 Labour Government *Equality for Women* is
curiously silent on social security issues, though presumably these
constitute one area where a Government has *direct* power to alter
the situation by legislation. Among generations of social workers
— trainers and trained — the majority of them women, only a
minority have recently started to become sufficiently aware and
vocal to bring out the sexist implications of statutory welfare
provisions (*Case Con* no. 15 1974; Wilson 1974). Land's paper is an
important contribution to the dialogue.

Jenny Shaw considers the organization of schools and their
curricula and points out some of the conflicts between the generally
accepted notions of the relations between education and social
mobility and the processes involved in supplying different kinds of
labour market. At several points she also raises the implications for
girls of the increase in co-education and suggests where gender
affects success by a process akin to streaming.

We have known for some time the differential chance of
educational mobility for the majority of boys as against the
majority of girls (an astounding discrepancy even in 1974), but
until recently few have begun to ask and systematically to
investigate how girls in particular are educated for low
performance and under-achievement. But this occurs, despite the
fact that the educational system is frequently, though not always,
assumed to have the opposite functions. Whilst much can be
explained by the class-based models of educational processsing,
there still remain large areas where none of us fully appreciates or
understands the meanings and implications of what happens in our
schools.

Shaw shows the extent to which the sociology of education has
left girls out of account. This may be explained in practical terms,
for example pressure from funding bodies to cut costs by means of
a sample avoiding the compounding sex variable, which
complicates all stages of the research process. This explanation
does not, however, account for the ignoring of gender in theoretical
models used in the sociology of education. It is interesting to note
that not one of the papers in the volume on *Knowledge, Education
and Cultural Change* in this series (Brown 1973), makes even a
mention of any aspect of education in relationship to sexual
divisions, though as Shaw points out, gender is at least as
important in many ways as class.[9] While we should not have

expected sexual divisions to be a major concern, some of the statements that are made call for at least a footnote to the effect that at present they apply only to boys' schools, male teachers, and so on.

We shall take but one example. In Davies (1973:271-3) the child is referred to continually as he, as is the teacher, though the author says that 'the basic decisions to be taken in education concern who is to be taught what? when? and how?'. It may well be agreed that in English 'he' includes 'she', but this will hardly meet the case where, although we do not know precisely the processes involved nor their extent, we *do* know enough to be certain that he does *not* include she in educational terms — whether at the level of labelling, allocating, or rewarding either teachers or taught.[10]

The reorientation of the sociology of education to take account of all instead of half those attending school and all instead of a quarter of school teachers, is a formidable task in itself; and thus Shaw's paper is tentative and selective in its explanation. We are, however, seeing the beginnings of a discussion of how this task can be undertaken, and a considerable body of material offering insights and ideas has already been produced by the women's movement — many of whose members, not surprisingly, are teachers or involved in the care of children.[11] These ideas and insights have yet to be taken up by sociologists of education, but Shaw's paper has indicated some of the ways in which work could proceed.

Sally MacIntyre's contribution raises what should, for sociologists be an obvious and valuable research area: 'normal' reproduction. The questions she asks are basic ones for an understanding of the cultural meanings attached to a biological process, and the ideological use of biology and 'natural instincts' to maintain particular social structures. Both she and Dezalay are concerned with social agencies' moulding of their clients into categories, and the extent to which outcomes are due to 'rate producing processes rather than to behaviour producing processes' (Kitsuse and Cicourel 1963). She brings into the open the cosy, reified presuppositions with which those in the medical and social work professions deny, obstruct, and oppress those they 'help', by their crude bracketting of sexual intercourse, marriage, reproduction, and by self-validating notions of maternal 'instincts'.

MacIntyre demonstrates from her own work that although there are some formidable obstacles of a practical nature involved in the research needed, these can be overcome sufficiently once the theoretical questions are raised and recognized within a sociological discourse.

Her paper relates at several points to the two which follow it —
by Brake, and Rose and Hanmer. All, in different ways, raise vital
issues of social definitions and of power relationships which have
largely been ignored in what are frequently thought of as intimate
'physical' inter-personal relationships. These are, however, in fact
subject to rigid external social control, whether of a traditional
folk-lore or a rational, scientific kind.[12]

Making individuals aware of the social origins of individual
problems has long been advocated as one of the tasks of sociology
(Wright Mills 1959; Rex 1974); and hopefully recognition that
private troubles are not necessarily due to individual faults and
failings is aided by sociological analysis. Similarly a questioning of
the 'reality' presented by society and the construction of new
consciousness and new realities has been the aim of the
consciousness-raising groups in the women's and gay movements.

Mike Brake considers the sexuality dimension of sexual divisions
in society along these lines. He argues that, 'The world of sexuality
is too often taken for granted as possessing definite forms and
patterns which have become reified into something which is
'normal' (p.174). By looking at comparative material on sexual
behaviour and interpretations of gender, he shows that sexual
meanings are socially constructed. He goes on to look at the
possibilities for achieved gender within a context of new forms of
consciousness, and gives an account of the various groups at
present to be found among homosexuals, transvestites, and
transexuals. He sees a potential for redefinitions of cultural
identities if such groups act collectively and resist the 'normalizing'
process of relegating them to pathological categories.

Brake links the heterosexual and the 'gay' world in terms of an
overall male hegemony and describes how gay people usually seek
their models in 'parodies of the heterosexual world'. He shows,
however, that the radical gay groupings are deliberately setting out
to resist such models, and thereby resisting the implied oppression.
While one may doubt the power of many of these groupings, even
if they overcame the obstacles that divide them among themselves,
he highlights in a crucial way the oppression of ascribed gender for
females, since it carries the sexist connotations of secondariness
(see Abrams and McCulloch's paper).

That sociologists have neglected sexuality as an area of enquiry
was obvious from the discussions at the conference. Their failure to
use or develop the anthropological material in a self critical way in
their own societies is perhaps fairly easily explained in terms of
taboos and consequent fears of the loss of hard-won respectability.

Indeed some anthropological material is only now becoming available, because it is only recently that anthropologists have felt free to publish in this country the material on sexuality which they had gathered. In addition to cross-cultural studies, we also need more information on changing sexual mores and thus on what conditions lead to the possibilities of the 'private troubles' of homosexuals becoming public issues — however circumscribed that public still is. It will be interesting to see how seriously the question of achieved gender and its economic and social underpinnings and social potential is taken by sociologists, and also if they choose to work on the 'politics of sexuality'.[13]

Scientific and technological advances in the field of reproduction have been seen by some radical feminists (Firestone 1971) as providing a 'technological fix' which will enable women no longer to bear, and thus to be seen to be 'naturally' required to rear, children. Hilary Rose and Jalna Hanmer argue in their paper that such utopianism is founded on a basic misunderstanding of institutionalized science, which has a male dominated culture, and technology, which is managed and controlled by the state and industry.

They also consider other alternative means of controlling reproduction 'to solve the contradictions of women's situation' which have been proposed by others within the women's movement. For instance the Italian radical feminists, Rivolte Feminale, argue that contraception and abortion are unnecessary, for they serve only to support men's advantages and the exploitation of women, since it is women who have to bear all the ill effects. They advocate lesbianism as the normal sexual relationship and consorting with men only for the purpose of breeding. Feminist Marxists are also considering the structures of reproduction, though they are hampered by the failure of orthodox Marxism to come to terms, in theory and practice, with the sex-class relationship. However Halpern *et al.* (1973) and Kendrick *et al.* (1974) have drawn together work on imperialism and population control in the third world, and Rose and Hanmer's paper itself analyses the relation between biological engineering and population control within contemporary capitalism. They discuss the possible social effects of some of the forms of biological engineering that are being envisaged — choosing the sex of children, breeding an almost entirely male population, quasi-sterilization via contraceptive time capsules, and cloning — none of which, they suggest, holds any good in store for women.

While some of the possibilities for biological engineering they describe do not seem likely to be put into operation by governments, aided by 'disinterested' scientists in the near future; and while crude eugenics are perhaps currently disfavoured (which is not to say they are not practised); eco-eugenics are seen as directed towards an increasingly legitimate goal — the control of 'over' population. Many states in the West, Eastern Europe, and the Third World have already tried various means to control family size and these methods have been applied with greater or lesser authoritarianism and varying (but usually little) consideration for the effects on women's lives. Rose and Hanmer suggest, however, that the schemes of biological engineering they describe afford the possibilities of much greater state control, through manipulation or outright intervention, and that these methods could reduce to a minimum the freedom of choice of when and if to have children.

Rose and Hanmer show that while potential technical advances *could* result in a reduction of the oppression of women, they are more likely, unless women come together to protect their own interests, to result in greater control. They conclude that the women's movement must confront the issues they raise and continue what has already been started: the demystification of science, technology, and medicine.[14]

The position of women in China, where around 400 million women, a quarter of all the women in the world, live, is of obvious sociological interest. Within the last fifty years their social position has changed from one that includes seclusion (among the elite), footbinding, female infanticide, beatings, concubinage, prostitution, child marriage, and selling into slavery, to something approaching equality before the law, and participation in social production, community activities, and the holding of public office. Much of the current interest in England comes from socialist women who can look to China with hope, while averting their gaze from the Soviet Union or Cuba — both of which indicate that revolution is not sufficient guarantee of change in family institutions, except perhaps in reducing the crudest forms of exploitation, which benefits all members of the family group. In China, by contrast, the 'women problem' has been accorded serious and continued consideration. Some of Mao's earliest and impassioned writings were on this subject and active policies have been pursued to change family relationships and to reduce sexual inequalities in wider spheres. China is of interest also because of the mix between legal changes and local action in the form of group meetings 'to exchange experiences' and to 'speak pains to recall pains', which have similarities to the consciousness-raising groups in the West. Together with the very effective use of women's cadres to help with women's problems, via word of mouth education and exemplary action (see Rose and Hanmer), and the emphasis on changes in basic attitudes by the use of a battery of devices to produce new role models (Croll 1974), the stress is currently on the need to talk over conflict and recognize difficulties between men and women as a first step to change, for 'without self-awareness or a new consciousness "a woman will be unwilling to fly though the sky is high" (Croll 1974:8).

Delia Davin suggests in her paper that some of the very early concern for the position of women in China arose among the young intellectuals in the 1920s (quite a number of whom were women) who sought to make 'free choice marriages', which led to problems of unattached student women with children, or abandoned village fiancées. She outlines the continued and determined efforts made to change the marriage laws of the People's Republic, and the changes of social and economic traditions that these required.

As she traces the development of official ideology at national level and the practice at village level, she gives due weight to the setbacks and compromises that were entailed. She thus makes a contribution to both the sociology of social change and to our understanding of the relationship of theory and practice in the particular case of marriage relations within a rural kinship context. The possibility of change from arranged to free choice marriage, the remarriage of widows, and the granting of divorces, involved the need not only for altering strongly entrenched attitudes, but also economic, particularly land, reform, as well as marriage reform.

The role of ideas and ideology in the process of social change and the question of what constitutes revolutionary change are raised by Davin's contribution. She gives her assessment of the possibilities and the limitations of the role of an officially adopted ideology with a clearly specified aim of equality between men and women. By examining what constituted revolutionary praxis at nation, district, and local levels within a society with a long history of the oppression of women, she adds to our understanding of the conditions and ways in which the struggle of the revolutionary and the traditional are mediated.

Philip Abrams and Andrew McCulloch's research into communes in contemporary Britain also examines the question of changes in gender relationships. They conclude that in 'so far as such relationships are concerned, communes in Britain cannot easily detach themselves from the constraints of a larger moral economy ...'; a not dissimilar conclusion from Davin's, except that the wider contexts differ and so in Britain the relationships 'remain a field of coercion' whereas in China a move towards a more egalitarian relationship is being facilitated.

Abrams and McCulloch see modern communes as aiming to be above all an alternative to the monogamous single household — a new setting for familism. This romantic-interactionist family can re-work gender relationships under certain conditions, but it need, and usually does, not. In this respect it is, they argue, no different from the conventional family.

The viability of communes and the possibilities for their re-working of gender relations seem to depend on the relationship they establish with the outside world — though this area is often fudged by the communards. A prime example of a commune they suggest is one where something like a society of free craftsmen (and craftswomen) has been created. These people, having had large amounts of capital available to them, have been able to 'repudiate the dominant social relation of the outside world, wage-labour'. Abrams and McCulloch rightly ask whether these can provide any sort of model for a wider construction of social relations. They set their scrutiny of communes within a context of a broadly defined petty bourgeois protest against the ills of contemporary society, and consider the 'practical' and 'interpersonal' difficulties that communes see themselves as facing. They conclude that the attempts to get away from the industrialized sector and into the traditional sector, and away from the modern family and into some kind of extended family, are undermined by the ideology of individual autonomy and the practice of individualism which motivates communards to choose communes initially.

But just as communes are not detached from the dominant economic system, even though they may manage to go far in *defining themselves* as so being, so they are not isolated from the societal hegemony of male-female relations, though they *may* go a long way by deliberately defining themselves as outside it (cf. many conventional marriages). However, Abrams and McCulloch found that in communes men still seem to reserve themselves the sexual initiative. In so far as a commune is part of a wider society, socio-economic pressures — for instance, the differential earning capacities of men and women and the organization of social security provisions (see Land's paper) — push them towards a conventional division of labour; and children at school experience pressures to have *a* mother and *a* father.

Their conclusions on gender relations lend remarkable support to Delphy's thesis, for they argue that women's 'social secondariness' derives not from the family (monogamous marriage) but from their responsibility for children.

> 'Of the three links that comprise the basic family unit — wife-husband, father-child, mother-child — the first two are often seriously opened-up in communes, but the third is hardly touched. Motherhood remains an all-demanding and totally female role. The notion that communal relationships are intentional and sustained only on the condition that both parties find the necesssary relationship-work gratifying, breaks down in the face of child-rearing' (pp. 270-1).

Communes are, after all, slightly easier to unscramble, both ideologically ('we all entered it freely accepting we could always split') and practically (there is less likely to be social worker intervention) than conventional families. Thus 'Any attempt by women in communes to assert themselves as women is more likely to lead to the departure of the men than to anything else' (p.270).[15]

The issue of the functional relevance of the nuclear family for capitalism is raised in Abrams and McCulloch's paper and they argue that it is diminishing. Frankenberg in this volume and Gardiner in the companion volume see it as a very economical way for any state to produce new members and service existing workers. We would also add that it has definite advantages for men (Delphy and Barker forthcoming). How far it is useful to regard communes and nuclear families as functional equivalents is an interesting question. However, certainly at the present time the nuclear family and the conventional sexual division of labour are strongly supported by governments, legal and economic practices, and potent ideologies of 'common-sense' and 'biological inevitability', whereas commune achieved gender, and egalitarian sexual division of labour and resources are not. But as the papers in this volume show in a variety of ways, the questions are now being raised and we hope sociologists in future will be concerned with much that they have hitherto excluded from their research and teaching — and even from their consciousness.

Notes

1 We think we should record the surprise (and even hostility and ribaldry) shown by some sociologists at the prospect of a BSA conference being devoted to sexual divisions and society. As far as we know, nothing similar was expressed about conferences on race and racialism, social stratification, or development. But all these areas are concerned with relationships between groups and how these relationships are determined in large part by control over economic and political resources; with explaining how ideologies that support them originate and develop; and under what conditions and by what means they are changed.

2 Sexism is a term as yet largely used as a political epithet. We suggest that as a sociological concept it indicates situations where the differences between men and women are not only emphasized, but consistently and systematically so, to the detriment of women, i.e. they are institutionalized. Such differences are frequently, though not exclusively, legitimated by biological assumptions. (See Allen 1973 for a comparison with racism.)

3 Family and kinship come in the bottom third of the interests of university sociologists and of articles published in the last twenty years. Sexual/gender divisions and sexuality are not even recorded as categories (Collison and Webber (1971) and Carter (1968)).

4 As he says, the main concern of most of those who have been reworking community studies has been with class, status, and power. Frankenberg does, however, omit mention of Klein (1965). This is, admittedly, a social psychological study, but it does look at community studies specifically in terms of the interrelationships within families, showing how 'modal personalities' are produced and in turn perpetuate themselves via social influences and child-rearing practices. In the process, Klein gives some attention to gender divisions, particularly in childhood.

5 For instance, Benston (1969), Dalla Costa (1972), Delmar (1974), Delphy (1970), Edwards (1971), Gerstein (1973), Mitchell (1966), and Vogel (1973). See also *Marxism Today* (1972:4).

6 In addition we might instance student grants, mortgage and hire purchase agreements, and tenancies. For further examples see Coote and Gill (1974). For instances of the bureaucratic impedence of attempted 'role reversals' in marriage see Coote (1974).

7 Although Land describes Ramsay MacDonald's opposition to

family allowances, members of the Labour Party have, from time to time, pointed to the fact that the provision of family allowances, school meals, maintenance allowances for older school children, etc. have, by relieving financial pressures on the husband/father, enabled him to participate more effectively in industrial disputes. This can be contrasted with the attempts to refuse social security rights to the families of strikers. For the the measures of protection — marriage settlements, allowances to married children, gifts to grandchildren — open to the middle class see Bell (1968), and Marceau (in the companion volume).

8   With the Health Service reorganization stressing 'community care', these obligations will, in default of community facilities, mean largely unpaid care by relatives, mainly women. Similarly, with the continuing lack of nursery places, care of young children will be restricted to their mothers in their homes. Since the carrying out of these activities is not 'work' it does not count for social security purposes, nor does it count as 'post-graduate experience' so far as, for instance, the Social Science Research Council, is concerned.

9   Indeed we could use any and all the volumes so far published in this series as examples of the virtual absence in sociological discourse of any awareness of gender as an organizing force in society.

10 It is worth noting that the same tendencies — an excessive use of male subjects, generalizing from these to whole populations (while carefully restricting findings on females to females only) and omitting mention in abstracts etc. that only males were used — have been remarked upon also in psychology (Schwabacher (1972), Prescott and Foster (mimeo)).

11 There has been a series of studies of children's books (see Hoffman (1973) and *Shrew* (1973) for details) showing the support these give to conventional sex divisions. Likewise consideration has been given to television programmes and advertisements (Comer 1974), education reports, (Moore 1973), constraints on classroom discussion (Elliott 1974), and the structure and ideologies of colleges of education (Loftus 1974).

12 Analyses of the family, such as those by Delphy, Dezalay, and Land suggest that there are, of course, also conflicts of interest between husband and wife, exploitation of women, and legal coercion by social workers in another area — marriage — commonly seen as voluntaristic and where the relationships are 'based on love'.

13 Such work has a long, if intermittent, interest for the Left. For
   recent examples see Reiche (1972) and Pearce and Roberts
   (1973).
14 Considerable attention has been given recently by those in the
   women's movement to demystifying psychiatry and medicine
   and their treatment of women's psyches and bodies. Recent
   books from the USA include Frankfort (1972) and Chesler
   (1974). In Britain, concern has been primarily with dissemina-
   ting information on contraception, abortion, and doctors'
   attutides towards 'women's rights to choose', with more limited
   attention to psychiatry. There is now a growing interest in self-
   help clinics (for fuller information see the 'Mind and Body'
   section in each issue of *Women's Report*). Following the discussion of Rose and Hanmer's paper (see their note 10) it is clear
   that attention must also be given to challenging the imperatives
   towards rationalization of obstetrics (see also Gillie and Gillie
   1974) which begin to make the natural childbirth advocacy of
   only a few years ago appear to be utopian or likely at best to be
   restricted in future to a favoured elite.
15 Abrams and McCulloch sample — drawn a few years ago — did
   not include any single sex communes, such as are currently
   being advocated and practised by some women. The WLM has
   been very critical of the institution of the family, but as yet has
   produced little by way of utopian suggestion as to alternatives.

References

Allen, S. 1973. The Institutionalization of Racism. *Race* XV (1):
   99-106. July.
Banks, J.A. and Banks O. 1964. Feminism and Social Change — A
   Case Study of a Social Movement, In G. Zollschen and W.
   Hirsch (eds), *Explorations in Social Change*. London:
   Routledge & Kegan Paul.
Bell, C.R. 1968. *Middle Class Families*. London: Routledge &
   Kegan Paul.
Benston, M. 1969. The Political Economy of Women's Liberation.
   Monthly Review 21(4) September.
Brown, R. (ed.) 1973. *Knowledge, Education, and Cultural
   Change*. London: Tavistock.
Carter, M.P. 1968. Report on a Survey of Sociological Research in
   Britain. *Sociological Review 16* (1) March.

Chesler, P. 1974. *Women and Madness*. London: Allen Lane.

Collison, P. and Webber, S. 1971. British Sociology 1950-1970: A Journal Analysis. *Sociological Review 19* (4) November.

Comer, L. 1974. *Wedlocked Women*. Leeds: Feminist Books.

Coote, A. 1974. Role of Law. *The Guardian*. Thursday, February 21:11.

Coote, A. and Gill, T. 1974. *Women's Rights: A Practical Guide*. Harmondsworth: Penguin.

Croll, W. 1974. Role Models in the People's Republic of China. Paper given to the BSA conference.

Dalla Costa, M. 1972. Women and the Subversion of the Community. In M. Dalla Costa and S. Jarus, *The Power of Women and the Subversion of the Community*. Bristol: Falling Wall Press.

Davies, I. 1973. Knowledge, Education, and Power. In R. Brown (ed.) *Knowledge, Education, and Cultural Change*. London: Tavistock.

Delmar, R. 1974. The Family and Capitalism. *Radical Philosophy*. Spring.

Delphy, C. 1970. L'Ennemmi principale. *Partisans* no. 54-55. Juillet-octobre (an English translation is available).

Delphy, C. and Leonard Barker, D. 1976. *Women in the Family*. London: Tavistock.

Edwards, H. 1971. Housework and Exploitation: A Marxist Analysis. *No More Fun and Games. A Journal of Female Liberation* no. 5.

Eekelaar, J. 1971. *Family Security and Family Breakdown*. Harmondsworth: Penguin.

Elliott, J. 1974. Sex Role Constraints on Freedom of Discussion. *The New Era*. Sepecial Issue on the Making of the Second Sex, *55* (6), July-August. (Also in *Spare Rib* no. 27).

Epstein, C. 1971 *Woman's Place*. London: University of California Press.

Firestone, S. 1971. *The Dialectic of Sex*. London: Cape.

Fletcher, R. 1966. *The Family and Marriage in Britain*. Harmondsworth: Penguin.

Fox, R. 1967. *Kinship and Marriage*. Harmondsworth: Penguin.

Frankenberg, R. 1966. *Communities in Britain*. Harmondsworth: Penguin.

Frankfort, E. 1972. *Vaginal Politics*. New York: Quadrangle

Freeman, J. 1973. The Origins of the Women's Liberation Movement. *American Journal of Sociology 78* (4). Reissued as J. Huber (ed.) *Changing Women in a Changing Society*. London: University of Chicago Press.

Gardiner, J. 1976. Political Economy of Domestic Labour in Capitalist Society. In D. Leonard Barker and S. Allen (eds.), *Dependence and Exploitation in Work and Marriage.* Harlow: Longman.

Gerstein, I. 1973. Domestic Work and Capitalism. *Radical America.* 7 (4 and 5) July-Oct.

Gillie, L. and Gillie, O. 1974. The Childbirth Revolution and The First Vital Hours. *Sunday Times Weekly Review.* October 13 and 20.

Halpern, P., Kenrick, J., and Segan B. 1973. Fertility: Economics and Ideology. In *Papers from the 2nd Women's Liberation and Socialism Conference.* London: Publishing Collective of the S.W.L.S.C.

H.M. Government, 1974. *Equality for Women.* Cmnd. 5724. London HMSO.

Hoffman, M. 1973. Children's Books. *Women Speaking 3* (4) Oct-Dec.

Huber, J. 1973. Introduction. In *Changing Women in a Changing Society.* London: University of Chicago Press.

Kendrick, J., Mettahedah, P., and Young, K. 1974. Bucharest: What *Kind* of Victory?: Ideological Uses of Concepts of Under- and Overpopulation in English History. Mimeo.

Kitsuse, J. and Cicourel, A.V. 1963. A Note on the Use of Official Statistics. *Social Problems 11.*

Klein, J. 1965. *Samples From English Culturs.* 2 Vols. London: Routledge & Kegan Paul.

Loftus, M. 1974. Learning, Sexism and Femininity. *Red Rag* 'A Magazine of Women's Liberation', no. 7.

McGregor, O.R. 1955. The Social Position of Women in England, 1850-1914: A Bibliography. *British Journal of Sociology 6.*

McIntosh, M. 1974. The Fifth Demand. *Red Rag,* no. 7.

Mair, L. 1971. *Marriage.* Harmondsworth: Penguin.

Marceau, F.J. 1976. Marriage, Role Division and Social Cohesion: The Case of Some French Upper-Middle Class Families. In D. Leonard Barker and S. Allen (eds.), *Dependence and Exploitation in Work and Marriage.* Harlow: Longman.

Mitchell, J. 1966. Women: The Longest Revolution. *New Left Review,* Dec. 11-37.

Moore, J. 1973. More Than Half Our Future. Mimeo.

Ortner, S.B. 1974. Is Female to Male as Nature to Culture? In M.Z. Rosaldo and L. Lamphere, *Woman, Culture and Society.* Stanford: Stanford University Press.

Pearce, F. and Roberts, A. 1973. The Social Regulation of Sexual

Behaviour and the Development of Industrial Capitalism in Britain. In R.V. Bailey and J. Young (eds.) *Contemporary Social Problems in Britain*. Farnborough: Saxon House.

Plummer, K. 1974. Some Relevant Directions for Research in the Sociology of Sex: An Interactionist Approach. BSA conference paper. Mimeo.

Prescott, S. and Foster, K. nd. Why Researchers Don't Study Women: The Responses of 67 Researchers. Mimeo.

Puxon, M. 1967. *The Family and the Law*. London: MacGibbon & Kee.

Rapoport, Rh. and Rapoport, R. 1971. *Dual-Career Families*. Harmondsworth: Penguin.

Reiche, R. 1972. *Sexuality and Class Struggle*. London: New Left Books.

Rex, J. 1974. *Sociology and the Demystification of the Modern World*. London: Routledge and Kegan Paul.

Syson, L. and Young, M. 1974. Poverty in Bethnal Green. In M. Young (ed.) *Poverty Report 1974*. London: Temple Smith.

Schwabacher, S. 1972. Male vs. Female Representation in Psychological Research. An Examination of the *Journal of Personality and Social Psychology*, 1970-71. *J. Supplement Abstract Service, 2*:20-21.

Vogel, L. 1973. The Earthly Family. *Radical America 7* (4 and 5) July-Oct.

Wedderburn, D. and Craig, C. 1974. Relative Deprivation in Work. In D. Wedderburn (ed.) *Poverty, Inequality and Class Structure*. London: Cambridge University Press.

Wilson, E. 1974. *Women and the Welfare State*. Red Rag Pamphlet no. 2.

Wright Mills, C. 1959. *The Sociological Imagination*. New York: Oxford University Press.

Young, M. and Willmott, P. 1973. *The Symmetrical Family*. London: Routledge and Kegan Paul.

Zubaida, S. (ed.) 1970. *Race and Racialism*. London: Tavistock.

Special Publications

Case Con. 1974. A Revolutionary Magazine for Social Workers. Women's Issue, no. 15. Spring.

Marxism Today. Theoretical Journal of the Communist Party. Following an article by R. Small on Marxism and the Family

(Dec. 1972), the journal carried contributions on this topic each month throughout 1973 and into 1974.

Shrew. 1973. Journal of the Women's Liberation Workshop, *5* (4), October. Children's Books Issue.

Women's Report. Bi-monthly round-up of news and reviews for women by women. Produced by a collective. Formerly associated with the Fawcett Society.

RONALD FRANKENBERG

In the Production of their Lives, Men (?)... Sex and Gender in British Community Studies

It is no new experience for community studies to be subjected to harsh criticism (Stacey 1969; Bell and Newby 1971), but to my knowledge no-one has so far looked at the British variety from the point of view of their adequacy in dealing with the relationships between the sexes and the significance of gender within society. To begin this critique I shall address my attention to the summary by Frankenberg (1966), a work to which I owe a great personal debt of gratitude (it might be said to have made me what I am today); and to a recent work of futuristic optimystology, *The Symmetrical Family* by Michael Young and Peter Willmott (1973). This latter illustrates in both its conscious/unconscious humour and its unconscious/conscious theory the deficiencies of the *genre* of community studies as well as the peculiarities of its *auteurs*.

Young and Willmott's first reference to the role of women in society comes on page 6.

[Towns in the outer metropolitan area] also had many commuters. Waiting for them when they returned at night from London were lines of cars stretching away from the stations, many with wives and dogs in the front seats. If he was not met by his wife a husband would walk down the line until he found a woman or a dog whom he recognised as a neighbour.'

Willmott and Young have always recognized the vital role of dogs in British middle-class culture (Willmott and Young 1960:1; see also 1973 table 50:247). They return to the identification six pages later.

'One wife was just about to say "working-class", her mouth half-open, when her husband, a printer, stopped it with a look and then said, "what a dumb wife I've got". She changed in mid-sentence and answered "middle class", whereupon he nodded, as if to a performing dog, to tell her, yes, that was the right answer.' (1973:12)

I have been less blatant, but a latent sexism (or at least a lack of consciousness) occasionally breaks through, as in my definition of role (Frankenberg 1966:16) — when social positions are seen as bringing *him* (new italics) into relation with the incumbents of other positions. It is characteristic of sociology as it has been, that Coulson and Riddell in criticizing my statement pick up the point of implied social consensus but do not notice the implicit gender assumptions (Coulson and Riddell 1970:39).

More serious than unconscious/conscious humour in Young and Willmott, and elsewhere, is the possible lack of theoretical sophistication in the treatment of relationships between the sexes. Although I would not fall into the elementary error of supposing that family relations are the be-all and end-all of sex role differentiation — the sociological etic equivalent of the emic statement that women's place is in the home — it is nevertheless there that one has to start.

Willmott and Young in previous works have seen themselves as allied with anthropology. They now argue that while this is appropriate for studies on the micro-scale, an alliance with history is needed to study the development of the family in a wider social context. They now see the family in capitalist society as having passed historically (like wages policy under the Heath government) through three phases.

In the first the family was the unit of production. The husband and wife and their children formed a unit which worked, prayed, and played together. Sex roles may have been segregated but they were complementary. In community studies an ideal type is found in the Co. Clare complete farm family (Arensberg 1939; Arensberg and Kimball 1940; Arensberg 1961; Frankenberg 1966), at least as seen by its ethnographers. Historically Edward Thompson (1963:416) has described (and Young and Willmott quote) the early industrial family working together in the fields or at home under the putting-out system. The putting-out system ended by the eviction of the people from the land. They were drawn or driven to town and city to work in the factories of the industrial revolution. The family (in this view) thus entered into stage two — disruption by the forces of industrial capitalism.

'While in the third stage the unity of the family has been restored around its functions as the unit not of production but of consumption' (Willmott and Young 1973:28).

I adopted this model, in what I hope, as a self-confessed Marxist, was a rare lapse, when I wrote of Bethnal Green and in criticism of Young and Willmott: 'Secondly, in economic terms, the immediate and extended family may consume as a unit but they do not necessarily or even usually produce as one' (Frankenberg 1966:194).

I would now argue however that the use of a consumption model of the modern family as an aid to understanding gender roles in society at large has two major and crippling defects which are bound to vitiate any analysis made with its use. First, it overlooks the continuing productive relations within the family and, second, it overlooks the fact that the family and the household are not the only stages on which interaction is influenced or determined by differences of sex and gender. Both my own earlier flirtation with history and Willmott and Young's later marriage with the same lady should have avoided the error, for it was exposed as long ago as 1894 as one into which sapient subjective sociologists might fall — and in Lenin's view into which Mikhailovsky (until recently perhaps still a hero of Oxford P.P.E.) had in fact fallen. Lenin pointed out a number of considerations at that time, and in doing so provides us with at least two levels of theory with which to analyse our problem in relation to community studies. First, in the same way that the social relations of production in the social formation as a whole provided a material base for superstructure of ideology, so the material basis of the family did likewise.

'But where have you read in the works of Marx or Engels that they necessarily spoke of economic materialism? When they described their world outlook they called it simply materialism. Their basic idea ... was that social relations are divided into material and ideological. The latter merely constitute a super-structure on the former, which take shape independent of the will and consciousness of man as (the result) the form of man's activity to maintain his existence. The explanation of political and legal forms — Marx says in the passage quoted — must be sought in the "material conditions of life". Mr. Mikhailovsky surely does not think that procreation relations are ideological?' (Lenin 1894:24)

The family then, and to this very day, is engaged in a process of *production*: of babies, of educated and growing children, of adults who will both produce more children and as adult workers produce not only commodities but also surplus value. Seen from this point of view, the family is a factory or a cottage industry for the production and reproduction of labour power. Capitalism cannot manage without it — it is not an accident of history — and very economical it is too, as even socialist countries who have tried to produce its services elsewhere have perhaps discovered (Sullerot 1971:80). Only the most philistine of bourgeois economists who, to quote a favourite Wildean epigram, know the price of everything and the value of nothing, can fail to see how much actual production of goods — from fried eggs and roast beef to decorated rooms and rebuilt garages — is involved in the reproduction of workers. And this of course is additional to and complicated by its role in the production of ideology.

It was this point that I was trying to make when I wrote in summary that Young and Willmott (1957) were illustrating 'the alienation of man's life from his productive activity at the same time as they discuss what is essentially the industrial sociology of the housewife and the effect of urbanisation on her conditions of work' (Frankenberg 1966:232). I formulated it badly, since I failed to emphasize (unlike Engels) that women are not only involved in the alienation but are often involved as proletarian workers in both micro and macro production systems, whereas it is often if not always the case that man is master in one while slave in the other.

Young and Willmott, however, see progress in terms of the effect of technology upon consumption. Surprisingly, or unsurprisingly, even the most apparently radical sociologists switch the emphasis from the effects of capitalism, through the effects of industrial capitalism, to the effects of industrialism, without apparently even noticing that they have diffused the argument and introduced a concealed principle of convergence at the same time as they have abandoned any pretence at the analysis of *social* relations. This enables them to postulate a direct and unmediated effect of technology on behaviour. In Young and Willmott this takes the form of a magical ideal: the 'Principle of stratified diffusion' (Young and Willmott 1973:19-22 et passim). They seem to see society as a vast Voortrekker column leading its covered wagons through a super supermarket. The middle and upper classes load their wagons with the latest wonders of consumer durable technology which (of course) makes their marriages more companionate. The working class do not need, however, either to struggle or to worry, their part of the column will eventually pass the same point — they too will then collect both hardware and (in the words of Eliza Doolittle's dustman father) middle-class morality. Of such is social progress made.

Communities revisited

If, however, we see progress, or rather social change, in less idealistic and optimistic terms — as a conflict between interest groups (classes, sexes) in interlocking processes of production — it becomes possible to see more sharply what my embryonic consciousness foreshadowed but did not delineate.

Revisiting the studies with consciousness raised by these theoretical considerations we may be able to make clearer even to such occasionally unimaginative positivists as Bell and Newby (1971:140, f.n. 27) that despite the studies' lack of (false) quantitative precision, they have some unity and that Bell and Newby's contention that 'Each has something to contribute to sociology yet, as it turns out, they contribute little to each other', generous as it is, is still an underestimate.

Rural Ireland

The pioneer study of rural Ireland (Arensberg 1939; Arensberg and Kimball 1940) still merits consideration, although its inclusion as a British community implies no recognition of the rightness of imperialistic claims to sovereignty over it. Nevertheless, as I pointed out, the productive relationships within the micro system of the farm family of County Clare are set in a wider context of exploitation which ultimately lies in England, consumer of Ireland's beef and labour-power.

> 'One must remember also that the small farmers are tied to the large farmers by economic necessity and divided from them by antagonistic interests. Like the Welsh parish ... the Irish town-lands maintain their single class appearance because their proletariat and their economic controllers are elsewhere.' (Frankenberg 1966:28)

Arensberg and Kimball did not see it as sharply, and in my earlier work I too failed to point out the functional interrelationships of the family organization and the supply of cheap labour to England. 'Keeping the name on the land' meant the surname, and despite the ideological adulation of motherhood (or perhaps by means of it — the shadow for the substance) only men, and a minority of them, could escape proletarianization.

> 'Mother similarly must watch the new mistress of the household feed the calves and make the butter, and usurp all her other authority. At first, again there is tension which if the daughter-in-law does not soon become pregnant, will mount and may even end in the wife being sent home and the farm passing to another of the husband's family who *can* make a fertile match. If,

however, signs of a baby appear, tension tends to go and the Irish bride is glad of her husband's mother's help with the baby. This leaves her free for her many tasks in the farm economy. The birth of sons to keep the name of the land will be greeted with especial joy'. (Frankenberg 1966:35)

When this is added to the woman's daily round (an almost fixed routine contrasted with the monthly, yearly, and life-cycle variation for men), it seems that it is her own particular brand of dependence rather than authority that mother loses to daughter-in-law. 'The women's daily round is easy to describe' I began, and went on to say that she is first up and last to bed and that unlike the men's day which ends at five, hers goes on until bed (1966:30). 'For tradition and proverb demand that "one woman in the home be always working" ' (Arensberg 1939:47).

'All this activity is directed and controlled by the head of the farm family. The father and husband is normally owner and director of the enterprise. The farm and its income are vested in him' (Arensberg 1939:54-55). Women are involved in the *mainstream* of social production — if (and only if) the uplands of County Clare are taken as being society. Within this narrow sphere women may also have their power, as Edna O'Brien and others (but not Arensberg) have shown. It may be exercized in Ireland as in other Catholic countries in alliance with an ideology and an institution whose guardians exert paternal authority while renouncing normal masculine roles. But this power of women is a brief and small scale island of authority in a sea of ascriptive dependence, to which even the achieved wage slavery of bedsitter Birmingham and labouring London have most often seemed preferable. The women do not always achieve micro-independence even there — see Edna O'Brien again and the coy, male, Levi-Straussian (?) humour of Young and Willmott:

'He spent a lot on Saturday nights when he drank until the pubs closed and then went off with a bunch of his Irish friends to one or other house occupied by a similar number of compatriot nurses or factory girls where they all drank together and moved from bedroom to bedroom, exchanging girls and laughter until it was time to get ready for mass on the Sunday morning.' (1973:154)

Arensberg tells us of a *man* and his friends with whom he co-operates, and of a man's group nicknamed the Dail. He describes how young men represent the village outside it. It is clear that women also co-operate in and outside production, like all subordinate workers, both in co-operation with and in antagonism to their employers, the men. But it is not brought out in Arensberg's work nor in my earlier comment upon it.

What was needed was an analysis in detail of relations of production — what was produced, how and for whose benefit. This would reveal for rural Ireland as for other migratory systems first, the degree to which women not only form a reserve of labour in their own right, but also by literally keeping the home fires burning, the cradles full, and the farm economy running, make possible the spasmodic employment of the men. Second, that the general family ideology is not accidental but an integral part of a system of acceptance of continued 'servility', bolstered (as Arensberg's functionalist approach enables him to demonstrate) by religion and folk belief. But the conditions under which the ethnographers are said to have entered the field — with hierarchical approval — made it unlikely that this would be brought to the fore.

Welsh countryside or Welsh village?

Rees's study of the central Wales parish of Llanfihangel-yng-Ngwynfa (1950) brings us nearer home, if still within an annexed province. Here on re-reading I wonder whether the whole basis of the analysis would not change if the community were seen from the point of view of women instead of men. For an essential point is made that the centre of social life is not a village but a network of scattered farmsteads. Is this equally true for the women? There is some evidence that it is not. In so far as women who have married (two-thirds) are still in contact with their kin, their social world may be wider; in so far as the industrial sociology of child rearing involves both shopping and taking children to school the hamlet may be more important to wives than to their husbands. Within the farm economy married women are particularly important in relation to eggs and dairy products, and they have a measure of economic independence. Daughters are also a potential means of movement eastwards and mobility upwards. A private education for a daughter in Oswestry is a useful investment for a farmer who wants to move into the high status and profitable farms of the Shropshire plain. However, Rees's description of the idea occupational unit (which I did not mention in 1966) is father, mother, one or two unmarried sons in their youth and early manhood, 'and perhaps a daughter' (Rees 1950:61).

There is clearly a sense in which women are kept under close surveillance all their lives. Rees explains how, while groups of young men are found about the area at night, girls are only permitted to go out when there is a specific reason. He sees significance in the fact that the Women's Institute of 1940 which has twenty-seven members, twenty-two of whom were unmarried women and girls of various ages, gave way to an aelwyd (branch) of the Urdd Gobaith Cymru, a mixed youth movement (Rees 1950:139). This at first met only in winter, until the girls asked that it could meet in summer too. 'Paradoxically, youth clubs, seen as a means of keeping young people off the streets in towns, provide an excuse to get on the street in Llanfihangel' (Frankenberg 1966:61).

The Young Men's group __ keeping women in their place

One of the most interesting institutions of Llan, mentioned by Rees and myself, and the subject of a paper belatedly published by Peters in 1972, is the group of young men licensed to retain public order through satirical disorder — a kind of good natured Ku Klux Klan. Re-reading this material now, it seems that a major function of this group may be to keep control of those women permanently or temporarily out of reach of either father or husband. Rees gives only three examples of their activities; preventing a widow 'enticing' a youth, punishing a man having an adulterous relationship with the wife of another, and preventing single girls from courting young men from other parishes. Peters adds two more examples from other parishes (Peters 1972:112-113). One is the disciplining of a prosperous farmer's son who had impregnated a local single girl.

> 'One night the youths removed the babe from its mother's care, took it to the farm of the mother's alleged lover and placed it in bed with him. The return of the child had to be made publicly, thereby forcing the man to acknowledge that his denial of paternity was not accepted by the majority of opinion in the community'.

Peter's second case 'concerns a woman who was known for her intolerable uppishness'. His analysis is long and complex (and comparative with Lebanese villages) but he makes a number of points that need mention here. 'The youth group garners the harvest of social relations which the formal institutions fail to contain' (Peters 1972:124). They assert 'their right of priority to their own girls', they discipline offenders against sexual (and gender) mores. They represent 'the entire male population of the right age and status for recruitment'. The evidence available is insufficient to carry this line of analysis any further, but it is clear at least, that for lack of the right theoretical framework, Rees and myself entirely and Peters partially fail to see the significance in social control of women.

I might say in my own defence that in my discussion of Williams's *Gosforth* (1956), I commented on the villagers tolerance of three 1950 survivors of the Women's Land Army. 'Local religious and fairy beliefs would have soon put a stop to that in County Clare. The young men's group in Llanfihangel would also have had something to say' (1966:81). The virtue gained by this insight is perhaps cancelled out by a petulant footnote, ten pages before, complaining of Williams's refusal to accept the convention that a woman's social class is that of her father or husband.

Gosforth need not detain us long — there is the same contradiction between the male forms in which gossip is first introduced, and the later analysis of women as carriers of gossip in the village and receivers of it on the farms. There is the same male emphasis among Gosforth farmers on surnames, although sometimes it is a father's or grandfather's surname that a woman keeps to hand on to a child. Williams is particularly strong on what he then called the analysis of social class. I said

> 'In fact, in all the organizations in which the gentry do take part their function is to suggest rather than to do. Williams tells the story of how at a church meeting a lady of the gentry proposed that the parish should be canvassed to find *people* to clean the church in preparation for the harvest festival. Another lady seconded the motion, but it was a working class woman who was asked to find volunteers. The eight *villagers* who carried out the task were all working class, while two single ladies from the gentry simultaneously decorated the pulpit with flowers.' (Frankenberg 1966:77)(italics added 1974).

Both Williams and I failed to draw explicit attention to the commonsense assumption that the work would be done by either ladies or women — divided by class but united by gender.

A Scottish village: Westrigg

Littlejohn (1963) is as highly sophisticated in his treatment of gender in Westrigg as he is of class and status. His book remains in my view the best community study yet published in Britain. His discussion of 'class and sex roles' begins with the disappointingly terse statement.

'The division of labour between them is the same in this
community as in the rest of the nation; after marriage men are
gainfully employed while women work in the house and tend the
children ... No extended description of it is given here as it is
common knowledge.' (Littlejohn 1963:122-3)

However, he has already made the point that women are more
likely to marry up than men, indeed marriage is the only channel of
mobility for women, and he goes on to point out, as few others
have, that it is women who are responsible for maintaining the
status of the children, especially in the working class.

'Because a woman's status derives from that of a man it might
seem as if the wife and mother had no responsibility for the
status of the family. In the working class this is not the case. The
wife can have no responsibility for gaining status for her family
but she has a great deal of responsibility for maintaining its
status and can be responsible for its downfall into the non
respectable "slum class".' (Littlejohn 1963:123)

He goes on to argue that the often quoted differences between
'rough' and 'respectable' working class — bare boards versus
cloth, china versus enamel, cooked meals, clean clothes, lack of
debt to salesmen — are all part of the *household* and therefore
female economy. It is true that women's skills at housework and
the like are portable — they can be carried across social class — but
only at one point of time — marriage. Once that is decided there is
no further possibility. Men's skills are perhaps sometimes more
diverse — but even a very good shepherd cannot by that token
become a farmer — although he may earn esteem over a wide area.
Littlejohn sees a main sex difference being between women's search
for status and men's for esteem. The former is derived from a
choice (more or less forced) of on whom to be dependent; the latter
is measured in the market place by the quality and sale price of
commodities produced. The woman pays for her dependence with
subordination, especially in the Westrigg working class. 'He refers
to her as "she" or "the wife", and she refers to him as "my man" or
"the man" and sometimes "he"' (1963:127). The fact that
Littlejohn regards this as aptly indicating the distance between the
sexes is perhaps worthy of more prolonged linguistic analysis!
However his other evidence is more internal — the censuring of
women by their husbands in front of the children and the facts that:

'Visitors in a working class house are usually offered the fireside chair the wife normally occupies while the husband stays put in his. If other men are in the house, the wife must either remain silent or join in the men's conversation which always centres around male topics particularly work, sport, politics or personal history.' (127)

Littlejohn argues that these differences are less marked in middle and upper middle-class families, amongst the young, and at later periods in history. In this he provides evidence for Young and Willmott's Principle of Stratified Diffusion, although I would wish to re-analyse Littlejohn's and similar material beginning with the question: what are the production relations that working-class and middle-class women are involved in — within and outside the family? Working-class *mothers* are perhaps producing workers and esteem for and through their children. Middle-class *wives* are producing esteem to confirm their husband's status. Opening the door for the wife to pass through, holding her chair, and permitting her to initiate conversation may be forms of conspicuous consumption; an indication by husbands that they can afford to relax the total subordination that the mere reproduction of labour power imposes on those of lower status.

A Welsh village without employment

In 1957 I published a report on my own fieldwork *Village on the Border* — a study of a village in which the production of commodities takes place for the most part elsewhere. The village produces children (for part of the time, they go away to school at eleven plus — a form of alienation that women resist) and prestige. I was then clear that I was writing about a sector of society in which women dominated because most of the time the men were not there. The choice of such a field of study was not coincidental — the research had started out to be a study of the West Indian (adult male deprived) family. The attempt to provide a Marxist analysis of this to counter both Herskovits (1941) and Henriques (1953) was frustrated by rapid deportation from the West Indies as a bad security risk. The principality of Wales was more hospitable (or had less legal power) than the Governors of Barbados and the Windward Islands.

The social and economic consequences of a Welsh village without paid work (except across the border in England) fell most sharply on the women who remained. For the most part they were married. The unmarried women and girls were exiled in domestic or health service slavery abroad in Liverpoool. Neither in 1957 nor in

1966 did I analyse the relationship between domestic dependence and village independence. Had I done so I might have commented on the lack of women as officials of village societies despite their informal leadership, and I might then have provided a more convincing analysis of both this and the defeat of the women's parish council candidate (1966:96-97 and 101). I did however suggest that there were, 'except for a period of courtship and early marriage', in effect two villages — one of women and one of men — which rarely mingled. I argued that women in this situation acted as a corporate group. I failed also to see the irony of my statement 'Glyn people are strongly egalitarian in outlook. Among themselves they consider every *man* is every bit as good as the next' (new italics).

I saw the apparently trivial division of opinion about the running of the football club as a microcosmic symbolic playing-out of sex roles in a society in which the total dependence of women, domestically, was made incomplete by the partial inability of men to earn their living. This was implicit, even perhaps cunningly concealed, but it was intended to be there as the West Indian background of the study shows.

> 'A village as small as Glynceiriog does not have enough talent to field an entirely local team that is capable of meeting and defeating those of a larger or less scrupulous village. The committee therefore had to decide whether it wanted a local team which would provide active recreation for village [male] youth, or a team including mainly outsiders which would maintain village prestige externally by its successes in the league. This was the chronic dilemma which also underlines the division between the interests of men and women in this situation. The women were organised into a supporters' club whose functions were to organise fund-raising whist drives, dances and other entertainments which the division of sex roles in Glyn precludes men from doing. Their interest was partly in doing these things for their own sake, and partly in seeing that the men did their reciprocal part in attending the social occasions organised. As far as the football itself was concerned, although they wanted the team to win, they also wanted to see and applaud their own sons and husbands in the action of winning.' (1966:103)

I would now criticize this passage and the analysis in general for failing to see that the independence of women is only being asserted through their simultaneous dependence as the last line quoted implied. This is further emphasized by the nature of the recreational tasks (sewing, making cakes) that they perform. Although (as Jane Fonda demonstrates in *Klute* and in *Steelyard Blues*) independent dependence may well be the first step to independent independence, I did not (either in 1957 or 1966) see the significance for the understanding of this dependence, of the replacement of the football team by a carnival built round a beauty queen, as Women's Liberation has now educated me to do.

Coal is whose life?

Coal is Our Life (1956), a study of the life in a Yorkshire mining village, had the benefit of an avowed Marxist amongst its authors in Cliff Slaughter, and the description of the production relations that determine the outline structure of a Yorkshire miners' life would be difficult to improve on (Chapter 2). But as Henriques points out in his introduction to the second edition (1969:9)

> 'When we described the many ways in which women were oppressed by the relationships imposed by the miner's work and dependence on wages we met the same kind of criticism. [i.e. a somewhat morbid preoccupation with the miner's past]. He continues 'Perhaps one statistic will serve to illustrate the effect of the kind of factors which we described in 1956: in 1969 the chance of a working-class girl entering university is one in 600'.

Quite so! I drew attention in 1966 (245) to Young and Willmott's criticism.

> 'Even though we may think the accounts overdrawn, and distrust the representativeness of the families they describe, we cannot ignore the historical evidence, all the more so since the notion still survives that the working class man is a sort of absentee husband, sharing with his wife neither responsibility nor affection, partner only of the bed. Such a view is in the tradition of research into working class family life.' (Young and Willmott 1957:19)

I do not think this gloomy picture accurately reflects *Coal is our Life* but it is not in any case the criticism that I would wish to make. The point is a major one to be directed not merely against Dennis, Henriques, and Slaughter but against the Left at large. The relations of production at work are lovingly and loathingly described; the relations of production in the home and community are ignored with equal determination.

The weakness of *Coal is Our Life* is not that it overdoes the oppression, but that it fails to take account of all of the fighting back at home or in the community at large. Indeed it even ignores its own evidence. The Yorkshire Miner of 1956 is seen and described as seeing in women only object and enemy — a passive object for the support of whom he is driven to unpleasant underground work. But the authors themselves see her in the same way: they accept their own miners' eye view.

I tried to make this point as far as the community is concerned when I wrote:

'The only voluntary association in which women participate fully in Ashton is the Women's section of the Labour Party, which has a hundred members. This meets fortnightly and draws twenty to forty middle-aged and elderly women to each meeting. Although its activities are mainly social, its core members are also the leading lights of Ashton Ladies Labour Choir; its activities have resulted in the election of two women district councillors. The Labour Party women's section is preoccupied with social activities which are tolerated by the men because men regard them as the sort of frivolities appropriate to women. Neverthe-less behind the facade, it seems to me possible that even in Ashton women are moving into a position where they will acquire the sort of importance in decision-making in the community which they have elsewhere. A comparative study of the linked question of the role of women and of clubs and welfare institutes in the various coalfields of Britain would be of great interest:' (1966:138)

Two comments come to mind. One is that Young and Willmott do not have a monopoly of facile optimistic liberalism. Second, that such a study as is suggested might well reveal that bingo is not the unimportant mindlessness that even women intellectuals dismiss it as being. It may be the thin edge of a thick wedge — asserting not only a right to share the gambling interests of the men, but also the right to a night out of the house, and to spend money as one pleases.

My criticisms of *Coal is Our Life* are now in fact twenty years old. I wrote them in a letter to one of the authors on seeing the typescript in 1954 — and his reply, while accepting the validity of the argument, sticks to a Yorkshire mining puritanical dismissal of trivial women's activity. He was also unwilling to accept at that time that the patterns of 'Callin' — visits for gossip — led to 'the formation of corporate activities or ideology, any more than *all* kinship relations do in primitive soceites'. Had either of us seen the question in terms of the industrial sociology of child rearing we might have distinguished what made some kinship or quasi-kinship relations more important than others.

Another observer of 'Ashton' at this time (and it is said of Cliff Slaughter too) was Clancy Sigal, whose book *Weekend in Dinlock* attracted the attention in *New Left Review* of both John Rex (1960:42-43), who taped a discussion with miners and their wives about it, and myself as South Wales Miners' Education Officer (Frankenberg 1960). Sigal, with non-sociological, literary, and American lack of reticence, suggests indirectly that women within the home revenged themselves in other ways — by retiring into a secret world with their sisters (and mothers) and by taking lovers. A hint by Henriques to this effect had caused him and Leeds University to be pilloried in the executive of the Yorkshire Miners Association and in the Yorkshire press. In fact in his (pre-Lessing?) male chauvinist (?) obsession with 'erotic leers', Sigal sees them as being taken rather than taking. I quoted:

"The women, and the lives they lead, what they talk about and think about, are still an impenetrable mystery. As soon as I touch on one of the thousand rawly sensitive subjects coveted and nourished by Dinlock females Loretta clams up; when I mention as lightly as possible family matters, she burrows as far back into herself as politeness allows, and further questions are useless. You LSE firsts in sociology, come on up here and find out what these women are thinking. Where are you?"' (1960:65)

and commented,

'Sociologists, even from LSE are surely interested in what people do and how they behave. It's a wise man or a psychologist who knows the thoughts that father his own actions, let alone those of the women of Dinlock.'

The assumption of both writers seems to be that LSE firsts are male — and they perhaps also share an awareness that the taboos on what sociologists can write condemn them to dullness, which when uninformed by theoretical understanding is doubly uninteresting.

One linked set of facts that does emerge clearly from *Coal is Our Life* is the contradiction implicit in the responsibility for child rearing and housekeeping — which in the depression made growing men and women dependent on their mothers rather than their fathers and engendered a loyalty that finds its most extreme form in the story of the three girls who beat up their father when he brought home a mistress. Sex solidarity works both ways.

Secondly, there is the impossibility for most Ashton women of escaping from dependence within the home — there were in 1951-2 196 jobs in Ashton for 4,826 women between the ages of fifteen and sixty-five. The prospects of paid work outside the home but within Ashton were decidedly poor.

The responsibility of women for housekeeping and childcaring, the solidarity of the male peer group reinforced by shared work hazards, shared pit language, shared clubs and shared interest in Rugby League, led to a situation in which men reacted to exploitation by fighting not as a class against capitalism, but as a gender group against women — or rather within a framework of sex solidarity against a specific woman chosen and caged for this express purpose. Ashton provides a magnifying and perhaps overdistorted model to use in the study of town-based communities elsewhere. At least in Ashton, however, women themselves show a sex solidarity, with which on the one hand they fight back, and which on the other enhances and reinforces the solidarity of the men.

Small towns: Glossop and Banbury

Studies of small towns are rarer in Britain than in the United States. It is perhaps unsurprising that the study of Glossop by Birch and his associates (1959) should, with the title *Small Town Politics*, say little about the position of women. It is clearly a significant omission, since they do reveal that more girls than boys stay in Glossop, that women's clubs — the Towns-Women's Guild and the Women's Institute — are the only ones with cross-class (or perhaps more properly cross-status group) membership and that there are four persons described as housewives on the magistrates bench. They do note about membership of the Conservative Party.

'The most striking characteristics of the members, as a group, are the paucity of women, not more than one-sixth of the total, and the large number of Anglicans. Only about a third of the members are not either active or nominal churchmen. The small number of women may be attributed to internal feuds, but it is much more obviously accounted for by the predominantly masculine character of the Conservative Club. The Anglican majority is not surprising in view of the history of the party in the town' (1959:50-51);

and again

> 'The Labour Party has thus been considerably more successful in attracting women members than the Conservative Party, less than a fifth of whose members are women, but not as successful as the Liberal Party, in which the sexes are about equally represented.' (1959:66)

Women are here seen to have a curiously moth-like quality of being 'attracted' somewhat passively to the Party whose light burns the brightest.

There is a Women's Liberal Association in Glossop which had on its rolls at the time of the study 220 people. But the authors point out that this like other Liberal Associations in the town

> 'tend to keep on their rolls any name that has once been entered on them as long as the person concerned remains a resident or (in the case of a man undergoing national service) connected with the town, and continues to show even a slight interest in the party — an interest which need not extend to the payment of a membership fee.' (1959:55)

The Liberal Association had a political talk 'either directly related to Liberalism or on a topic of general interest. Speeches on Liberal policy take their place alongside talks on such subjects as the British system of government, racial problems in Africa, or the place of women in public life' (1959:59).

Clearly in Birch's book, as in Glossop Liberal Party, the place of women is one of many eclectic specks. Margaret Stacey's study of Banbury in *Tradition and Change* (1960) is of course quite different, although it should be remembered that she was, especially in the discussion of the family, editing and interpreting material collected by others. I ended my chapter on Banbury by saying 'No-one in Banbury doubts that they live in a class society. Banburians only differ in whether or not they accept the situation' (Frankenberg 1966:173). The lines of sex division are equally clear, and Stacey is clear about the mechanism that brings them about. I summarized her account:

> 'Few married women work for wages outside the home in Banbury. When they do it is often as secretaries or teachers — jobs in which they remain in the traditional female roles of help-mate to men or in charge of children. Most Banbury women are housewives only, and of them it is true that a wife cannot resign from her work without breaking from her husband and children, nor can she leave her husband without losing her job. Her

occupation is rightly returned as "married woman". *This is a unique status in a society otherwise based on individual contract, specialisation, and separation of function.*' (Stacey 1960:136. Italics added in Frankenberg 1966:161)

I then concluded, 'the norms of the married women's social life lag behind' and rapidly returned to my major interest in class and status, modified by considerations local and cosmopolitan. Stacey, however, albeit implicitly and ahead of her time, applies the theoretical approach that I am now advocating.

'Therefore it is not perhaps surprising that women, compared with men, tend to show group characteristics regardless of other social factors like class. Their training from childhood sets them apart from boys and together as potential wives and mothers. A concept of what is appropriate to the female runs from the nursery through education to employment. The girls are sent more often to private schools and less often have higher education. They hold less responsible posts than men when they are in paid employment (those in occupational status 1 in Banbury can be counted on the fingers of one hand) and of the more responsible posts they do hold, the more important ones, e.g. secretaries and school teachers, are associated with their traditional status, as helpmates to men or in charge of children. When they work in industry they do the cleaner, lighter jobs.

Work for women being looked upon as filling in time before marriage or as an unfortunate necessity in a bad or broken marriage, it is the wife-mother role that stamps women's attitudes above other sectional interests. The role of keeping the family together spills over into their attitudes in wider fields, for they have been shown in previous chapters to be more traditional on balance than men. They are more religious and more conservative in politics. Maintenance of the institution of the family apparently leads them to show more concern about maintaining established institutions generally.' (Stacey 1960:136)

One could adapt Althusser's view on intellectuals and workers substituting men and women proletarians of the home, even without making the assumption that women are a class.

'Class instinct is subjective and spontaneous. Class position is objective and rational. To arrive at proletarian class positions, the class instinct of proletarians only needs to be *educated*, the class instinct of the petty bourgeoisie, and hence of intellectuals, has, on the contrary, to be revolutionised. This education and

this revolution are, in the best analysis, determined by proletarian class struggle on the basis of the principles of Marxist
Leninist theory.' (Althusser 1971:16-17)

Stacey, then, took easily to this education provided by life and the
data collected by Cyril Smith.

However, despite this and her recognition of the necessity of kin
and neighbour co-operation in productive and reproductive crises,
like myself in 1966, her main concern was with the categories of
class and status, traditional and non-traditional. The group
characteristics she quotes are not used analytically in order to
understand Banbury as a whole, only that section of Banbury —
women — which holds them. Perhaps the forthcoming re-study will
redress the balance.

Bethnal Green and Mum

I must turn now to the studies that put working-class mums on the
middle-class map. The Institute of Community Studies in Bethnal
Green did for sociologically-minded social workers what John
Bowlby had done for their psychoanalytically-oriented predeces-
sors, and concern with the Virgin Mary for their religious
ancestors.

The arguments of Young and Willmott (1957) and above all most
cogently Townsend (1957) are too familiar to need exposition here.
They have been critically examined in Platt (1971) and uncritically
in most 0-level, A-level, and degree examinations for some years.

Here I reiterate some aspects of their context, neglect of which
has led Young and Willmott since then along less convincing paths.
These are, as I have already stressed, that: (a) the family is a
productive system in which the work of producing and socializing
ideologically (Hunt and Hunt 1974) the commodity of labour
power (Secombe 1974) is carried out by women, under the direction
of, and dependent on, men and the financing they supply; (b) that
this financing is inadequate and is supplemented either by co-
operation amongst the workers — the mother-daughter tie — and
mutual aid by sisters of both kinds, biological and social, or by the
women entering, not instead but as well, into the wider productive
system. Nineteen of the forty-five wives in Young and Willmott's
marriage sample, all of whom had young children, were in paid
employment, inside or outside the home — the putting out system is
not dead (cf. Macciochi 1973 and Hope, *et al.* in the companion
volume); (c) that the family as a productive unit, although it has
become more capital intensive, has become less co-operative. While

the production of most commodities takes place in larger and larger production units, the production of labour power has become individuated. The housing-estate where elementary families, as Bell suggested (1968:147), in one respect ironically resemble Marx's nineteenth century 'sack of potatoes' French peasants, is the culmination of the process.

> 'The small holding peasants form a vast mass, the members of which live in similar conditions but without entering into manifold relations with one another. Their mode of production isolates them from one another instead of bringing them into mutual intercourse ... Their field of production, the small holding, admits of no division of labour in its cultivation, no application of science and, therefore no diversity of development, no variety of talent, no wealth of social relationships.'
> (Marx 1885)

Housing Estates

The study of housing estates, from Durant's account of Watling (1939) onwards, suggests this tendency towards individuation of the elementary family unit. Durant fully recognizes that by changing their place of residence women also changed their place of work, both as housewives and in the 1930s as a reserve of cheap labour for the suburban, tube-railway equivalent of the South Wales 'Doll's Eye Factory'. The ascriptive kin-based 'trade union of women' described by Young and Willmott for the East End disappeared and there was an attempt to recreate it in Watling by the formation of voluntary associations. These associations only took on life and became wider in scale when Watling estate was attacked and criticized by the inhabitants of the established village. This brought in the men, for in the housing estate home it is the women who have the instrumental and men the expressive roles. It is, however, true that while women predominated among office holders, they were not a random or representative group. They were not drawn from the poor, the ill, or the overworked — and they had neither large families nor full-time jobs (Frankenberg 1966:211, summarizing Durant 1939).

Housing estate studies that have followed Durant have confirmed her findings.

> 'Now I shall consider the theme that the Englishwoman's home is her factory. The housing estate very often cuts married women off from outside paid work and hence from their contact with the

wider world. Thus, in the traditional housing area of St Ebbes in Central Oxford (Mogey, 1956) thirty householders yielded twenty-two working wives and five retired from paid employment. In the new housing estate which Mogey compared with it there were only twelve working wives in thirty households ... a move to a housing estate for a woman may mean being cut off from her kin, from her mother, and from her work. Each of these presents a narrowing of the scale of social relationships.' (Frankenberg 1966:225)

and later ...

'All this has a profound effect on the relationships of men and women. In Bethnal Green there was a community of women which was almost self-sufficient. Men, except the retired, were cut off from it by their daily exile at work. When they came home the women included them in the community by passing on gossip. In Greenleigh it is the women's work of raising children and keeping house which cuts them off. This activity which was a "factory industry" in Bethnal Green has become a cottage industry in Greenleigh. Like all cottage industries child rearing and home building tend to encompass all the family. The man is drawn in as well. Here is the mechanism of changing networks, changing roles in action. Men spend more time doing jobs in the house and garden and watching telly than they do in the pub and at the football ground. (229)

I developed Mogey's suggestion that women in new housing estates were unwilling to be identified with any group or to enter into relationships which might impose reciprocal obligations. The Irish farmer and his wife and the housing estate family are at opposite poles. Men and women in rural Ireland were willing and indeed unable to avoid, even by emigration, far-reaching social obligations with their peers: they were equally determined to avoid commercial contacts with companies or suppliers other than those who represented in the town the same social stratum as they did in the country. I would now emphasize that these relationships were, although the participants appeared unaware of it, firmly embedded in contractual impersonal relationships with English capitalism. By contrast the housing estate housewife is ultra-cautious in her dealings with neighbours, but often an easy prey for the impersonal, commercial nexus with hire purchase company or mail order house. A coffee morning organized by Tupperware or Avon may be acceptable whereas pure sociability is not.

The difference perhaps lies in the certainty of expectations in the

former; the uncertainty in the latter. It was this uncertainty about
the 'correct' reaction which I saw as a major dimension of the
social isolation which the housewife suffers.

Young and Willmott bring this out clearly in Greenleigh. I
summarized as follows:

'Although active interaction with neighbours is at a minimum,
their presence is felt. They are perceived as watchful eyes looking
for faults in the housewife's craftsmanship as a wife, housekeeper, and mother. The husband's job, often far removed from
the estate, is no longer the main criterion of status. A family is
judged by the appearance and affluence of her home and her
children's appearance. The standards to which the neighbours
are thought to impel one are paradoxically not local but national
— the standards of the women's magazines, newspaper, and
television commercials.

Consumer goods are acquired because they are useful and
because others have them. Some, like cars and telephones, are a
means of retaining contact with the old way of life in the context
of the new. Visiting sisters on other housing estates may only be
possible by car. Urban public transport tends to go from periphery
to centre rather than linking places on the periphery.

I have suggested ... that conflict within consensus is an
essential part of community. In Bethnal Green I described the
friendly rivalry between streets and sub-districts. In Greenleigh
the only possible basis for such unity creating conflict are the
nuclear families in their "little boxes". As Young and Willmott
suggest, relationships are often window-to-window rather than
face-to-face (1957:163). The neighbours are ubiquitous but
anonymous.

Though people stay in their houses, they do in a sense belong
to a strong and compelling group. They do not know their judge
personally but her influence is continuously felt. One might even
suggest, to generalize, that the less the personal respect received
in small group relationships, the greater is the striving for the
kind of impersonal respect embodied in a status judgement. The
lonely man, fearing he is looked down on, becomes the
acquisitive man: possession the balm of anxiety; anxiety the spur
to unfriendliness.' (Young and Willmott 1957:164 quoted in
Frankenberg 1966:231-2)

I have already commented on the use of 'man' by Young and
Willmott in this passage. I would now wish not to abandon this
analysis entirely but to put it more sharply into context.

The future — demographic change and social action

Rising political consciousness amongst women perhaps goes some way to stifle the pessimistic wail on which I ended in 1966: 'Must life become poorer as it becomes richer?' I would not however go so far as to accept the over-optimism of Young and Willmott (1973) who see a bright future in the technologically re-united, durable, consuming unit of consumer durables — the companionate family. This problem seems to me to have two keys. The first derives from Rosser and Harris (1965), Bell (1968), and ultimately McGregor and Rowntree (1962), and Titmuss (1958) and lies in the harsh facts of demographic change. The second derives from the increasing possibility of social action, not in the Parsonian but in the collective committed sense (rent strikes, squatting etc). A major weakness of all the studies I have discussed was the lack of commitment of their godlike authors. They observed, they commented, occasionally they advised; never did they participate in a real active sense.

To consider the demographic point first; Rosser and Harris in particular refer to 'the revolution which has taken place in the position and roles of women'. These changes (essentially demographic) can be summarized by saying that women can expect to live longer, and to spend a much shorter period of time 'concerned with childbearing and maternal care in infancy'. In discussing Myrdal and Klein (1956), Rosser and Harris point out that the functions of the family, whoever fulfills them, are not confined to the care of children. The care of the aged and infirm is also (in our terms) part of the familial productive processes. What they do not point out is that a change in the facts of life (vital statistics) do not necessarily and automatically lead to a change in the facts of life (social interaction). Nor does a mysterious Principle of Stratified Diffusion. Demographic change may be a necessary, but not a sufficient cause. The nature of social interaction changes when individuals or groups decide to change it, and set about dong so, overcoming the opposition of other individuals and groups. This requires both consciousness and theoretical understanding. The housing estate little box may provide the beginnings of consciousness (as Betty Friedan (1963) suggests), despite the barriers to communication which it also offers. The debate about theoretical understanding (in which I have found Hunt and Hunt (1974), Secombe (1974), and Gardner (in the companion volume) most recently stimulating) to which this paper is intended to be a contribution, neither begins nor ends here. Nor can it be seen in isolation from the actions people themselves like to bring about personal and social change.

The crucial theoretical issue, however, is whether emancipation in the fields of sex and gender in the family, in industry, and in general social life can be achieved independently of a general emancipation which only the destruction of capitalist social relations would make possible. I choose my words carefully — I write 'make possible' not 'bring about'. I hope I have gone beyond my own earlier well meaning unclarities and the near-sighted futurology if not blind optimism of what in the United States would be called liberal sociology.

I believe that sexual differences and our particular form of family are an integral part of a particular social formation dominated by the capitalist mode of production. If I am correct it should nevertheless not be taken to mean that sociologists can, with a sigh of relief, return to class, let alone status, as the sole driving mechanism of society; still less can they return to micro studies of the family and kinship torn from context, and popular criticism.

Women as a group, like Blacks in the recent past and workers in the recent future, have begun to answer the sociologists back; to claim the right not to be inferior objects of study, but equal subjects of dialogue. The future of sociology does not lie either in arid mechanical determinisms, nor in reflexive navel contemplating, but, in my view, precisely in the dialectics of a dialogue that unites theory and practice, students and subjects of study. This is at the basis of our present methodological disputes. Despite the philistine question of a senior sociological colleague recently 'what understanding of society could Mao Tsetung get from talking to peasants', it seems to me that for sociologists, like infants, 'listen and learn' is still a good motto. It is the theoretical understanding of what one hears that provides not a conclusion to, but the basis for, the sociological side of the dialogue. I hope that what I have heard and read since 1966 has improved the theoretical understanding of this paper, itself improved by discussion at the BSA conference at Aberdeen. I am sure that in future people will go on talking sufficiently loudly to ensure that professional sociologists like myself can still hear them even over the sound of our own voices.

References

Althusser, 1971. Philosophy as a Revolutionary Weapon. In *Lenin and Philosophy*. London: New Left Books.

Arensberg, C.M. 1961. The Community as Object and as Sample. *American Anthropologist 63* (2):241-264. Pt. 1. April.

Arensberg, C.M. and Kimball, S.T. 1940. *Family and Community in Ireland*. London: Peter Smith.

Bell, C. 1968. *Middle Class Families*. London: Routledge & Kegan *American Anthropologist 63* (2):241-264. Pt. 1. April.

Bell, 1968. *Middle Class Families*. London: Routledge & Kegan Paul.

Bell, C. and Newby, H. 1971. *Community Studies*. London: Allen and Unwin.

Birch, A.N. 1959. *Small Town Politics: A Study of Political Life in Glossop*. Oxford: Oxford University Press.

Coulson, M. and Riddell, D. 1970. *Approaching Sociology: A Critical Introduction*. Students Library of Sociology. London: Routledge & Kegan Paul.

Dennis, N., Henriques, F., and Slaughter, C. 1956. *Coal is our Life*. London: Eyre and Spottiswood. Second edition with new introduction by Henriques, 1969. London: Tavistock.

Durant, R. 1939. *Watling: A Survey of Social Life on a New Housing Estate*. London: P.S. King.

Frankenberg, R. 1957. *Village on the Border*. London: Cohen and West.

— 1960. First Thoughts on Dinlock. *New Left Review* No. 2:65 March/April.

— 1966. *Communities in Britain*. Harmondsworth: Penguin Books.

Friedan, B. 1965. *The Feminine Mystique*. Harmondsworth: Penguin Books.

Gardner, J. forthcoming. Political Economy of Domestic Labour in Capitalist Society. In D. Leonard Barker and S. Allen (eds.), *Dependence and Exploitation in Work and Marriage.* Harlow: Longman.

Henriques, F. M. 1953. *Family and Colour in Jamaica*. London: Eyre and Spottiswoode.

— 1969. Introduction. In *Coal is Our Life* (2nd edn). London: Tavistock Publications.

Herskovits, J. 1941. *The Myth of the Negro Past*. New York.

Hope, E. 1976. Homeworkers in North London. In D. Leonard Barker and S. Allen (eds.) *Dependence and Exploitation in*

Work and Marriage. Harlow: Longman.

Hunt, J. and Hunt, A. 1974. Marxism and the Family. *Marxism Today* February: 59-64.

Lenin V.I. 1894. *What the 'Friends of the People' Are and How They Fight the Social Democrats*. Moscow: Progress Publishers (1970).

Littlejohn, J. 1963. *Westrigg: The Sociology of a Cheviot Parish*. London: Routledge & Kegan Paul.

Macciochi. M.-A. 1973. *Letters from Inside the Italian Communist Party to Louis Althusser*. London: New Left Books.

McGregor, O.R. and Rowntree, G. 1962. The Family In A.T. Welford *et al. Society: Problems and Methods of Study*. London: Routledge & Kegan Paul.

Marx, K. 1885. *The 18th Brumaire of Louis Bonaparte* in *Marx and Engels Selected Works*. Edition 1970 (one volume). London: Lawrence and Wishart.

Mogey, J.M. 1956. *Family and Neighbourhood: Two studies in Oxford*. Oxford: Oxford University Press.

Myrdal, A. and Klein, V. 1956. *Women's Two Roles*. London: Routledge and Kegan Paul.

Peters, E.L. 1972. Aspects of the control of moral ambiguities: A comparative analysis of two culturally disparate modes of social control. In M. Gluckman (ed.), *The Allocation of Responsibility*. Manchester: Manchester U.P.

Platt, J. 1971. *Social Research in Bethnal Green*. London: Macmillan.

Rees, A.D. 1950. *Life in a Welsh Countryside*. Cardiff: University of Wales Press.

Rex, J. 1960. *Weekend in Dinlock* : a discussion. *New Left Review* No. 3:42-45 May/June.

Rosser, C. and Harris, C.C. 1965. *The Family and Social Change: A Study of Family and Kinship in a South Wales Town* London: Routledge & Kegan Paul.

Secombe, W. 1974. Housework under Capitalism. *New Left Review* 83:3-24. January-February.

Sigal, C. 1962. Weekend in Dinlock: Harmondsworth: Penguin.

Stacey, M. 1960. *Tradition and Change: A study of Banbury*. Oxford: Oxford University Press.

— 1969. The Myth of Community Studies. *British Journal of Sociology* xx (2): 178-192. June.

Sullerot, E. 1971. *Woman, Society and Change*. World University Library. London: Weidenfeld and Nicolson.

Thompson, E.P. 1963. *The Making of the English Working Class*.

London: Gollancz (Penguin edition 1968).

Titmuss, R.M. 1958. The Position of Women. In *Essays on the Welfare State*. London: George Allen and Unwin.

Townsend, P. 1957. *The Family Life of Old People*. London: Routledge & Kegan Paul (Penguin edition 1963).

Williams, W.M. 1956. *The Sociology of an English Village: Gosforth*. London: Routledge and Kegan Paul.

Willmott, P. and Young, M. 1960. *Family and Class in a London Suburb*. London: Routledge & Kegan Paul.

Young, M. and Willmott, P. 1957. *Family and Kinship in East London*. London: Routledge & Kegan Paul (Penguin edition 1962).

— 1973. *The Symmetrical Family: A Study of Work and Leisure in the London Region*. London: Routledge & Kegan Paul.

VANESSA MAHER

Kin, Clients, and Accomplices: Relationships among Women in Morocco

This paper will deal with instrumental relationships among women mainly in Morocco, but also in other Mediterranean areas. My primary aim is to provide evidence that such relationships exist, contrary to the Parsonian dictum that women's roles are mainly 'expressive', and to that of a Moroccan acquaintance who claimed, 'Women are made for love'. Yet even to those of us who are not taken in by such ideology, it is difficult to think of relationships *among women* as being instrumental or to imagine what political or economic repercussions they might have, for our interest in them has generally been limited to the mother-in-law problem or the functions of gossip. I shall show, however, that relationships among women carry considerable weight in Moroccan society.

In the second part of the paper I will try to analyse the ways in which the specific forms these relationships take, and the structures they compose, affect socio-political developments on the national scale. Although this study is strictly regional, it may provide insight into a broader range of social situations than the one I describe. Particularly where there is an impoverished rural semi-proletariat with a high rate of migration, on the one hand, and on the other a strict segregation of sex-roles such that women are subordinate in political and economic terms to men but retain rights in their family of origin, we may find an 'informal structure' of instrumental relationships among women, for example in parts of North Africa and the Middle East. In parts of Southern Europe we find similar instrumentality but exercised within the family of procreation.[1]

The 'Woman Network'

Moroccan women engage in a series of relationships with other women which assure to them and their children the minimum requirements for life and help in crises, whether such crises are of a social or an economic kind. I will refer to the connections so established as the 'woman network'. Such association is typical of any politically deprived social group, whether they are migrants in West African towns or ethnic and religious minorities in Britain. Since these groups are socially stratified, some members may get more out of these contacts than others, satisfying more complex cultural wants, such as the desire for power and prestige; or they may even provide themselves with a docile and dependent labour force, exploiting the ethic of mutual loyalty that binds the members of the group. And so it is among women.

The 'woman network' is not some hypothetical web that links all Moroccan women in mysterious solidarity, but an institution like 'kinship' or 'marriage' that affects the life of every Moroccan woman. It is a response to several factors that condition the lives of most of them.

Chief of these are their. lack of economic autonomy and the segregation of women's activities from those of men. In itself the second factor need not be damaging to women, but where there is private property it must give rise to the oppression of women by men. In Morocco, the public sphere, that of legal and commercial transactions, wage work and political affairs, is reserved for men. Women should occupy themselves with domestic matters and the care of children. For most townswomen and the wives of rural 'notables' this means a life of severe seclusion, with occasional visits to the Turkish baths, or to the houses of kinswomen — the latter a privilege of older women. Rural women, however, must take care of the animals and work in the fields, so that they cannot live in seclusion, and whereas the only men a townswoman should talk to are her husband and close kinsmen, a rural woman lives among men whom she calls her paternal cousins, whom she may greet and pass the time of day with, even if she should not receive them in the absence of her husband.

The economic background

Yet it is considered just as shameful for rural women as for townswomen to work for wages where there are 'stranger men', and there are few places of work where there are only women. Further, women should not buy or sell, and indeed they conform closely to the ideal in the latter case. So women tend to have only mediated access to the market economy, which, together with its companion, secular education, has considerably modified their social environment in such a way as to place at a severe disadvantage those groups that are unable to operate its terms to their own benefit. Although we are concerned here with women, we could cite rural small-holders or the populations of shanty-towns as examples of the chronic loser in the face of advancing capitalism.

Both colonization and the development of foreign and local capital have contributed to this situation. The French, by seizing extensive tracts of pastureland put an end to transhumant pastoralism in southern Morocco. By introducing the registration of land, they opened the way to the expropriation of illiterate peasants by powerful notables. By imposing taxes they exacerbated the difficulties of many Moroccan households, who already had to deal with the impossibility of producing many consumer goods at home (such as woollen clothing) and of deriving a living from their miserable land-holdings. The scarcity was answered only by a flood of French products and Moroccans were forced to seek paid work. The French promoted migration by recruiting Moroccans to fight in both World Wars and in Indochina, as well as employing them in mines and factories at home and abroad.

Finally, the colonial practice of rewarding Moroccan collaborators with land and capital stocks paved the way to the formation of a ruling class hopelessly entangled with the imperatives of international capitalism, one of which is a continuous supply of cheap labour; and to the construction of a state machine which often fails to operate in the best interests of the mass of Moroccans. So the flow of migrants continues.

Having hinted at the convulsions of history, I wish before passing to the discussion of relations among women to stress three major aspects of their present-day economic environment. First, there is the economic non-viability of most peasant households in Morocco. For these households with less than twenty hectares (77 per cent of all land-owning households) the average area under cultivation is 2.7 hectares; this is without taking into account the 80,000 rural households that cultivate no land at all (Villeneuve 1971:90).

Second, there exists the phenomenon of mass migration to the cities. The urban population has increased five times between 1930 and 1964 although it is still only 30 per cent of the total. Of urban household heads, 60 per cent were not born in the town in which they live (Résultats de l'Enquête à Objectifs Multiples, 1964: 135-141, Section D).

Third, the presence of urbanization without industrialization means widespread and chronic unemployment and the mushrooming of shanty-towns. In 1960 20 per cent of Moroccan men between the ages of twenty and sixty were unemployed, and the urban proportion was higher (Résultats du Recensement de 1960, Vol.II:177-180).

It seems, therefore, that many men cannot provide for themselves or their families either by staying at home, or by migrating to a Moroccan city, and there are fixed quotas for external emigration. The woman network acts as a buffer against the vicissitudes of the market, and in a minor way it channels the means of subsistence from the richer to the poorer members of kinship-based communities. But women cannot rely on men.

The instability of relationships between men and women

In none of their family roles can men be seen as a reliable source of economic and social support for women. As husbands they may vanish by divorce, for the divorce rate as a percentage of all marriages was between 28 per cent in the towns and 50 per cent among migrants and in rural areas, in the region of the Middle Atlas where I worked (Maher 1974). Husbands may die, for where I worked they were, on average, at least ten years older than their wives, with extremes of thirty years. Since widows without children should not remarry, and those past the menopause are unlikely to in any case, this leaves many women to fend for themselves. In fact the proportion of widows in the female population was 9.3 per cent between 1961-3, and the proportion of divorcees 2.7 per cent. The divorcees are likely to be mainly older women, for younger ones remarry very quickly. The corresponding percentages for men are 1 per cent and 1 per cent, suggesting that men remarry at any age, but also that they die before their wives. (Résultats de l'Enquête à Objectifs Multiples 1964:41). Finally husbands may go away. Until the beginning of the century, they would be away fighting feuds, or visiting distant markets. Now they migrate to the industrial cities of North Morocco, or to Western Europe, or, in the not so distant past, they left to fight the wars of their colonial masters. It is true that the rate of annual migration is much higher for the plains than for the mountain areas with which we will mainly be dealing, and that women leave the countryside nearly as often as men, except when they are over sixty. However the fact remains that emigration from the countryside is estimated at an annual weighted minimum of eighteen per thousand and a maximum of forty per thousand, and that women leave probably as often as widows and divorcees in order to be the dependants of male or female kin in the towns, as with their husbands (Résultats de l'Enquête à Objectifs Multiples

1964:83). In fact, in a town sample I took the majority of collateral or more remote kin staying in town households were women.

Men as fathers, and particular as brothers or sons, are slightly more reliable, but they are logically as likely to migrate as husbands. Further, women marry virilocally, leaving fathers and brothers behind, and they are likely to receive visits from them less often than from their female kin.

Finally, women can expect help from men, neither in their daily tasks nor in pregnancy, illness, or childbirth, for the segregation of men from women in most areas prevents this.

Town and hamlets

My fieldwork was carried out in a series of Berber-speaking hamlets in the Middle Atlas and in the small town, which I will call Akhdar, whose satellites they are. The most distant hamlet is fifteen kms away from the town, the nearest a mere two, but town and hamlets are culturally worlds apart, differentiated by language, social organization, and religious practices. Yet there were migrant groups in the town who shared the culture of the local hamlets, and a few hamlet notables who were integrated into the town in all but residence. Both town and hamlets showed marked economic stratification, and only a tenth of hamlet inhabitants could be said to own enough land to provide for their subsistence needs.

Moroccan towns are Arabic speaking. All political, educational, and legal affairs are conducted in classical Arabic, a fairly close relative of the Moroccan spoken language, but unintelligible to the illiterate. Townsmen adhere to orthodox Maliki Islam and seclude their women. The majority of technical and professional posts in Akhdar are held by Arabic speakers from the more developed north-west and the Marrakesh region, which before the Protectorate formed part of the Makhzen or government controlled area. Joseph writes of the *bled-el-makhzen*: 'a central political body integrated the economy, extracting taxes, channelling production, and supervising trade. The central government ran the economy which, with its large estates, absentee landowners and tax-supported upper class, presented a classical example of an Oriental style of economic integration' (Joseph 1967:109). The Berbers of Akhdar originated in great part from the Central High Atlas and the Tafilalet, the arid region to Akhdar's south, which were part of the dissident, stateless *bled-el-siba*. 'The *bled-el-siba* presents quite another form of political integration and economic organisation' consisting of 'a number of small sub-units, each autonomous from the rest, and each relying only on its own power for maintaining its political integrity and economic well-being' (Joseph 1967:109). (Nevertheless the tribes of *siba* did acknowledge the Sultan as spiritual leader even if they did not accept his temporal government.)

This history of tribal resistance to Makhzen hegemony haunts the relationship between town and country even today, at least in the south of Morocco. Relations between Akhdar and the hamlets are further complicated by the fact that Akhdar was founded by the French as a military outpost, from which they attempted to gain a foot-hold in the hinterland. Today it is a town of 9,000 people, from which is administered a district of 70,000 inhabitants. It is a commercial, educational, and political centre. It provides medical services, US Aid, postal services, and is a recruiting centre for labourers to work in the nearby French owned lead-mines. Clearly the hamlets, in spite of their cultural defences depend on the town quite considerably in economic and social terms, for the town represents participation in the market economy and state institutions.

A successful participant in the market economy needs to be able to manage Arab cultural modes, and in fact most Berbers, including all but elderly women, are bilingual. But language is not enough, and hamlet-dwellers, especially women, use their contacts and classificatory kin in the town to gain access to town facilities. For example, a hamlet woman who needs to go to the hospital will seek out a kinswoman in the town who has a nurse acquaintance, for the nurses control the tickets that allow entry to see a doctor. Or a hamlet woman will obtain goods on credit from a shopkeeper kinsman. I say a kinsman but this may be a fictitious claim on the part of the client, whose relationships outside the home should be limited to those people she calls kin, a category she extends as convenient. However, the reconstitution under the banner of kinship of communities whose members have obligations of mutual support, is a process in which women play a significant part.

Land and the definition of kin

The question which presents itself to any market-minded enquirer is, 'If peasants are so hard up, and jobs so hard to come by, how do they manage not to sell their land?' It is easier to see *why* they do not than how, for land and the community relationships it represents clearly provide a minimum of security against the vacillations of the labour and commodity markets and a guarantee of minimum social satisfactions. It is well known that land and labour are the last items to become commodities in an economy where capitalism has gained a foothold but does not yet prevail over other modes of production. The mechanisms that inhibit their sale are less familiar, and may vary from society to society. Dobb writes of the seventeenth-century proletariat in England, 'Its numbers remained small, and its mobility was restricted both by legal restrictions designed to protect the estates and the larger yeoman farms against the loss of their labour supply, and because so much of the work for wages was done by those who still retained an attachment to the land, even though a slender and precarious one' (Dobb 1963:230). He suggests that the development of cottage industry brought to small land-holders the additional income that allowed them to maintain this 'precarious attachment', thus inhibiting the formation of a mobile labour supply and the growth of factory industry. 'Not until the period of the industrial revolution was this rural semi-proletariat to be finally uprooted from the land and the obstacles to labour mobility from village to town removed' (Dobb 1963:231).

In Morocco, the sale of land was prohibited by the French, but that was twenty-five years ago. Today its alienation is slowed up partly by the customary requirement that a field should be offered to close and classificatory agnates then to friends in the hamlet and hamlet members in general before it can come onto the open market. And the price increases according to the social distance between buyer and seller.

The most important mechanisms against the sale of land, are those that operate through the 'woman network'. These work in three ways. First, the community of putative kin, linked more by their common geographical origin than by real blood ties, is perpetually reconstituted by community-endogamous marriages, which are arranged by women. Adam (1968:739) points out that in a Casablanca shanty town 64 per cent of the men had married a girl from their home region and 33 per cent had married a relative. In one hamlet near Akhdar 78 per cent of hamlet members over three generations had married spouses living less than five kms away, and 22 per cent had married a relative. The community is reinforced by continuous association among its women members, who attend each other's feasts, and, in the case of migrants return to their region of origin to have their children, to attend weddings and funerals, visit mothers, and look for prospective brides for their sons.

Second, patron-client relations within the kinship-based

community, contracted by women, provide for the subsistence needs of the poorer families and supply the extra domestic labour required by the richer families, so that the buying and selling of labour power at exploitative rates is to some extent avoided.

Third, women do not have economic autonomy, but they do have the right to inherit half a male share in their father's patrimony, and an eighth of that of their husband. Since they are so liable to widowhood and divorce, it is important for them to be able to count on at least the usufruct of this land which they leave otherwise in the hands of their male agnates. Uterine kinswomen are closely bound not only emotionally but by their common interest in validating these minimal claims of the female members of a patrilineal kinship group.

To sell property, whether land or houses, would be to resign the benefits of belonging to the community whose foundation is a common interest in property. Thus we find that 80 per cent of a hamlet's houses are owned by their occupiers, that only 40 per cent of town houses are owned by their occupiers and these all belong to southern migrants, and that migrants retain their property interest in the home region when they migrate. In Morocco as a whole, 53 per cent of shanty-town migrants, 34 per cent of those in the *medinas*, and 45 per cent of those in the modern parts of towns possessed rights in fields and houses, or in a single house in their home region (Résultats de l'Enquête à Objectifs Multiples, 1964:135-41).

Patron-client relations among women

The adhesion of hamlet people and town migrants to such a group gives them a special claim on those members who are socially mobile, who have influence and know-how to use on their behalf, and who can offer protection and occasional maintenance in exchange for the services of those who, in effect, are their clients. Often the difference between patron and client is merely a matter of a fixed job. But a job means, more often than not, living in the town and familiarity with commercial and bureaucratic procedures and contacts. The patron-client relation is between women, for there are few services that men can render each other and their meetings tend to depend on chance, for they generally visit each other's homes only by invitation. Yet a man's wife's bounty to her clients derives from him, and he relates directly to some of his wife's clients who treat him in a friendly, mocking way, and may ask his help. Further, their services, especially of mediation with the outside world and other members of the group enables him to seclude his wife more completely, and thereby gain prestige.

Patron-client relations among women, based on the home and depending to some degree on the cultural skills and economic power of men, may be almost as widespread as domestic service. Joyce Riegelhaupt, writing about Portuguese women in a village near Lisbon comments

> 'The people for whom (the village girls) have worked become important links for the *saloio* (rural village) in their interaction with the larger society. As we will see, these are often the people who will provide the all important *conhecimentos* (contacts) that the *saloio*, faced with the various demands of modern society — ranging from a driver's licence to finding a medical specialist — must depend upon. Often the employer of one of a family's daughters finds himself in this role and in later years access to these "patrons" is through the women. Moreover service in middle class or upper class households brings the women into contact with urban life, an experience for which men (full-time cultivators in the village fields, V.M.) have no parallel.' (Riegelhaupt 1967:118)

In Morocco, however, patrons and clients are involved in a series of overlapping networks. One of the migrant networks I knew best consisted of the families of two sets of siblings, some of whom were more prosperous than others, two client families represented by their women members, and three widows. The patron families, except for that of one of the poorer siblings, all lived in Akhdar, but three of the clients came from various hamlets. Not all the clients of a patron family were the clients also of the other families, although most of the patrons and clients knew of each other's existence and background. The patrons, in particular, would attend one another's feasts and keep in touch through the clients who moved between them; but I also knew of several friendships among clients who would visit each other, find each other jobs spinning wool for a common 'putter-out', and could not be said to be in competition for the patrons' favours. Both patrons and clients in the network I mentioned had migrated from the adjacent valleys in the Central High Atlas where they still held land, and where the clients had yet other patrons. Patrons and clients called one another 'sister' or 'mother's sister' according to whether there was a large or a small age difference between the speakers.

A woman client, apart from providing the extra labour resources that a patroness needed to maintain the scale and quality of domestic arrangements proper to a person of her standing and hospitability, enabled her to overcome the restrictions of seclusion, to which the poorer hamlet-dweller was not subject, nor the older widow. The client was able to make purchases for the patron, to convey gifts to her friends, to entertain her, and above all, to act as a node of communication between the various patrons and their clients.

The client, on the other hand, received gifts of clothes, meals for herself and any children she brought with her, invitations to the feasts she helped to prepare, presents of delicacies such as cakes or dates, and the right to ask favours.

A client may ask to borrow large sums of money. In one case it was the price of a radio, in another the deposit on a small gas-stove, in a third, the price of the sheep which every Muslim should kill at the annual feast of Aid-el-Kbir. By providing thus for their needy 'kin', the patron earns the praise and blessings of the entire community. The money is obtained from the patron's salaried husband but it is she who makes the transfer and gains merit in the eyes of her women friends.

Women and the market economy

Because the condition for the formation of this type of relationship is that the patron's husband should have a salaried position, or be a successful trader or artisan with connections among public officials, the patron-client link tends to mediate between the market economy and that economic sphere whose currency is in social relationships. Here people depend on credit, for few have any cash to spend on consumer goods. They are even hard put to it to pay taxes and to buy subsistence goods (such as firewood, sugar, tea, oil) which they cannot produce or obtain from kin. Unstinting hospitality (often paradoxically extended to their creditors) is however a striking feature of this scene.

Since women neither earn nor control property, the possibility of gaining access to the market via the patron-client relations signifies a new level of economic participation which appears to terrify some husbands. One complained that women only wanted enough money to accumulate enough gold to enable them to leave their husbands. Few women nowadays resign themselves to insolvency, even if they must intrigue, lie to their husbands, or sell personal trinkets one by one to other women, in order to invest in the object of their choice.

Yet even if the patron-client relation, based on common origin, may give women access to consumer goods (both poor and rich, for the latter may send the client to buy things rather than subject her purchases to her husband's censorship), it has never, as far as I know, affected social mobility for the client or any member of her family. The social and economic distance between patron and client is too small for the former, a mere clerk or artisan, to achieve anything in the latter's favour. This means that the patron and client always remain, in the absence of great strokes of fortune, in the same respective positions. Yet the relationship is conducted in the idiom of equality. The patron works in the house with her client, calls her 'sister', treats her with respect and affection, accepts on rare occasions her pressing invitations to meals — they are to all intents and purposes close friends.

Exploitative patrons

There are two other kinds of patron-client relations in which necessitous women may be involved. The first is one in which the client seeks help or intervention from a powerful person, a big land-owner, or public official. She calls him her father's brother but he has no reciprocal kinship term, for he wishes to recognize no obligation towards her. He may give her husband a job as labourer on his land, or call on her to help his wife, in exchange for food and clothes. But the relationship is exploitative and humiliating, and those women who resort to activating it can be said to be on the verge of wage-labour. The patron sees it as a short term commitment, useful as long as it lasts. Poncet (1971:199) has reported this kind of casual employment of landless peasants by established land-owners in nineteenth-century Tunisia, and indeed it is as common among men as among women, so I will not dwell on it here.

  More significant for women are those patron-client relations that are contracted within a framework of 'estates'. I use the term 'estate system' to refer to a hierarchy of social categories, differentiated by ritual status. Membership of these estates is by ascription (inherited patrilineally) and they are ideally endogamous but in fact exercise asymmetrical marriage rights. The term 'class' is inappropriate for they are not defined by their relation to the means of production, although the highest estate, the *shurfa*, do profit in political and economic terms from their status, and the majority of the lowest estate, the *haratn*, are poorer than the majority of any other.

  The *shurfa* are held to be the descendants of the *Prophet*, to be the source of blessing and sanctity, and to merit service and homage. In times of *siba* they often acted as political mediators. Next in status are Arabs because they are more learned and orthodox Muslims than Berbers who, by living in towns and following their example, can also become Arabs, with whom they intermarry anyway. 'Every Arab has a Berber grandfather' I was told. These two groups could be termed lay and free groups. The *haratn*, on the other hand, are descendents of West African slaves, brought into Morocco in the eighth century. Their ritual duty is to serve the other estates, with whom many have a joking relationship. At feasts they are expected to take the undignified roles, to serve, sing, and clown for the company. They should and generally do marry among themselves.

Patron-client relations between either *haratn* or *shurfa* and members of any of the other estates are permanent and often inherited. It is women, with their devotion to ascriptive statuses who adhere most closely to the forms of estate membership. This is especially obvious at feasts but is apparent in many daily gestures. It is common to find *hartani* girls working as servants in Arab households where they are said to be 'fostered'. Sometimes they are treated harshly, sometimes affectionately, but their kin-group cannot modify the behaviour of members of a higher estate, and as they grow up they become clients of a particularly modest kind, who do not pretend to the egalitarian relationship I described earlier.

This subordination could be attributed not only to their estate but to the fact that they have not arrived at being clients by means of a certain sloughing of male control, as the other women have. Even patronesses are only fully effective after a decade or so of marriage during which they have become *mtafqin* 'mutually trusting' with their husbands, who are then willing to let them have money and to leave them full discretion in the matter of their clients.

Divorce and property

The third mechanism, mentioned previously, by which the sale of land is inhibited operates through the inheritance of women. The property and guardianship of a woman are in the hands of her father, and after his death pass to her nearest male agnate, her son, then her full brother, and so on. Her property consists of a share inherited from her father equal to half that inherited by each of her brothers, after an eighth of the total has been set aside for the father's widow.

This property should legally pass under the control of her husband when she marries, but the majority (estimated by an Akhdar lawyer at 80 per cent) of women who inherit land, rather than saleable property, leave it in the hands of their brothers or other male agnates. Indeed, the occasional attempt by a hamlet woman, definitively established far from her kin, to claim her rightful share ended in bitter family feuds. Yet the male kinsman generally acknowledges his 'sister's' claim, by sending periodic gifts to her husband and a token share of the harvest. Further, the 'sister/daughter' may reactivate rights of usufruct by returning to her family of origin, a factor that plays no small part in determining the fragility of marriage and a high level of interaction among female kin.

It is rare for bridewealth to be paid in the hamlets and rural areas, but if a woman marries a salaried townsman, she will generally receive a certain amount of money on marriage, and a further amount should be paid on divorce, if it is none of her fault. Thus she forfeits temporarily her kinship rights and obligations and acquires a considerable economic and social stake in her conjugal unit. In fact the rate of divorce among couples married with bridewealth appears to be just over half the rate for the hamlets and the town migrant community. Divorces in bridewealth marriages are generally initiated by the man after many years of marriage and the birth of several children, so that divorce in the town is much more severely censured than in the countryside, for it leaves wife and children in a very difficult position. Divorces in the hamlets are generally initiated in the first couple of years of marriage by the women, who run home 'to be with their mothers and sisters'. The legal procedures for obtaining divorce are then undertaken by the husband under pressure from the woman's kinsmen. It is worth noting that in the hamlets a woman's status as a sister/daughter has many advantages over that as a wife, for as a wife she is often a mere labourer for scant reward, and in a strange environment, whereas at home she can work with her mother and sisters, protest if the burden is too heavy and be indulged. This is not true of the pampered town wife, who was often worse off in her family of origin.

The fostering of children among women kin

It is the 'woman network' that must deal with the continuous stream of social casualties resulting from the high divorce rate (one in two marriages in the hamlets and one in four in bridewealth marriages), which may itself be regarded as an indirect product of the economic and political subordination of women to men. On divorce a woman generally keeps young daughters and children who have not been weaned, but the father may claim them later if he contributes enough to their maintenance in the interim.

When she remarries a mother cannot take her children into her new household and they must be left to be brought up by a female relative. Uterine kin actually have priority over the father's kin in the exercise of *hadhana*, which has been defined by Pesle (1946:94) as 'l'accomplissement du devoir d'éducation dont la famille est tenue envers l'enfant'. Note that the bringing-up of the child is considered a right of the foster-mother, to be exercised or not as she pleases, not as a right of the child. This explains in part the low status of foster-children, their difficulties in social relations, and the tendency for them to be sent to school rather than to receive the affection which is lavished on other children.

The divorce of a mother, or her death, may represent a real crisis for her kin. The fostering of children is conspicuously rare in the poorer hamlets, but from a survey I made in Akhdar it appeared that a quarter of the households in the sample contained a foster child. Two-thirds of these children were girls and two-thirds of these were the product of broken marriages. The remainder of the girls had been fostered voluntarily by childless or secluded women who needed a small minion to run errands and keep them company. The boys, only a third of the total, were in a slightly better situation, half of them having come to town to go to school or learn a trade, but half were, nevertheless, the product of marriages broken by death or divorce. It is clear then that the relationships among women are important and reinforced because of the necessity to provide children with mothers, and mothers, in this society where childbearing is so important, with children.

Women who are 'like men'

Although young widows with children may return with them to their family of origin, it is not uncommon for older widows to take over the management of the patrimony, especially if they have sons old enough or near enough to do so. Sometimes they are seconded by male-in-laws, but the ones I knew went it alone. This situation resembles closely that described by Barbara Aswad in a plains village on the Turkish-Syrian border. Here, too, land cannot be alienated, and women give up their share in order to retain the protection of their patrilineage (see Rosenfeld 1960). They return to their family of origin on divorce, but some widows who are relatives of their husbands, stay in their husband's homes to administer the household land. 'Approximately 6 per cent of women in the patrilineage have performed this function' (Aswad 1967:147). Here, too, there seems to be a 'woman network', vitalized mainly by the activities of 'peripheral women' — for this is a stratified society. Of 'peripheral women' she says (Aswad 1967:147): 'The communication network is more informal, they gossip freely and move more freely between various sections of the village and kinship structure than men may.'

The responsibility Moroccan widows assume involves taking over many tasks normally carried out by men. In the hamlets, it means renting out fields, or making contracts with a sharecropper. It involves sowing, finding a *fellah* to plough, battling for irrigation water, employing harvesters, as well as carrying out with the daughters of the household all the domestic and women's field jobs. It means arranging marriage for one's children, protecting the honour of one's daughters and educating one's sons, and, last but not least, finding a source of occasional cash income that is not dishonourable. For capable widows do not 'become men', and they experience shame if they are forced to do conspicuous buying or selling, and avoid being seen in male occupations. They seek work where other women work; for instance I knew three in the weaving atelier of some nuns, a fourth in the public baths for women, and two wove carpets at home.

Intermediaries

These women have a type of access to the public space and to the opinions aired there which is exceptional among women, while at the same time they can build up a network of relations among women in the private space. Aswad (1967:150) calls them 'sub-culture brokers'. These are excellent qualifications for being the intermediary who helps to arrange marriages. By working in the match-making area widows create relations of indebtedness which are more honourable and cost less labour than clientship, while solving many problems of liquidity. In arranging marriages, widows link themselves with three or more households in one blow. These new friends will treat her as a kinswoman, ask her to feasts, lend her the labour-power of their male members if she wants a field ploughed, grain carried to the mill, or a room built on to her house. One hamlet widow had fostered two boys, thus providing herself with help, company, and links with many households.

Most townswomen are incapacitated by years of seclusion and a more complete domination of their initiatives than hamlet women experience. Those who do not belong to a migrant network may be quite isolated, and it is these who tend to foster their kinswomen's children from other areas, and to adopt *hartani* children to help with the labour-intensive domestic tasks. If they have recently come (that is in the last ten years) their contacts will be more limited to their real kinswomen with whom they will exchange visits. The wives of opulent professionals often make their friends among the wives and daughters of their husbands colleagues, as well as keeping in close touch with their own female kin. Such women are psychologically and socially more dependent on their husbands than the women of the hamlets or the southern migrant communities. Belghiti quotes (1969:346) the comments of a normally cloistered woman in the Marrakech region: *'Moi, quand il m'arrive d'aller en ville, je suis tellement troublée que mes jambes tremblent et je ne sais où aller.'*

The 'sine qua non' of the 'woman network'

Apart from the uses made by women of the variety of social and economic fortunes to be found within a community of putative kin or even within a single family, there are certain claims that a woman holds against all women of her acquaintance or even outside. Those who do not respond are put rather in the position of the 'bad fairy' who figures in so many folk-tales.

A woman can expect help and participation from other women in all those areas that concern women more closely than men, and from which men are often excluded by custom or ritual taboo. Among these are pregnancy, childbirth, and the death of children — a harrowingly frequent occurrence where the infant mortality rate is 186 per thousand and 70 per cent of all deaths occur among children under fourteen. Since these areas are so heavily loaded for women, their participation in each other's joys and griefs is partly a demonstration of their goodwill towards one another and proof that they are not likely to regard each other, or have not regarded anyone, with an 'evil eye'.

However the configuration of demands that a woman makes at such times have their own significance, and contain the usual mixture of the friendly-sentimental and the instrumental. Many women have elaborate pregnancy cravings, looked upon by men with fear ('if you refuse to satisfy them some ill fortune will come upon you') and by women with indulgence ('if you refuse the child will be blemished'), for the latter have an interest in giving high value to their reproductive powers. A nice example of an instrumental craving was the passion that a teacher's wife developed for ice, in the middle of a rainy spring. She thought that this could be most conveniently found two miles away in the fridge of the wife of her husband's far removed superior. This relationship she pursued after the birth, asking the lady to machine some clothes for the baby, thus establishing both herself and her husband on the fringe of an influential social circle.

Instrumentality and the safety-net

It is important to recognize that the mode of relationship in which women combine sentiment and instrumentality is dictated by a discriminatory social system that deprives them of economic and political autonomy; thus each is impelled to create her own guarantees of security based on inducing a sense of personal indebtedness in those on whom she depends. In Morocco women do not expect men (apart from their brothers and sons in some cases) to be reliable sources of support. To preserve themselves from disaster women retain economic rights in their family of origin, distribute responsibility for their children among their kin, keep up useful contacts among women, and in the last resort, administer the household property themselves.

In Italy, by contrast, marriage is for ever, and a woman's property, like that of town Moroccans, is saleable and is therefore transferable to her conjugal unit, where it is administered by her husband. Women who do not work and have few extra-familial relationships depend much more directly on men, but especially on their children for comfort and security in their old age in the eventuality of a breakdown of relations in their marriage, and, of course, in widowhood.

Women tend to exercise control over their children by means of what is known in Italy as 'emotional blackmail'. The Sicilian writer Leonardo Sciascia in a recent interview with the Italian weekly *L'Espresso* observed with some misogyny that Sicilian women take ages to do things. 'They want to make their very laboriousness weigh with other people. It is a way for the Sicilian woman to sell her goods at a higher price and to exercise power' (Sciascia 1974).

Friedl has also commented on the tendency of women in Greece to create obligation in others by stressing the hardships they undergo in their service.

> 'What is expressed by women to the men in the privacy of the household is a constant reminder of the lengths to which the women go in the toil and the trouble which they take in the performance of those household tasks which enable the men of the family to preserve their public honour. ... For the weaker partner in a social structure, the ability to create and maintain such a sense of obligation in the stronger is a real exercise of power.' (Friedl 1967:108).

Note that here, too, husbands control their wives' property and marriage is permanent, so that women are much more subject to men than they are in Morocco where their women kin and contacts supply many alternatives to their conjugal situation, both socially and economically.

How women's dependence and instrumental approach to relationships affect the political structure

In both the Moroccan and European cases, each woman's success in creating a sense of obligation in others, and in getting guarantees of security through personal relationships, is a purely individual matter, although as we have observed the ideological infrastructure is often ready and waiting. Thus, Sciascia, in the same interview, points out how Sicilian women associate themselves in general terms with suffering, particularly in their dramatization of mourning rites: 'The Sicilian woman administers death, she manages it, manipulates it as if she was immune to its effects. As I remember it (perhaps it is not so now) the three days of mourning, the so-called "visit", were her stage and apotheosis' (Sciascia 1974, my translation).

Women reproduce these cultural attitudes, especially in their children on whom they must rely. Men, even if they operate more in terms of social categories created by the market, i.e. in the class struggle, tend to fall back on this clientistic, person-to-person model of relationship especially where there is a fierce competition for jobs and civil rights. Such competition induces employers and bureaucrats to offer, and their 'dependents' to seek, preferential treatment which distinguishes them from other members of their social category or class. In the mass society where it is difficult to work through kinship all the time, this is done through bribes, which are the only way of establishing a special relationship with a person with whom you have no previous connection.

Graziano points out that the patron-client system is an inefficient way of articulating and aggregating interests in a mass society, for such a system is hierarchically, dyadically, and informally organized and cannot, by definition, give rise to more categorical attitudes and structures. He says 'Generalising, it can be said that any patron-client system undermines the autonomy of the social groups and organisations involved, and tends to absorb them in a political game managed by the groups in power' (Graziano, 1973:234, my translation).

Particularly in the case of women, patron-client relations under various mystifying labels, such as those of kinship, obscure the real boundaries of class and enable certain groups to exploit the labour of others, who receive very little in exchange and remain permanently dependent and subordinated. The sinister influence of this tendency is to be seen in the fact that even when women work for wages, they tend on the whole to perceive their relations with members of another class in 'particularistic' terms (Graziano's word). Maria Macciocchi cites the example of a woman out-worker in Naples, who earned a miserable wage making umbrellas at home. She:

> 'expressed gratitude to the "teacher" who might have chosen another in that alley to work in her stead, and who yet trusted *her*. She defined herself as the 'putter-out's favourite "disciple" ... "Teacher" the one who hands out the umbrellas for sewing, "Pupil" the one who sews them. So in the alley rise the "chairs" of this refined school of super-exploitation of human labour.' (Macciocchi 1969:50, my translation).

It is a school which affects a minimum of one and a half million Italian women.

In conclusion, we may observe that the prohibition of social space to women, their political and economic deprivation and subordination to men, merely inhibits the development of class consciousness, promoting exploitation and the abuse of power.

A note on methodology

The conclusions I wish to draw from this paper make up a little essay on their own. They are both methodological and theoretical, since the first type are difficult to separate from the second.

Looking for the Links

First of all it is clear that what goes on among women has no official recognition, nor is considered to be subversive of the 'real society'. The relationships which I have described would come under Wolf's rubric of 'informal structure' (Wolf 1966:2). But Wolf regards such 'informal structures' as 'interstitial, supplementary parallel' to 'the formal framework of economic and political power'. The implied association of 'formal' with 'important' and 'informal' with 'unimportant' does not seem to me to help us with the identification of social facts, still less with the analysis of the relations that exist between them. Wolf's formula needs a dose of dialectic: 'informal structures' may be the substance of which the 'formal framework' is merely a facade.

Certainly the structures that involve women have been wrongly considered 'supplementary' for a long time, as I hope my study has shown. Friedl, for example writes, 'If ... the women in a Greek village hold a position of real power in the family, and, as I have shown earlier, the life of the family is the most significant structural and cultural element of the Greek village, then there is unmistakable need for a reassessment of the role of the Greek woman in village life' (Friedl: 1967:97). On the other hand, I do not think there is a case for a battle over 'who counts more, women or men', which tends to be the problematic of studies that treat society as if only women were involved, and which can hardly correct the current tendency to discuss theoretical questions in sociology and anthropology as if only men were involved. Some of the bias derives from the different opportunities of men and women fieldworkers. It might be worth mentioning a few that occur to me when I consider my own fieldwork experience.

In most Middle-East societies, with an agricultural base, women anthropologists, like widows, are 'like men' in that they can move to some extent among men, and to a great extent among women whether they are secluded or not. This offers not-to-be-missed opportunities for studying the sexual and other divisions of society and the relations of the various parts. However certain areas are as closed to women anthropologists, for all their foreignness, as they are to widows — for example, the mosque, the law courts, and the cafés where the men play cards, although it is possible to know individual lawyers and prayer-leaders in their homes. Propriety for women and its dispensability for men is the first law of social relations in segregated societies, and the anthropologist risks losing all her friends if she defies it. Thus the whole area of illicit unions, whether common-law or otherwise, is more accessible to men fieldworkers than to women fieldworkers who are thus deprived of important insights into counter-culture areas of society. However, this can hardly compensate men for the difficulty that they may have in getting to know people, especially women, in their homes.

On the other hand, in many parts of urban Italy, for example, there is no accepted role of 'highly mobile autonomous woman' and here the woman anthropologist is likely to be in serious difficulties, particularly as there is no 'woman network' to speak of, and women tend to be extremely closely linked to their families of origin and of procreation, attempting to secure their uncertain future through binding their children to them rather than through other women.

Information or participation observation
But there is a serious indictment of anthropological method which must be made: the use of informants to obtain knowledge of a society. Informants who are old, male, or of high status have been particularly trusted, but it is these who are likely to take part in the exercise of a certain cultural hegemony. In Morocco I was told by men and educated women, 'We have a lot of trouble because men are always divorcing women', or 'We Moroccans pay a brideprice', or 'My father told me to marry Y', or 'X is holding a circumcision ceremony', or 'Women never go to market'.

Such statements arouse little suspicion and many similar have been taken at face-value and recorded for the benefit of anthropology students and enquiring minds all over the world. Only after a substantial, polemical, and varied experience of the society in question is it possible to discover that these statements, so gravely and precisely articulated, are statements of ideology, reflecting either the behaviour of the dominant social group, which may be the minority, or the ideological tendency to confuse the substance of an act with its legal enactment, thus attributing the agency of all significant social processes to men.

Through my association with women, who had few ready theories but many observations to make about social relationships, I learnt that most divorces happened after women ran home, that many Moroccans pay a bride-price only on paper, and Y was chosen for her husband by his mother or sister, and X barely appeared at his son's circumcision. Finally, I learnt that categorical statements like 'Women never go to market' cover a range of actual practice, whose variety is calculated in surprising percentages by Belghiti in her admirable article about women of the Marrakech region of Morocco (Belghiti 1969).

Sex-roles, language and relationship

The corollary of the suggestion that men, the old, and high status people are likely to make statements that represent the dominant value-system rather than describing actual behaviour, is that a special approach is needed when learning about society from women or from an oppressed group.

Since the contradictions between women's actual experience and the reported or prescribed version are often flagrant, women tend to give an ambiguous version of social facts, whose best medium of expression is the ritual or multivalent symbolic one. In contrast to men who generally agree on the meaning of a ritual (especially petit-bourgeois men) women's accounts tend to differ and to seem idiosyncratic.

Women seem in their relations with each other to be less dominated by a concern to adhere to the models proposed by the dominant ideology than men are, for women have no 'public image'. This makes for more direct and emotionally relaxed relations than are common among men. Aswad remarks of the Turkish-Syrian village she describes

'Men are restricted in visiting and speech patterns [using formulae and proverbs, V.M.] in accordance with political alliances and coalitions, women's relations with each other are somewhat freer from these restraints, partially because of the more heterogeneous background of the women with whom they live and work, i.e. including in-marrying women.' (Aswad 1967: 149)

I would endorse the first part of the explanation, but the second part does not help us to understand why Moroccan brothers and fathers treat each other with exaggerated respect and avoid each other, while the relations among sisters and mothers are marked by friendliness and plain speech. Schneider, quoting several authors on the Middle East and Southern Europe, writes:

'It is typical of the Mediterranean that the father-son relationship is somewhat strained and potentially competitive; that brothers are not emotionally close after they marry; that the most enduring and solidary bonds are those uniting a mother and her children and, in lesser degree, those between cross-cousins and between a mother's brother and his sister's son.' (Schneider 1971:11).

I think the market and property context of the first set of relationships, and the social security functions of the second are crucial in explaining their content.

Notes

1   References to Europe in a paper on Morocco may be puzzling.
    To a certain extent I have given in to the temptation to compare
    the data of one piece of research I have carried out with those of
    another; a temptation that every fieldworker experiences. While
    I am not convinced by the 'Mediterranean area as a cultural
    entity' thesis, I wish to point out that my yielding to the tempta-
    tion of comparison, or, more often, of contrast, has been
    judicious and based on certain objective considerations.

    The Mediterranean countries I mention in this paper,
    however culturally heterogeneous, have shared some historical
    experiences, and even today there are some broad economic and
    political similarities among them; e.g. the existence of pools of
    high unemployment, the importance of internal and external
    migration and of patronage in public life. There is a superficial
    similarity in the situation of women in these countries. Women
    are not generally engaged in public wage labour and they do not
    often control cash or property even if they own it. The segrega-
    tion of men's and women's roles is highly developed, with child-
    bearing and -rearing playing an important part in a woman's
    role-set. However, the contrasts are equally interesting; the
    permanence of marriage in the European countries and its
    instability in North Africa being only one example.

    In this paper whatever comparisons I make are intended to be
    extremely loose and provisional. My purpose is to suggest that,
    in variously defined circumstances of oppression and insecurity,
    women will tend to turn close and kin relationships to political
    and economic ends, and that this tendency has causes and reper-
    cussions far outside the family.

References

Adam, A., 1968. *Casablanca.* Paris: Editions du C.N.R.S.

Aswad, B.C. 1967. Key and peripheral roles of Noblewomen in a
    Middle Eastern Plains Village. *The Anthropological Quarterly,
    40* (3) 139-151.

Belghiti, M. 1969. Les Relations Féminines et le Statut de la Femme
    dans la Famille Rurale — dans trois Villages de la Tessaout. In,
    Abdelkabir Khatibi (ed.) *Etudes Sociologiques sur le Maroc.*
    Rabat.

Dobb, M. 1963. *Studies in the Development of Capitalism*. London: Routledge & Kegan Paul.

Friedl, E. 1967. The Position of Women — Appearance and Reality. *The Anthropological Quarterly 40* (3): 97-108.

Graziano, L. 1973. Clientela e Politica nel Mezzogiorno. In P. Farneti (ed.), *Il Sistema Politica Italiano*. Bologna: Il Mulino.

Joseph, R. 1967. Rituals and Relatives: a Study of the Social Uses of Wealth in Morocco. Ph. D. thesis, Univ. of California.

La Division du Plan et des Statistiques, 1961-3. *Résultats de l'Enquête à Objectifs Multiples*. Rabat.

— 1964. *Résultats du Recensement de 1960. Vol. II, Population Active*. Rabat.

Macciocchi, M. 1969. *Lettere dall' Interno del Partito Comunisto Italiano a Louis Althusser*. Milano: Feltrinelli.

Maher, V. 1974. Divorce and Property in the Middle Atlas. *Man. 9* (1).

Pesle, O. 1946. *La Femme Musulmane dans le Droit, la Religion et les Moeurs*. Rabat: Editions La Porte.

Poncet, J. 1971. Statut Foncier et Rapports Sociaux dans la Tunisie d'avant 1881. In, *Sur le Féodalisme*. Paris: Editions Sociales.

Riegelhaupt, J.F. 1967: Saloio Women: an analysis of informal and formal political roles of Portuguese peasant women. *The Anthropological Quarterly*. 40 (3):109-125.

Rosenfeld, H. 1960. On Determinants of the Status of Arab Village Women. *Man. 15*: 66-70.

Sciascia, L. 1974. Le Zie di Sicilia: colloquio con L.S. *L'Espresso* 27 January:19.

Schneider, J. 1971. Of Vigilance and Virgins: Honor, shame, and access to resources in Mediterranean societies. *Ethnology 10:* 1-24.

Villeneuve, M. 1971. *La Situation de l'Agriculture et son Avenir dans l'Economie Marocaine*. Paris: Editions du C.N.R.S.

Wolf, E. 1966. Kinship, friendship and patron-client relations in complex societies. In Banton M. (ed.), *The Social Anthropology of Complex Societies*. London: Tavistock.

CHRISTINE DELPHY

Continuities and Discontinuities in Marriage and Divorce

Studies devoted to divorce in the past have presented it as the sum of individual divorce situations, they have not defined it (e.g. Goode 1956; Chester 1973; Kooy 1959). This is doubtless because the definition of divorce and its sociological significance are taken for granted; divorce means the breakdown and failure of marriage. These are the words used by the individuals concerned and sociologists have implicitly approached the problem from the same point of view. Even if they have apparently (but not always) refrained from direct value judgements and emotionally laden terms such as 'failure', they have still considered that the definition of divorce as the end of marriage, its revocation, or as the opposite of marriage, was a satisfactory one.

A great deal of attention has been paid to the individual causes of divorce. Here, in contrast, it is evident that sociologists have not limited themselves to the reasons advanced by the protagonists, nor to their psychological 'motivations', but have included in their studies more objective data: for instance, social characteristics such as class origin and educational level. But in every case they have directed their attention to the 'couple' or the individual union. This method may have enabled them to pinpoint the differences — if indeed there are any — between couples and/or individuals who are divorced on the one hand and those who are not, on the other. But it cannot teach us about the institution of divorce, for this is not just a multitude of individual accidents.

Were a similar method of analysis to be applied to marriage as has been with divorce (and indeed this has unfortunately often been the way sociologists have approached marriage, unlike anthropologists) we would look for — and would in all probability find — differences between married and non-married individuals. But marriage is an institution and merely to look at those who enter or leave it, cannot shed light on the institution or why it exists. Similarly with divorce. It can be established that divorce obeys certain rules, it is codified and subject to controls, ranging from the implicit but unformulated social control to penal control.

Furthermore divorce is organically related to the institution of marriage. In an old American film the heroine asks what the grounds for divorce are in the state where she lives, and the lawyer replies, 'being married'. But we would go further and argue that not only is marriage the necessary condition for divorce; but also that divorce is not inconsistent with marriage. For while a divorce signifies the end of *a* marriage (marriage meaning here a particular union), it by no means implies the end of *marriage* as an institution. Divorce was not invented to destroy marriage since divorce is only necessary if marriage continues to exist. Indeed, it is often argued that the increase in the incidence of divorce can be interpreted as proof, not that the institution of marriage is sick, but on the contrary that it is thriving.

Further, divorce reveals and throws into relief certain institutional aspects of marriage, and it shows what is otherwise latent. Conversely marriage sheds light on divorce. Not only do certain aspects of marriage make the institution of divorce more intelligible; what is more noteworthy is that they are carried over and perpetuated in divorce.

The institution of marriage is, of course, complex and it is imperative to specify which aspect and which function is being studied. This paper will focus attention exclusively on the economic aspect of marriage, and to make clear what this means. We will first summarize briefly the approach that is used.[1]

A theory of marriage

The proposition is that marriage is the institution by which gratuitous work is extorted from a particular category of the population, women-wives.[2] This work is gratuitous for it does not give rise to a wage but simply to upkeep. These very peculiar relations of production in a society that is defined by the sale of work (wage-labour) and products, are not determined by the type of work accomplished. Indeed they are not even limited to the production of household work and the raising of children, but extend to include *all* the production accomplished by women (and also by children) within the home and in small-scale manufacturing, shop-keeping, or farming, if the husband is a craftsman, tradesman, or farmer; or various professional services if the husband is a doctor or lawyer, etc. In France, for example, the official census classes one adult woman in ten under the heading 'family helper': an unpaid worker.

Moreover, the domestic goods and services produced by the

married women are of the same kind as others produced and used by the family. For example, the raising of pigs for the family's own use is, unlike domestic work, considered to be productive, and as such is invested with value since it is taken into account in the evaluation of the national revenue. Finally, domestic services can be bought on the market — they have a value — when they are not produced within the framework of marriage by married women.

The fact that domestic work is gratuitous is not inherent to this particular type of work, since when it is done *outside the family* it is paid for. The same work acquires value — is remunerated — as long as the woman furnishes it to people to whom she *is not related or married.*

It can therefore be seen that the valuelessness of domestic work performed by married women is derived institutionally from the marriage contract, which is in fact a work contract. To be more precise, it is a contract by which the head of the family — the husband — appropriates all the work done in the family by his children, his younger siblings, and especially by his wife, since he can sell it on the market as his own if he is, for example, a craftsman or farmer or doctor. Conversely, the wife's labour has no value because it cannot be put on the market, and it cannot be put on the market because of the contract by which her labour power is appropriated by her husband. Since the production intended for exchange — on the market — is accomplished outside the family in the wage-earning system, and since the married man sells his work and not a product, the gratuitous work of women cannot be incorporated in the production intended for exchange. It has therefore become limited to those productions which are intended for the family's internal use: domestic services and the raising of children.

Of course, with the increase of industrial production (and hence of the number of wage-earners) and the decrease in family production, many women-wives work for money, largely outside the home. They are nonetheless expected to do the household work. It would appear that their labour power is not totally appropriated since they divert a part of it for their paid work. Yet since they work they provide their own upkeep. While one could, with a touch of bad faith, consider the marriage contract as an *exchange* contract when women work only within the household, with married women providing domestic work in exchange for upkeep; when married women earn their own living that illusion disappears altogether. It is clear that the domestic work is given for nothing and the feature of appropriation is even more conspicuous.

However, the modes of appropriation differ depending on whether the woman has a paid job or not. When she does not her total work power is appropriated, and this thus determines the type of work she will do — if her husband is a doctor she will make appointments for the patients; if he has a garage she will type the bills, etc. It also determines the nature of the relations of production under which she operates — her economic dependency and the non-value of her work — for while she may accomplish exactly the same tasks as her well-to-do neighbour, the upkeep she receives will be different if her huband's financial status is not as good. When she has a job, however, she recuperates part of her labour power in exchange for the accomplishment of a precise and specific type of work: housework. Legally any woman can choose this second solution, although in France the law requiring a husband's authorization for his wife to work outside of the home was abolished only some ten years ago. In point of fact, however, it seems reasonable to suggest that the only women who work outside the home are those whose husbands give their consent if they consider that they do not need all their wife's time. Equally, in France, the obligation to do housework is not written in any law; all that is said in the Code Civil (1974) is that the wife's contribution to the 'household charges' can be in kind if she has no dowry or independent income. But this obligation is inscribed negatively, so to speak, in the sense that failure to assume it is sanctioned. Some of the possible sanctions are social worker intervention or divorce (as is shown in the paper by Yves Dezalay).

When the social control agents intervene, whether it be in the person of the children's judge, the social worker, or the court, and if a divorce ensues or the family budget comes under the control of the social workers, the obligations of marriage are officially expressed and in particular the differential duties of the husband and the wife. This precision and differentiation contrasts markedly with the vague legal formulation of marriage contracts, which suggest an apparent reciprocity in the respective duties of the partners (notably the wife's contribution in kind and the husband's in money are represented as having the same value and producing a similar status for both partners).

Conclusions following from this theory of marriage

It is clear that the position of women on the labour market and the discrimination that they suffer are the result — and not the cause as certain authors would have us believe — of the marriage contract as we have described it.[3]

If it is accepted that marriage gives rise to the exploitation of women, then it would be logical to suppose that pressure is brought to bear on women to persuade them to marry. Of course there are various sorts of pressure — cultural, emotional-relational, and material-economic — and one could argue that the last is not the most important, or that it is not perceived as a pressure at the time of marriage, or that it is not operational at this time. However, if we compare the standard of living to which a woman can aspire if she remains single and the standard which she can reasonably expect from being married, it seems certain that relative economic deprivation will be experienced by single women as time goes on. We are confronted with a paradox: on the one hand marriage is the (institutional) situation where women are exploited; and on the other hand, precisely because of this, the potential market situation for women's labour (which is that of all women, not just those who are actually married (see Barron and Norris in the companion volume)) is such that marriage still offers them the best career, economically speaking. If the initial or potential situation is bad, it will simply be aggravated by the married state, which becomes even more necessary than ever. The economic pressure, in other words, the difference between the potential 'single' standard of living and the actual 'married' standard of living, simply increases as time goes on.

Marriage as a self-perpetuating state

When women marry or have a child they often stop working or indeed studying; or even occasionally among the middle class — the American model is becoming generalized in France [4] — they stop studying in order to put their husband through college, by means of a job that has no future and they stop working as soon as their husband has obtained his degree. If they continue working, they do so at the cost of enormous sacrifices of time and energy and even then they still are not as free to devote themselves to their work. As a result they cannot aspire to the promotion which they might have had if they had not had to look after materially a husband and children as well as themselves. Ten years after the wedding day, marriage is even more necessary than before because of the dual process whereby women lose ground or at best remain at the same place in the labour market, while married men make great progress in their work as they are not hampered by household obligations. Of course individual husbands are not responsible for this situation but all men benefit from a situation that is taken to be normal. A 'normal' day's work is that of a person who does not have to do his own domestic work. But even though this is the norm, it is nonetheless made possible only by the fact that the household tasks are assumed by others, almost exclusively women. It is evident that the career of a married man must not be compared for our purposes with that of other men, but with the life he would have led if he had remained single, or if he had had to share the household tasks including the raising of children. This dual process is particularly evident in the case where the wife gives up her own studies in order to finance her husband's. Here, even though both begin in more or less the same position (not taking discrimination into account) marriage results in the wife moving down the economic ladder and the husband moving up, and these changes combine to create an important gap between the economic possibilities of the two partners.

Thus it can be said that, from the woman's standpoint, marriage creates the conditions for its own continuation and encourages entry into a second marriage if a particular union comes to an end.

In this respect statistics are ambiguous, or, more precisely, are difficult to interpret. There are generally more divorced women at work than married women (Ministere de la Justice 1973). This could be taken as confirmation that their economic situation, notably the absence of an independent income, discourages full-time housewives from getting divorced. But on the other hand many women begin to work just because they are in a divorce situation — they start the moment they decide to get a divorce, long before the decree is issued. This explains why they are registered as 'working' at that particular time. Having a job enables some women to envisage divorce while others in the same situation but lacking a job have to 'make a go' of their marriage. A large number of women who are divorced or about to be divorced come on the labour market in the worst possible conditions (as do widows), with no qualifications, no experience, and no seniority. They find themselves relegated to the most poorly-paid jobs. This situation is often in contrast with the level of their education and the careers they envisaged or could have envisaged before their marriage, the social rank of their parents, and not only the initial social rank of their husband but, more pertinently, the rank he has attained when they divorce, some five, ten, or twenty years after the beginning of their marriage. In addition, those with dependent children have to look after them financially, and this new responsibility is added to the domestic work which they were already providing before divorce. For the majority of women the contrast between the standard of living that they enjoy while married and that which they can expect after divorce simply redoubles the pressures in favour of marriage or remarriage depending on the circumstances.

The state of divorce as a continuation of the state of marriage

The fact that the material responsibility for children is assumed by the woman after divorce confirms the hypothesis concerning the appropriation by the husband of his wife's work, but it suggests as well that the appropriation which is a characteristic of marriage persists even after the marriage has been dissolved. This leads us to contend that divorce is not the opposite of marriage, nor even its end, but simply a change or a transformation of marriage.

At the beginning of a marriage this appropriation is legally masked; it is a matter of custom in the sense that the legal framework which underlines it is vague and unused and even useless. It only begins to operate — by means of the intervention of the judicial system — when the marriage comes to an end. Even then its apparent purpose is not to burden the wife with the entire responsibility for the children nor to exempt the husband totally. It *permits* such an outcome, but by omission rather than by a positive action. There *is* positive action, however, in the official guide line of considering 'the child's interest'.

Unofficially custody of the children is considered to be a privilege and even a compensation for the woman who may be left badly off in other respects. A real battle is staged to make the two spouses turn against each other and to keep them uncertain as to the outcome of the conflict as long as possible. The custody of the children [5] becomes the main issue, and at the end of the battle the spouse who obtains this custody considers that he or she has won the war. But in fact when the children are young they are almost always entrusted to their mother. Officially both parents share the responsibility for the cost of looking after the children. But the woman's income after divorce is always very much lower than that of her former husband, and the allowance for the children decided by the courts is always ridiculously low.[6] The woman's financial contribution is thus of necessity greater in absolute value than her husband's, even though her income is lower. As a result her participation and her sacrifices are relatively much greater. Furthermore 80 per cent of all allowances are never paid (Boigeol, Commaille, and Roussel 1975). But even if the official directives are respected and the allowance is paid, the amount agreed never takes into account the woman's time and work in the material upkeep of the children.[7]

Thus the courts ratify the exclusive responsibility of women both by positive actions, granting of custody to the mother and assigning a low allowance for the children; and by negative action, failing to ensure the payment of the allowance. The 'child's interest' makes it imperative for him to be entrusted to his mother, be she poor, 'immoral', or sick, as long as he requires considerable material care: as long as there are nappies to wash, feeds to prepare and special clothes, toys, medicaments, lessons, etc. to pay for. As soon as the child reaches the age of fifteen the courts usually regard the father more favourably than the mother:[8] she is thought to be unable to provide the child with as many advantages as the father, who is better off (for a very good reason). A child who has been entrusted to his mother can then be handed back to his father, again in the 'child's interest'. And yet, curiously enough, this aspect of the child's interest — the parent's wealth — did not come into play when the child was younger. Objectively the child's interest[9] has served to make his mother poorer and his father richer, creating thereby the conditions in which it will be 'in his interest' later on to return to his father.

Two conclusions can be drawn: in divorce, as in marriage, the work involved in raising children is carried out by the woman *gratuitously* and the husband is exempted from this charge as part of the normal process. Furthermore, the financial care of the children which was shared by the couple or assumed by the husband alone in the marriage situation is hereafter assumed predominantly or exclusively by the woman.

In compensation the woman no longer has to carry domestic responsibility for her husband. This casts a special light on the marriage contract. Indeed, when the married state is compared with the official as well as real divorced state, it becomes clear that the material responsibility for the children is the woman's 'privilege' in both cases; while in marriage, in contrast to divorce, the wife provides for her husband's material upkeep in exchange for his participation towards the financial upkeep of the children.

Marriage and responsibility for children: A question of theoretical antecedence

Our overriding concern in this paper so far has been to re-think the economic aspects of the institutions of marriage and to give them the definition that they have lacked.

Comparing marriage to divorce, it seems that the material upkeep of the husband by the wife is related to the participation of the husband in the financial upkeep of children. This can provide grounds for viewing marriage differently. This approach is consistent with the contention that whereas marriage sheds light on divorce, the reverse is also true. So far this has meant only that divorce reveals the nature of the marriage contract, but it can also be taken to mean that divorce can shed light on what made this contract possible in the first place.

We would contend that these conclusions allow us to see childcare (from the analytical not from the empirical point of view) as separate from the rest of domestic work. The obligation of childcare may have to be viewed as not so much perpetuating the husband's appropriation of his wife's labour, as making it possible in the first place. Or, to put it slightly differently, these conclusions compel us to consider the possibility that the continuation of the obligation of child care is a continuation of the marriage contract, *in so far as* the appropriation of the wife's labour includes the obligation of child care; but that this obligation, while *carried out* in marriage, does not necessarily *stem* from it; that it might be antecedent to it, and might even be one of the factors that makes the appropriation of wives' labour — the free giving by them of the rest of housework — possible.

If marriage is considered as giving rise to the appropriation of the woman-wife's work, the position of married women who work outside of the home suggests that this total appropriation can be transformed into a partial appropriation, bearing no longer on their time or work power as a whole but on a specific task, the household work, that can eventually be replaced by an equivalent sum of money.[10] The evolution of the system of appropriation of the wives' labour may at first sight call to mind the evolution of the appropriation of the labour of slaves between the Roman Empire and the late Middle Ages. The appropriation by the seigneur of the slave's total work power became a partial appropriation, approximately half of his time, three days work per week (Bloch 1964) when the slave became a 'serf' and was 'settled'. He then worked part-time for his own profit on a piece of land which he rented from the seigneur. The time debt to the siegneur was later itself transformed into the obligation to accomplish a specific task, the *corvée*, which later on could be commuted into a money payment.

However, this way of formulating the problem is perhaps false because the partial appropriation of the married woman's labour on this analogy should be counter-balanced by the woman partially recuperating her work power, when in fact she pays for the freedom to work outside, and to have an independent income, with a double day's work. It cannot be said that she recuperates either a period of time or a value. On the other hand she does partially escape from a relation of production characterized by dependency.

Furthermore, if marriage as a state is characterized and differentiated from divorce by the 'contract' of appropriation, marriage and divorce can be considered as two ways of obtaining a similar result: the collective attribution to women of the care of children and the collective exemption of men from the same responsibility.

Seen from this angle, not only the married and the divorced states but also the state of concubinage, in short all the situations in which children exist and are cared for, have similar characteristics and are different forms of one and the same institution, which could be called X. The situation of the unmarried mother can be taken to be its extreme form and at the same time its most typical form, since the basic dyad is the mother and child. Marriage could be seen as being one of the possible forms of X in which the basic couple is joined by a man who temporarily participates in the financial upkeep of the child and in return appropriates the woman's labour power.

This view is similar to that of those anthropologists (Adams 1971; Zelditch 1964) who criticize Murdock (1949) and say that the family defined as a trio proceeding from the husband and wife couple (taken to be the fundamental dyad) is not a universal type, whereas the mother-child association is. This point of view may become a new element in the study of Western societies where it has generally been taken for granted that the family is patrifocal. This element may be new but it is not contradictory; for if the family, considered as *the place where children are produced*, can be viewed as matrifocal, even in our own societies, it remains none the less true that as an *economic production unit* (for exchange or for its own use) it is defined, as during the Roman era (Engels 1884), as the group of relatives and servants who give work to the head of the family: the father.

Going a step further, the state of marriage-with-children appears as the meeting place for two institutions: on the one hand the institution relating to the woman's exclusive responsibility for child care, on the other hand the institution relating to the appropriation by the husband of his wife's labour power.

Indeed if one considers marriage alone it will appear that the care of children, their upkeep, which is no different from the material upkeep of the husband by the wife and which is carried out in the same manner — the gratuitous execution of work in exchange for financial upkeep — partakes of and flows from the appropriation of the wife's labour power by her husband. As long as there are two parents it can be postulated that the children, in accordance with the legal terms, are their common property, possession, and responsibility. In this case, in the marriage situation half of the work involved in the upkeep of the children is appropriated by the husband-father, and continues to be so after the divorce. But the children do not always have two owners. In the absence of the father, their upkeep by the mother or even half of this upkeep is obviously of no benefit to any particular man. Besides even in marriage or divorce it is doubtful whether the parents are the only ones, excluding society as a whole, to benefit from the children and consequently it is not at all certain that the husband-father should be considered as the only one to benefit from his half of the work involved in looking after the children, or as the only one to appropriate his wife's work, since he does not carry it out with her. If this is accepted, then the raising of the children will have to be considered apart from the woman's family work (household or other) and the exclusive responsibility of women concerning the children will have to be treated as a relatively autonomous institution with respect to marriage.

If the relationship between marriage and divorce is viewed in this way it will appear slightly different from what was suggested at the beginning of this paper. The husband's appropriation of his wife's work ceases, in part or completely (depending on whether or not the husband is considered as continuing to benefit from the children (and from their upkeep) either partly or not at all) as soon as the marriage comes to an end. In this sense then divorce is not the continuation of marriage. On the other hand, the divorce situation, in which the responsibility for the children is an important aspect, constitutes a strong economic incentive to remarriage for women.

When there are children, the responsibility for their care continues to be borne exclusively by the woman after the divorce, and this burden is increased by the financial cost. However, rather than considering that this illustrates a continuation of the husband's appropriation of his wife's work, it would now seem more exact to say that it illustrates a new form of women's responsibility for children, which exists before the marriage, is carried on in the marriage, and continues afterwards. This responsibility can be defined as the collective exploitation of women by men, and correlated with this, the collective exemption of men from the cost of reproduction. The individual appropriation of a particular wife's labour by her husband comes over and above this collective appropriation. It is derived from, or at least made possible by, the collective appropriation which acts in favour of marriage, since if the husband appropriates his wife's work power, in return he contributes to her financial upkeep and the children's, and in this way he 'lightens' her burden by partially assuming a responsibility from which society exempts him. In other words, the institutional exemption from which he benefits allows him to claim his wife's total labour power in exchange for his contribution to the children's financial upkeep.

Notes

1   This is elaborated in Delphy (1970).
2   I use the expression woman-wife to stress that the one is a person and the other a role. This ontological distinction is blurred by the fact that the social role is so widely associated with a biological category that they have become equivalent.
3   The thesis of Blood and Wolfe (1960), for example, is that no model exists, let alone a patriarchal one. If more married women do the housework than married men, it is because they have more time to do it and their husbands less since they work outside(!). And if married women are of less weight in making decisions, it is owing to the fact that since they do not work outside (this being compensated by the extra time they have to do the housework) their contribution to the domestic economy is less important.
4   See, for example, the couples where the husbands are at business school, described by Jane Marceau in the companion volume.
5   This is a legal notion which officially denotes official responsibility and, unofficially, the right to dispose of and enjoy as one may dispose of and enjoy any possession.
6   In one provincial court we found that the ex-wife was awarded a *mean* of £10 per month per child. In general, courts in France will never instruct the exhusband to pay more than one-third of his income to his ex-wife and children.
7   I distinguish the financial and material upkeep of a family. The first is the part of the consumption that is bought. The second consists of services, or labour applied to goods bought by the wage.

88 — Christine Delphy

8 This is based on statistics from the Ministere de la Justice (1973) and oral communications from a lawyer.
9 That this is a mere legal fiction is clear if we consider the result to which it leads, and that from the very beginning it is the judges and not the children who talk of their 'interest'.
10 When for example the woman buys off her obligation by paying for a nurse or a public nursery, etc. out of her salary.

References

Adams, R.N. 1971. The Nature of the Family. In J. Goody (ed.), *Kinship*. Harmondsworth: Penguin.
Barron, R. and Norris, G. 1976. Sexual Divisions and the Dual Labour Market. In D. Leonard Barker and S. Allen (eds.), *Dependence and Exploitation in Work and Marriage*. Harlow: Longman.
Bloch, M. 1964. *Les caractères originales de l'histoire rurale française*. Paris: Armand Colin.
Blood, R.O. and Wolfe, D.M. 1960. *Husbands and Wives: The Dynamics of Married Living*. Glencoe: Free Press.
Boigeol, A. Commaille, J., and Roussel, L. 1975. Enquieter sur 1000 divorcés. *Population*.
Chester, R. 1973. Divorce and the Family Life Cycle in Great Britain. Paper presented to the 13th Annual Seminar of the Committee on Family Research of the I.S.A. Paris. mimeo.
Code Civil Francais. Paris: Librairie Dalloz.
Delphy, C. 1970. L'Ennemmi principal. In *Partisans* no. 54-55. An English translation is available.
Engels, F. 1884/1972. *The origin of the Family, Private Property and the State*. Edited and with an introduction by E.B. Leacock. London: Lawrence & Wishart.
Goode, W.J. 1956. *Women in Divorce*. New York: Free Press.
Kooy, G.A. 1959. *Echtscheidingstendenties in 20ste eeuws Nederland inzonderheid ten plattelande*. (Divorce trends in the rural areas of the Netherlands in the 20th century) Assen: Van Gorcum.
Marceau, J. 1976. Marriage, Role Division and Social Cohesion: The Case of Some French Middle Class Families. In D. Leonard Barker and S. Allen (eds.), *Dependence and Exploitation in Work and Marriage*. Harlow: Longman.
Murdock, G.P. 1949. *Social Structure*. New York: Macmillan.

Zelditch, M. 1964. Family, Marriage and Kinship. In R.E.L. Faris (ed.), *Handbook of Modern Sociology*. Chicago: Rand McNally.

YVES DEZALAY

French Judicial Ideology
in Working-Class Divorce

Research workers who approach a subject that touches on or which
is in any way related to the judicial system, inevitably risk falling
into the trap laid for them by the very institution that they are
observing. For, while it is constantly creating its own ideology in
order to justify itself and its actions, it differs from other
institutions in so far as it does this not as a subordinate or parallel
activity, but as part of its everyday functioning.

To understand this it is helpful to use the analysis of mythology
formulated by Barthes (Guillaume 1974:19). He suggests that a
myth is a semiological system with two components: one having a
restricted but precise meaning, the other a vague but broader
one.[1] If we use this approach and apply it to legal accounts, we
regard each legal statement about events as carrying two meanings:
one which is narrow, technical, and operational; and the other
vague, manipulable, and supportive of an ideology. This second
meaning often serves to hide and divert attention from the first. In
this way the authoritarian nature of legal institutions is
camouflaged under a pretext of assistance to children in danger,
help for the weak and even for the poor.[2]

The preceding paper by Christine Delphy shows how the civil law
in France gives the impression that in marriage both partners give
and take equally and how it thus effectively hides the extortion of
the woman's unpaid work. The object of this paper is to show,
using examples drawn from observation of divorce cases, how the
judicial machinery also covertly contributes to this same end.

First, however, we must point out more fully how the
fundamental ambiguity of legal statements has led many previous
observers of divorce astray. Those sociologists and psychologists
who take as their point of departure the legal definition of divorce,
lose any chance they might have had of understanding the process
by which people getting divorced are moulded into a category by
the legal system and how they themselves contribute to the creation
and maintenance of a stereotype of divorce.[3] (This is a point
made by various people who have worked in the general area of

'deviancy', including Chapman (1968) of juvenile delinquency. [4]) This stereotype affirms that divorce is a distinct form of behaviour and that divorcees themselves are the product of physical, psychological, or social factors.

We would suggest that this blindness on the part of 'scientific' observers with regard to the role the legal system plays in moulding and defining the stereotype of divorce, prevents them from seeing how divorce acts as a scapegoat for marital problems.[5] The stigmatization of certain individuals by the judicial system in the course of divorce proceedings can be interpreted as an attempt to hide the conflicts consequent on the exploitation of women. Some may dispute this view of divorce as the sacrifice of a few scapegoats, though the miseries that follow a divorce — the disputes between parents and resultant traumatic effects on children — get so much publicity that they cannot be ignored. And at the same time it is interesting to note that the majority of people who lay emphasis on these miseries seem to be unaware that these difficulties are more often than not the result of the authoritarian intervention of judicial agents. They fall, consciously or not, into the ideological trap laid by the legal system, and accept its presentation of itself as an unbiased and disinterested helper of couples in difficulties; while the divorcees are seen as themselves responsible for their own unhappiness. Once the confidence trick is put across, the process of stigmatization can then be used to dissuade other couples from following the same route in an attempt to solve the conflicts inherent in their situation of exploitation.

To study divorce from this point of view means that any approach that is essentially statistical and uses official sources and definitions is out of the question, since by entering into the game of legal definitions and categories it is impossible not to reproduce the ideological presuppositions of the system. Only a detailed description in the style of, for example, Goffman allows us

'to avoid the ideological rationalisation created by the Judiciary, in short to go over and above the official concept without looking at them through the deformed prism of institutional statements, where they are reduced to symbols which serve merely to justify social intervention.' (Castel 1968:10)

The case studies used in this paper come from a study of divorce in a town in western France. They were collected in order to describe judicial intervention more from the point of view of those who are subjected to it than that of those who impose it. In order to see the ways in which legal ideology is used by social control agents and by those who are its victims, we limited ourselves to the observation of a single small provincial court.[6] We first interviewed the social control agents — lawyers, police, psychiatrists, the Director of Social Work (Directeur du service des tutelles aux allocations familiales) and social workers — and we studied divorce dossiers. These agents and the dossiers guided us in the choice of cases to be observed and interviewed. In this way, before we met a family, we knew the opinions of the authorities, who outlined the case to us and explained their intervention. We felt this method presented the most interesting and effective way of breaking down 'divorce' as a socio-legal artifact by putting the institutional account against that of the individuals concerned.

From this extensive material we have chosen a few examples to try to show the way in which the process of stigmatization, controlled by the legal system, contributes to the maintenance of female exploitation in marriage and at the same time diverts attention from this by having it believed that it is women who are responsible for the exploitation of their husbands at work.

One does not need to look hard to see the difference between myth and reality in judicial statements. By merely glancing over the dossiers of applicants for divorce, one can make a list of conjugal misdemeanors which differ from those forecast in the law texts; and the actual picture of marriage itself is the reverse of the supposed balance of conjugal relations which the law pretends.

The two grievances most frequently advanced by women in the dossiers are: the drunkenness of the husband who spends all his pay at the café, comes home drunk, and threatens or even beats his wife; and the husbands irregularity at work which is used as a pretext for refusing to give his wife the money needed for housekeeping. In both cases the women complain of being obliged to work outside the home in order 'to make ends meet'.

On the other hand, to add weight to *their* claims, husbands state that their wives neglect their families. In one case the dossier said she 'refuses to prepare his meals and he has to wash his own clothes'; in another, the wife 'shows no affection for her husband and leaves the children revoltingly filthy'.

Obviously we are not dealing here with the actual opinions of the parties concerned — the husbands and wives. The grievances listed in divorce dossiers have been selected because they are liable to be received favourably by the courts and to produce the desired effect; the granting of a divorce. The model of marriage of the courts emerges even more explicitly when we turn to the accounts given to us by those whose task it is to formulate the grievances officially, that is to say the lawyers and other agents of the judicial system. For example, one social worker said that

> 'A good husband is one who works regularly and seriously and gives his wife whatever money she needs to look after the house and family. A good wife is one who spends the couple's income wisely to set up a home, decorate it and make it pleasant to live in; moreover she must do this with affection and pleasure since then her husband will prefer to stay at home with her rather than go out drinking.'

For these legal agents it is not difficult to explain divorce; one lawyer summarized the causes: 'The typical case is the one where the husband drinks and the wife gives herself a good time.'

But even when the wrongdoings of one spouse are not seen as justifying and counter-balancing the wrongdoings of the other, the judicial agents see divorces as originating in the refusal of one of the parties to be satisfied with what the marriage contract allows him or her. For example, a psychiatrist who treated a tradesman's wife for some ten years (in the process ruining the tradesman), spoke of her in the following terms: 'You can't imagine what a terrible time she gave her husband, that man must be amazingly stable, she always wanted something new, absolutely ruined him. She's nothing but an insatiable little bourgeoise.' A social worker who carried out inquiries among broken families went so far as to say that this dissatisfaction is one of the major causes of the increase in the number of divorces. She claimed wives who have jobs push their husbands to be ambitious, and if their husbands do not look for better jobs or fail to get them, the wives quit.

> 'My experience has shown me that women who have outside jobs are ambitious. They want to rise in the world, they want to have an excellent position, lots of money, to have a better home, more freedom, spare time, they want their children to be better off. The husband is usually an honest fellow, hard-working but modest. He goes his own way. He meets his friends regularly. He has no ambition at work at all. Naturally he'll rise. If he's a civil servant, or if he works in a factory, the promotions will come regularly, so why bother tiring himself out? Everything's fine, he's very happy, he has a lovely wife, lovely house, beautiful children, he's very happy, everything's perfect. But she chooses that very moment to say to him: "Take it or leave it, either you get a move on or I will. I'm warning you, we're going to do this

or that." He says he's not interested and so that's it. There isn't
another woman behind it all; it's his wife who, faced with the
apathy of her husband, says to herself "I'm thirty years old; I'm
not going to spend my life beating my head against a brick wall.
Its over. I'm going."'

When officials of the judiciary give examples of divorce cases
they always emphasize the active role of the woman.[7] There is
nothing paradoxical in this: rather, the husband, when faced with
marital problems, because of his greater economic independence, is
able simply to take liberties with the marriage contract. Very rarely
does he need to appeal to the courts to have his wife's part of the
contract respected. All he has to do is leave, stop giving money to
his wife and take a mistress. In the words of one of the husbands we
met, 'Whenever there's a crisis, I leave'.

We were struck when we looked at the judiciary officials'
accounts that men did not seem to be judged on their capacity as
husbands; their only qualities or faults were of a vocational nature
and all that was expected of them was to be 'good workers'. On the
other hand women were expected to fulfill their household,
maternal, and conjugal tasks, and it was on these points alone that
they were judged. This duality shows the falseness of the equal
nature of the contribution brought by each partner to the marriage
as it is set out by the civil law for, in the event of trouble, the
husband is held to almost nothing outside his professional
obligations while the wife is held to everything else.

To get a clear idea of the effect of the judiciary system, it is
necessary to look at it in action and this is best done by looking at it
as an authoritarian system and as a deterrent system.

The law as an authoritarian system

Because divorce is classified as in the civil domain, it is easy to
forget that one is dealing with an authoritarian situation. In
France, divorce legislation is based on the concept of marital fault:
the divorce decree rewards the innocent party by punishing the
guilty one. Since magistrates refer to the grievances already briefly
outlined to determine the outcome of the trial, it is evident that
what is punished is failure to conform to a particular model of
marital behaviour.[8] But penalties do not stop at a mere statement
of guilt.

Not only is it often a dishonour to have a divorce pronounced
against one; it is also dangerous, since the custody of children,

maintenance, and damages are to varying degrees at stake during the trial.[9] Since it is unusual for couples to have no conflict of interest, cases of agreement are rare. One lawyer estimated that they represent perhaps about ten per cent of all cases and, what is more important, agreements can always be rescinded. Another lawyer explained to us why he did not like to issue divorces 'by mutual consent', by outlining the case of a woman who had arranged to have the courts give credence to a 'phoney' adultery, thus winning the divorce at her husband's expense. But two years later she sued him for maintenance and damages amounting to five thousand pounds. Thus it is impossible to avoid the notion of conflict, and magistrates arbitrate this conflict according to their idea of marriage.

If this is true of the outcome of the trial, it is even more true of the way the trial takes place in court. There is no need to reiterate the financial costs of a divorce — in France currently from £300 to £500 — nor the cost in time, more than a year, for these have often been discussed. On the other hand, it is worth drawing attention to the implications of the divorce procedure's inquisitorial character, as this aspect is becoming more and more dominant in France. The divorce-duel at the end of which the loser is punished, is frequently replaced by a divorce-inquisition which leads to the wife and children being placed under 'tutelary authority' (social work guardianship) — the judge's authority replacing that of the absent husband. Because of this, the number of social inquiries ordered by judges, ostensibly to assure the children's protection, is increasing rapidly.[10] They are used almost as a matter of course in the 'Family Courts' and these have often been presented as showing the way to the future in family law. A deeper understanding of what these inquiries can be like is therefore useful.

As their name implies, they are searches for information, and as the following excerpt from an interview with a social worker illustrates, the end often justifies the means:

'Generally speaking you can get a lot of information about people that way. You go to their house, without warning; you've already made inquiries in the village: the baker's a good person as he usually knows everybody, sometimes the mayor, always the local school-teacher. It's always better to arrive unexpectedly. It's not very nice for them, but you get a good picture of the situation. Once I went to see a woman like that; I didn't warn her. I arrived at ten in the morning. She made a really wry face; she wasn't pleased (laugh). She was cross because she was busy getting fancy-dress costumes ready for her children so there was paper all over the place. It was a real mess, you can hardly imagine. I said to her, "but Madam, that doesn't bother me at all". There's just one thing I wanted to see, if by chance there was a man in the house — there wasn't anyone. Then she said to me "Excuse me, I'm not very polite ..." I said, "You're very polite, you're not pleased at all, I saw that from the very beginning, I understand how you feel, if I were you I'm not so sure I would have let *me* in (laugh laugh)." Then she said, "Excuse me, I understand why you do this ...."'

It is interesting to compare what this social worker says about her 'investigation methods' with the account given by one of the women she visited:

'So, one day, I saw her arrive, she hadn't warned me, she just walked in; she was a tall woman with a big fur coat, and I said to myself she must be really well paid to have a coat like that. We were having a meal, luckily that day there was a gorgeous roast chicken on the table, lots of chips and salad. So right away she went to look in my bed, she opened everything up, the children's beds, the cupboards, ransacked everything without saying a word. So I said to her, "Hey, what are you doing?" She replied, "Be quiet, I've got a court order" and she showed me a little pink slip ...'

Again one notices that in their authoritarian activities, the agents of the judiciary system contribute towards the control and the maintenance of the domestic exploitation of women. In the reports made out by these investigators the husband's work outside the home and his financial contribution to the household; and the care the woman takes in looking after and cleaning her home and her children, are the points which come up most often. For example:

'Mr. P. is a respectable person, temperate, calm, a very steady worker. He gives entire satisfaction to his employer.
Mme. P. strikes one as "agitated". She must be quite violent, and does not seem to be fundamentally sincere; she is quite hard to get along with. She takes good care of her daughters, her home is very clean, her children are always perfectly well dressed.'

An unfavourable judgement with an implicit condemnation is made of the woman who does not accept the situation that her marriages creates. Hence the C. family:

'The wife, intelligent but wily, has a notoriously bad reputation;

she often leaves her children by themselves, has no scruples about taking a taxi when she goes out, doesn't seem to worry about whether her children have everything they need.

The husband — extremely retarded, harmless and defenceless, cannot read or write ... In conclusion, the family has been broken up by the immoral behaviour of the mother who is certainly intelligent but completely amoral and wily ... The children are in unquestionable moral danger if they stay with their mother and her lovers; it appears most urgent to remove them from her noxious influence.'

In the last analysis these reports are not very different from the ones made by the police. In connection with the same woman, the police officers had simply noted under the heading concerning domestic work: 'Does the housework, but goes often in to L' (near-by city). And it is certainly no coincidence that in one Family Court in the north of France, social inquiries into divorce cases are, for reasons of economy, systematically entrusted to former police officers.[11]

The Law as a deterrent system

The main point of judicial intervention does not lie in the immediate and direct expression of its authority. It functions above all as a deterrent system with a multiplicity of agents and a whole hierarchy of punishments aimed at bringing about a 're-education'. These deterrents range from decrees prescribing a social work guardianship for family income and allowances, to imprisonment.

In principle, the objective behind social work guardianship (*mise en tutelle*) is to make sure that financial resources are effectively used for the children. In point of fact a study has shown that in almost all cases it is mainly used to guarantee the payment of rent in state housing estates, where it is difficult to turn out the families of defaulting tenants and to ensure payment of household bills (Lucconi 1972). The Director of the Tutelage Department in the town where we worked recognized this: 'Often it is the H.L.M.[12] office or the local shopkeepers who draw attention to non-payments — but the real causes may be conjugal disagreements which lead one or the other to look for compensation elsewhere ... a car, drinking for the man, clothes for the woman.'

By this device social workers can control the total income of a household. He said:

'At the beginning of the month we decide with the family what we're going to do with the money, we make a list of what everyone needs; we have them note down exactly what wages and family allowances bring in; then, for example, we may decide on a television set so that the father and children will stay at home in the evening.'

The objective is re-education and reorientation and a whole sex role philosophy is implicit in these interventions.

'We want to modify our action so that it will not be intrinsically an action which relies on the payment of debts, but an action which is more educative and all enveloping. For example we shouldn't let the mother buy herself a dress because that is the easy way out. She should make it herself and so it's better to get her to take sewing lessons. If the husband drinks we help the wife ask herself the question as to why he drinks; some women decide to reorganize their domestic arrangements to help hold on to their husbands.'

However, one cannot attempt to judge the efficacy of just one element of the system of social control by itself. The various sub-systems — social worker control of family incomes, the educative action or surveillance by social workers, the institution of moral and social re-education etc. — are closely linked together so that there are frequent transfers from one sub-system to another. The Director of the Tutelage Department said: 'It often happens that parents come to talk about the problems they're having with their children, so we refer them to an educational psychologist who in turn consults the children's judge ...'

The essential characteristic of the judicial system's manner of operating lies in this close interrelationship between the various departments and in the graded nature of their interventions: they form a graded penalty system and its counterpart, an incitement to accept moral and social re-education. Two quite ordinary examples bear witness to this. One is the story of a couple where the husband was an alcoholic who beat his wife when drunk. She tried to bring pressure to bear on him by having the local police commissariat certify that she had received a number of blows. Finding that this had little or no effect she went further and sued her husband for divorce. At this point the Children's Judge came onto the scene and threatened the husband that he would take away his children unless he agreed to undergo treatment for alcoholism. In another case, there was an 'amputation of the sick member' [13] when all attempts at re-education had failed. The story began in the same way as the preceding one, but after the divorce had been pronounced against the husband, as due entirely to his faults, his behaviour became more and more that of a vagrant. He spent half his time in prison, the other half wandering aimlessly about. In this case, the law acted to 'separate the wheat from the tares'.

The judicial system is also, of course, a dissuasive system directed against women and children. In one case, after twenty years of married life, an engineer ran off with his young mistress. His wife, a school-teacher, won the divorce but in spite of that continued to feel 'spied upon' and 'watched'. In her own words she was afraid that her husband's family would try to take the children away from her. So she forced them to be brilliant at school. Once, during a teachers meeting, a colleague told us she refused all idea of her children receiving the school-prizes they had quite deservedly won, as 'it would go to their heads'. She cut her hair and that of her children very short, and each Sunday she paraded them down the main street so that 'every one would be able to see how well brought up they are'.

Divorce as a process of stigmatization

The great strength of judicial intervention is its public character. The ambiguity of judicial statements makes it possible for the law to disguise the fact that it is an authoritarian system of dissuasion, and, on the contrary, allows it to get a process of stigmatization endorsed by the population as a whole and even accepted by those who themselves are the victims. In this way, the small number of cases in which the law does intervene serve as scapegoats, and are given a great deal more 'publicity' than their numerical importance justifies.

Judicial intervention relies quite often on the co-operation of one of the couple or on that of their relatives. Marital grievances have to be known and public to be accepted by the courts. It is a cliche that one can beat one's wife, but in private only, and provided it leaves no traces; but a study showed that physical violence was present in more than half of the families considered (Steinmetz and Strauss 1974). In France, marital 'faults' are made public — at *l'enquête de temoins*, when the grievances stated by the lawyers are proved at a hearing during which the friends, neighbours, or work colleagues come to testify to the reality of the misdeeds. This procedure, however, is not a primitive sort of popular justice; on the contrary, the witnesses can only accept or refuse to substantiate those grievances which have been formulated by the judiciary officials. Nonetheless, this procedure ensures that the condemnation which the court pronounces is helped, even guaranteed, by those close to the couple, and this support provides it with a great deal of its force.

Further, the law finds its most important collaborators in the spouses themselves. It is they who institute proceedings and they present, or accept interpretations of 'faults' which fit the stereotype. The following case illustrates this quite clearly. The wife of a doctor, a former nurse, sued for legal separation following the court-ordered confiscation of all the couple's furniture owing to the husband's refusal to pay his debts. The lawyers presented a dossier which was ratified by the court and showed Mme B. to be a 'hard worker, methodical, and a good mother' whereas Doctor B. had 'an unconventional character, was lazy, kept his patients waiting because he got up late, was forever contracting debts, and even went so far as to refuse to pay his doctors' pension plan subscriptions ...' But particularly note-worthy is the fact that numerous and repeated instances of infidelity were mentioned particularly in connection with his professional activities: 'Because of his frequent absences at night he was often unable to look after his patients when they needed him.'

This woman was held to be — as are all women — fully justified when she demanded that her husband work and support her, and when the court granted alimony at the end of the proceedings, they acknowledged this fact. The greater part of the pressure brought to bear on the husband concerned his professional behaviour and not his behaviour towards his wife. One is tempted to say that the courts go through the divorce demands and choose those which are likely to best serve the interests of emphasizing the domestic responsibility of women and the financial responsibilities of men. In this type of collaboration the judge has the last word. He decides who will be the scapegoat and why.[14]

The sex role stereotyping is even clearer when the wife makes what are considered as unacceptable demands.

'Right at the beginning, as soon as I was married, I became preg-nant and I thought that this must be true happiness. But all the same he bored me, and I began to find that sexual relations weren't all that good. Besides I cried each time afterwards, but as far as he was concerned that's what I was there for and that's all there was to it; he didn't give me a moment's thought once he was satisfied, everything was fine and he looked happy. So one day I said to myself, there's something very wrong, if that's what being married means; I certainly didn't expect it to be like that.

But my husband didn't have the slightest idea. I was there, I looked after the children, did the cooking, kept the house tidy, answered the telephone, he was satisfied. But I had the feeling that I didn't even exist. One day I became hysterical because I had already tried to make him understand that it couldn't go on like that ...'

This is the same woman who was described by her psychiatrist as an 'insatiable little bourgeoisie'. His opinion justified the following treatment: repeated internments in psychiatric hospitals, many sessions of electro-therapy, and a regular and massive administration of tranquillizers.

Many other examples could be given: For instance, a working-class woman married to a peasant farmer said:

'In the beginning I was still working and everything was alright, but as soon as I stopped working after the birth of Nathalie I was at home all the time, I was just a maid. I didn't have any money and I never went out. His peasant mentality really got on my nerves, he never wanted to go out. On bank holidays he would just go and work on the farm, and besides, he told his mother everything, always hanging onto her apron-strings. We had arguments all the time. And so I got really fed-up and I said to him "It's your mother or me". I didn't like that country mentality at all; they're dirty and it's no joke for a woman ... Now I'm alright, I work in town at the factory and nobody bothers me ...'

This woman in fact obtained her divorce, but while the courts agreed to a confirmation of the separation, they at the same time condemned her explicitly; she was found to be the guilty party and she lost the custody of her son in spite of her claims, and was left with only her two daughters.

A woman is liable to be more or less penalised depending on the degree to which she has deviated from the proposed marital ideal. The present encouragement of rural emigration in France makes it acceptable for a peasant farmer's wife to wish to improve her situation, but it is out of the question that she deny her maternal or conjugal duties. Another couple were tradespeople, the husband was Italian, a grocer. He treated his wife as an inferior, making her work doubly hard as servant and as employee. He quarrelled with her in front of the staff — accusing her of not working hard enough in the store, not looking after their home properly and of having continual love affairs. The woman dared to rebel against the kind of life to which she was subjected and refused to work without being paid. But worst of all she left her home and her children. The judicial system pronounced against her: 'She's a bad mother ...'; 'She's more woman than mother ...'.

The severity of these condemnations of women who dare to refuse their maternal obligations shows that in the eyes of the law and society these obligations are precisely their fundamental and exclusive responsibility. This point becomes more evident when we compare the severity of the law with regard to women, with the relative tolerance and near comprehension which is so often shown husbands who fail to carry out their part of the contract. The Director of tutelage of family allowances pointed out that frequently when a family is under guardianship:

> 'The salary is monopolized by the father who refuses to put it on the table so that it can be used for the whole family's needs. He tends to say, "You have your guardian, shift for yourselves." That is why', the Director concluded, 'we should also try to work with the husbands whereas in the past we would only see the wives ...'

These last examples show that the obligations binding the men-husbands and the women-wives in marriage are fundamentally different from the informal legal viewpoint, not only in degree but also in kind. One is tempted to formulate the hypothesis that there are in fact two systems juxtaposed, each having it's own specific objectives; one belongs to the legal control of work relations whilst the other concerns conjugal relations proper. Confusion stems from the fact that the judicial system gives the appearance of being coherent when it intervenes in matters relating to the family. But might this not be a mere facade whose function is precisely to dissimulate that all the specifically marital obligations rest on the woman? If this is so, it is consistent with the fact that it is the wife who most often sets the judicial intervention into the family in motion, running the risk of having it turn against her — her resources or children may be put under tutelary authority, and she is the only partner whose behaviour *towards her family* is likely to be blamed for she may be condemned as a bad wife or, worse still, a bad mother.

The man as husband rarely brings in outside agents and is, by comparison, ignored by the legal agents when they do intervene. The interventions or pressures brought to bear on him are directed more at his capacity as a wage earner: the 'bad husband' being above all a 'bad worker'. A large part of what is observed during divorce or other similar proceedings may be at the moment incorrectly classified as 'family intervention' when it should rather be entered under 'work relations'.

The conclusions that one can draw having observed the actual functioning of the judicial machine are not very different from the avowed purposes of the institution as they appear in the legislative debates which preceded the vote on the divorce laws of 1884.

Those in favour of the law claimed that a 'Restricted and difficult divorce would be more moral for the lower classes than a *de facto* separation. The alternative to divorce being bigamy and illegitimate births' (*Journal Officiel* 1884). The purpose behind the law was to offer the working classes a more realistic and satisfactory model of marriage which would contribute towards limiting concubinage and the very high rate of illegitimate births (40 per cent in Paris in the first half of the nineteenth century). It was an attempt to moralize and stabilize the working class, with much emphasis on the family and thrift — both of which helped to discipline workers by encouraging them to work regularly and steadily.

Again this ambiguity of judicial statements, the mixing of the professional control of men and the conjugal control of women, involves an ideology that the reciprocal obligations of the two parties are equal. A lot of men in fact consider that it is because of their wives that they are forced to 'kill' themselves working and this, in their eyes, makes up for whatever sacrifices their wife is obliged to make in marriage.

One could in fact ask whether our social system's great strength has not been to propagate this ideology/myth, which is dissembling the exploitation of women in marriage, makes women appear responsible for the exploitation of men in the labour market. The dual nature of legal discourse thus contributes to the division/opposition of the exploited work force.

Notes

1   The following example from Barthes (1972) may help to indicate his line of thought.

In an article in a woman's magazine on French women novelists, individuals were introduced as 'Jacqueline L. (two daughters, one novel), Marina B. (one son, two novels)' etc. The information about the women's children is both a limited, precise fact about each of them and also a particular broad vague representation of the woman novelist — as preeminently a wife/woman/mother.

2   On England and America see Handler (1969 and 1974). In
    France, children in 'moral danger' and juvenile delinquents are
    often classed together, treated in a similar manner and put into
    the same institutions.

3   See, for instance, Goode (1956) and I.N.E.D. (1974).

4   ' ... much of the work done by social scientists in the field of
    Criminology has been unprofitable because it has begun with
    definitions — stereotypes — which have determined the course
    of the inquiry and the conclusions that have emerged'
    (Chapman 1968:ix).

5   'It is surely not implausible to see here one more ambivalence in
    the culture, the practice of the sacrifice of the scapegoat as
    solving the emotional maladjustment of the great mass of
    society and theories of crime and punishment as providing a
    "rational" basis for the practice' (Chapman 1968:246).

6   The fieldwork was carried out in the area under the jurisdiction
    of the County Court (Tribunal de Grande Instance) of Laval,
    between June 1973 and February 1974. All the divorce cases
    which had come before the courts during 1970, '71, and '72
    were considered, but the main effort was directed towards a
    detailed study of a dozen cases and their relationships with the
    judicial agencies.
        The sample was chosen for us by the court clerks, judges,
    lawyers, and social workers as being those which best illustrated
    and *justified* their intervention. For these dozen cases we had
    the accounts of the judicial agencies and the dossiers of the
    court, the lawyers and the assistance éducatrice. We also met
    the (ex)spouses several times.
        The data were collected by Manuela Vincente and Anne
    Biadi.

7   A local lawyer, commenting on the increasing ease with which
    divorces are granted by the courts, said

    'In the past in rural areas women put up with their husband's
    drunkenness and no one ever thought of dividing the livestock,
    since even the winning partner would find it impossible to
    survive. Nowadays women demand more from their
    husbands ... They're even beginning to realise that men can
    be clean ...'

8   However, the notion of divorce as punishment is being seriously
    challenged by a new idea of divorce as the failure of a marriage.
    Projects for a reform in divorce legislation confirm this change
    and it is common knowledge that in large cities many divorce

proceedings are pure legal farces.
9 Christine Delphy (in this volume) makes the point that the battle over custody is 'staged' and whoever gets the custody believes he — or more usually she — has won the war.
10 Whilst there is no actual measure of this increase available, various things point in this direction:
   — the very large number of such enquiries (9400 in 1971);
   — the development of the family courts (Chambres de la Famille) which undertake this sort of investigation;
   — the doubling in the number of social workers between 1962 and 1972 (*Esprit* 1972).
11 The divorce cases cited so far have involved only the working class. But this should not be taken to imply that divorce is non-existent in the upper classes; only that their proceedings are very different and as a general rule far more discreet. The public part of the trial is often much shorter: an exaggerated example being that of a well known politician whose trial lasted only eight days. Even without going to such extremes it can be observed that separations involving members of the upper classes are studied and briefed behind the closed doors of lawyers' and notaries' chambers, and that the conflicts involved are resolved by a kind of amicable arrangement, as acknowledged by one notary we interviewed: 'Right now we have the case of a husband and wife who are personal friends of my father; in this case he is the one who more or less acts as arbitrator, his privileged position enables him to obtain concessions from each of the parties.' It is therefore difficult to study this type of separation, but one can be sure that financial matters predominate.

   If, in such circles, the law loses part of its authoritarian character, very often another person takes over the authoritarian role: the psychiatrist. It is no exaggeration to say that working-class women deviate from the marital ideal by getting into debt, having love affairs, or simply by disappearing, whereas middle-class women have nervous breakdowns. In both cases the same escape from conjugal duties is involved. Simply the forms are adapted to the particular situations and the prophylaxis is different. Instead of getting an affidavit of adultery or a search warrant, the middle-class husband tends to have his wife committed to an asylum or, less extreme, he will get the family doctor to prescribe her chemical sedatives (Chesler 1974). In one dossier we found the expression 'neurotic disorders with a tendency to depression related to conjugal conflict'. A 'diagnosis' such as this can eventually justify treatment by internment or electro-therapy.

In France, advertisements produced by drug merchants extol the merits of sedatives which are presented as being especially indispensable for housewives living in large apartment buildings (which are the normal housing for the French middle-classes).

12 *Habitations à Loyer Modéré.*

13 The 'amputation' can be obtained physically by putting the children into a home, or by placing them with a geographically distant family; or it can be achieved by putting the adult into prison or a hospital. For further details see Mayer (1974).

14 Thus in a case where the husband agreed to let his wife go off on trips with her lovers because he preferred her being 'unfaithful' to leaving him altogether, the court decreed that: 'the husband may appear to have consented to the situation but in fact he was simply submitting to something he could not prevent ... and the moral depravity of Mme G. makes it impossible to entrust her with the child.'

References

Barthes, P. 1972. *Mythologies* (trans. A. Lavers). London: Jonathan Cape.

Castel, R. 1968. Preface to the French edition of E. Goffman's *Asylums/Asiles.* Paris: Editions de Minuit.

Chapman, D. 1968. *Sociology and the Stereotypes of the Criminal.* London: Tavistock.

Chesler, P. 1974. *Women and Madness.* London: Allen Lane.

Esprit. 1972. Numero spécial sur le travail social. Mai.

Goode, W.J. 1956. *Women in Divorce.* New York. Free Press.

Guillaume, M. 1974. Mythologies de la science économique. *Projet.* January.

Handler, J.F. 1969. The Coercive Children's Officer. *New Society.* October.

— 1974. *The Coercive Social Worker.* London: Academic Press.

I.N.E.D. 1974. *Le Divorce et les Français.* Cahiers de l'I.N.E.D. Paris: P.U.F.

Editions du Journal Officiel. 1884. *Journal officiel.* Debats parlementaires. 27 Juillet.

Luccioni, 1972. *Rapport sur les tutelles aux prestations sociales.* Caisse Nationale d'Allocations Familiales. Paris: C.N.A.F.

Mayer, P. 1974. *Rapport au C.O.R.D.E.S. sur le controle social.* Paris: C.O.R.D.E.S.

Steinmetz, S. and Strauss, M. 1974. *Violence in the Family.* New York: Dodds Mead.

HILARY LAND

Women:
Supporters or Supported?

The social security system of any country is based on beliefs and assumptions about human nature, social relationships, and the forces which mould and maintain these relationships. The inequalities and anomalies in a social security system cannot be understood or challenged unless these underlying values and assumptions are examined, for they are crucial determinants not only of the nature and level of benefit to which an individual may be entitled, but also of his or her access to social security. Some of these assumptions have been established over many decades and will have been used continuously by dominant groups to legitimize and maintain the power they exercise over weaker sections of society. Often remaining implicit, they are also firmly embedded in the system of family law and taxation, and are remarkably persistent in the face of major social, economic, and demographic changes. This can be illustrated by looking at how women benefit from the British social security system and the extent to which their unequal treatment reflects society's attitudes towards marriage, women, and the poor.

Men and women do not receive identical treatment under our present social security system, for a woman's rights to benefit are determined by her marital status to an extent to which a man's entitlement is not. To understand why this is so and how far these inequalities reflect real differences in need, it is necessary first to look at the development of social security provisions for women, particularly those for wives and mothers; second to examine the assumptions underlying these provisions; and third to explore how far the assumptions incorporated in the *Beveridge Report* (Beveridge 1942), which formed the basis of the legislation passed twenty-five years ago, have been preserved in the first major restructuring of our social security system to take place since that time; namely, those changes incorporated in the Social Security Act 1973 and the tax-credit proposals (Select Committee on Tax-credits 1973). It will then become clear that the British social security system, by perpetuating inegalitarian family relationships, is a means of reinforcing, rather than compensating for, economic inequalities.

The Beveridge plan for women as wives, mothers, and workers

In 1942, when William Beveridge was writing his report, all women, whether single or married, received lower social insurance and means-tested assistance benefits. Every woman insured under the state health and unemployment insurance scheme paid slightly lower contributions than a man and received a disproportionately lower rate of sickness and unemployment benefit.[1] It was argued that the incidence of absence due to sickness was higher among women than men, particularly among married women (largely due to ill-health associated with childbirth)[2] and therefore actuarial principles dictated that women should receive a lower benefit, the married woman getting even less than her single sister.[3] There was no attempt to differentiate between sections of male workers, some of whom had higher risks of illness or disability than women: their risks were pooled. Actuarial principles were ignored, however, in unemployment insurance where they would have justified higher benefits for women than men as the incidence of unemployment amongst insured and registered women was far less than among insured men (Labour Party's Advisory Committee 1935:9). In addition, the means-tested public assistance scale rates gave less to the single female householder than to the single male householder. Presumably this was because it had been estimated that her nutritional requirements were less, although nutritionists then, or indeed now, were not capable of estimating nutritional requirements expressed in money terms very accurately and there were, and are, considerable individual variations.

Beveridge removed the anomalies concerning single women and under his scheme, in terms of benefit, they were to get the same as men. Their contributions to the national insurance scheme were to be lower, however, on the grounds that a man, unlike a woman, was making contributions 'on behalf of himself and his wife, as for a team' (Beveridge 1942:49). He did not use the argument that on grounds of equity a woman should contribute at a lower rate because her earnings on average were so much lower than a man's.

Housewives

Married women were regarded differently from single women. Their status in the national insurance scheme was based on a picture of 'the great majority of married women ... occupied on work which is vital though unpaid, without which their husbands could not do their paid work and without which the nation could not continue' (Beveridge 1942:50). In other words Beveridge regarded the family as an economic unit and the distinctive economic role of the wife was to service the existing work force and produce the next generation of workers. In return for this 'vital work' husbands had a moral and legal duty to provide their wives with the means of subsistence and Beveridge wanted to ensure that they were able to do so when they were sick, unemployed, or old. By treating housewives in his national insurance scheme as a special class, a dependent class, Beveridge was faithfully reflecting and reinforcing women's economic dependence on their husbands which Gardiner (1975) argues places women engaged in domestic labour in a distinctive class in the Marxist sense.

The direct participation of married women in the labour market as workers was ignored and Beveridge assumed that the majority were totally dependent on a male wage earner. He wrote:

> 'During marriage most women will not be gainfully employed. The small minority of women who undertake paid employment or other gainful occupations after marriage require special treatment differing from that of a single woman. Such paid work will in many cases be intermittent, it should be open to any married woman to undertake it as an exempt person, paying no contributions of her own and acquiring no claim to benefit in unemployment or sickness. If she prefers to contribute and to requalify for unemployment and disability benefit she may do so, but will receive benefits at a reduced rate.' (Beveridge 1942:50)

He argued (1942:51) that the case for lower benefits was strong 'both on practical grounds and on grounds of equity'. He gave three reasons. First, a married woman had a husband's earnings on which to depend and as household costs, particularly rent, were shared she needed less benefit. Of course this applies equally to anyone who shares a household. The only difference is that a husband has a legal obligation to maintain his wife which friends living together may not have. In practice this may offer very little financial security to the wife. Second, repeating the arguments used since the beginning of the National Health insurance scheme, in 1911, he argued that a married woman's earnings were more likely to be interrupted by sickness than a single woman's. Therefore 'the rate of benefit for married women was reduced because as matters stood single women, whose needs during sickness were greater, appeared to be paying more than their share' (1942:51). However, it was also the case that lower paid workers of either sex were more prone to illness than higher paid workers. There was no suggestion that they should receive lower benefits. Indeed, Beveridge had defined 'social insurance' to mean 'the pooling of risks'. This implied, he wrote, (1942:13) that 'none should claim to pay less because he is healthier' and 'men should stand together with their fellows'. Yet he differentiated between women. Third, a married woman's earnings were more likely to be interrupted through childbirth and 'in the national interest it is important that the interruption by childbirth should be as complete as possible; the expectant mother should be under no economic pressure to continue at work as long as she can and return to it as soon as she can' (1942:49). He therefore proposed that maternity benefit should be 50 per cent higher than the man or single woman's unemployment benefit. Thus 'on grounds of equity a proposal to pay lower unemployment and disability benefit to married women is right in view both of the special maternity benefit proposed and of the general balance of contributions and benefits' (1942:51).

Beveridge's plans for a marriage grant to mark the beginning of a woman's 'new life in relation to a social insurance' (1942:50) and an end-of-marriage benefit along the lines of widow's benefits were never implemented but otherwise his proposals concerning married women were incorporated in the subsequent National Insurance Acts.

Mothers
At the time Beveridge was writing there was widespread concern both inside and outside government about population trends. It was feared that Britain's population would decline unless the birth rate was increased. 'In the next thirty years housewives as mothers have vital work to do in ensuring the adequate continuance of the British race and of British ideals in the world' (Beveridge 1942:43). The married women's role as a paid worker was underestimated by those concerned with social policy twenty-five years ago because it was believed 'maternity is the principal object of marriage' (Beveridge 1942:50). The possibility that women might wish to, and be capable of combining motherhood with paid employment, as many in fact were already doing, was both disapproved of and ignored. Beveridge wrote: 'the attitude of the housewife to gainful employment outside the home is not and *should* not be the same as that of a single woman. She has other duties' (1942:51). How then were the needs of mothers recognized in Beveridge's scheme and in the subsequent legislation?

The first underlying assumption of Beveridge's plan for social security was that children's allowances would be paid to all families with at least two children irrespective of the employment or marital status of the parents. This was the first of his proposals to be implemented and in fact the Family Allowance Act was passed in 1945 by the war-time coalition government. The rest of the national insurance and assistance legislation were passed by the succeeding Labour Government. Family allowances were not a new idea and the government had accepted in principle a universal scheme of cash allowances before Beveridge published his report. When family allowances were threatened with abolition in the tax credit proposals recently, it was argued that they were important because the 'Family Allowance is the only form of income all women with two or more children are entitled to; however inadequate it may be, it is for many mothers the only source of money of their own. It is also the only recognition they get for work they do in looking after children' (Women's Family Allowance Campaign 1973:384). This is true but it would be a mistake to think that the introduction of family allowances in 1946 was *predominantly* a triumph for women's rights. On the contrary, only a minority supported family allowances as a means of recognizing and improving the status of mothers as a worthy end in itself. It was only when family allowances were widely believed to be a means of achieving other ends, in particular economic ends, that they acquired sufficient support to be introduced.

The arguments in favour of the state maintenance of children which later took the form of a universal scheme of cash family allowances, were initially couched in terms of improving the welfare and status of mothers and children, particularly those who were poor. Serious discussions of the idea this century started among predominantly left-wing or feminist circles. Before the First World War trade unionists, for example, particularly members of the Social Democratic Federation (a Marxist organization) saw the introduction of local authority financed school meals as the first step towards full state maintenance. Their proposals were very vague and it was generally believed, even among trade union members, that such proposals 'would excite great prejudice and alarm' (National Labour Conference 1905:15). At this time leading Fabians became interested in the subject not only because they wanted to reduce women's economic dependence on their husbands but also because they were worried about the falling birth rate particularly among those whom Sidney Webb (1907) called 'the self controlled and far seeing members of each class'. During this period there was considerable concern about the 'physical efficiency' of the British population and it was feared that the less intelligent and less healthy sections of society were breeding at a

faster rate than those of better stock, thus bringing about a decline
in the physical and intellectual standards of the British nation. At
the end of the First World War, when the campaign for the
introduction of a scheme of cash family allowances began in
earnest with the formation of the Family Endowment Society led
by Eleanor Rathbone, it was argued that family allowances would
not only enhance the status of women as mothers but also as
workers by removing a barrier against equal pay. It was argued at
the time, and is still argued by many at least implicitly, that men
should be paid more than women because unlike women, men have
families to support.

   Support for family allowances made little headway outside of the
suffragette or Labour movement in the twenties, not least because
it was believed Britain was already overpopulated, as demonstrated
by the high level of unemployment. However in the thirties the
demographic situation was believed to have changed and there was
increasing concern that if the birth rate continued to fall Britain
was faced with the prospect of a declining population. Moreover
there was evidence of extensive poverty and malnutrition
particularly among children. This, against a background of a
dwindling number of children, posed a real threat to the military
and economic strength of the country. For the first time
Conservatives, notably Leo Amery, Duncan Sandys, and Robert
Boothby, took up the cause for family allowances as a means of
encouraging the birth of more children and preventing poverty.
Meanwhile, Beveridge, as chairman of the Unemployment
Insurance Committee, was having increasing difficulty in paying
adequate benefits to the unemployed man, whose allowances since
1921 had taken into account the size of his family, without making
him better off than he was in work. 'It is dangerous to allow benefit
during unemployment or disability to equal or exceed earnings
during work', so in order that 'the gap between income during
earning and during interruptions of earnings should be as large as
possible for every man' (Beveridge 1942:154), his family needs
should be considered at all times. In other words family allowances
were a means of preserving the work incentive for men.

   The argument which finally convinced a government to consider
a proposal for a state family allowance scheme was that used by
Keynes at the beginning of the Second World War (Keynes:
1940). This too, relates to the level of men's wages. The control
of inflation was one of the most important economic issues facing
the war-time coalition government. Keynes argued that the
introduction of a universal scheme of family allowances, together

with rationing and food subsidies, would protect poor families against rising prices and reduce the need and demand for overall wage increases. Family allowances, therefore, were taken seriously only when they were seen to be relevant to the government's economic policy.

The arguments against family allowances have also been varied. At times of concern about overpopulation, universal cash family allowances are always less popular, for it is believed, although there is little evidence to support the belief, that family allowances encourage larger families. Another fear which has rather more substance if family allowances are financed by the employers, is that such allowances depress wage rates. This was the argument used against family allowances in the inter-war years by some trade unionists and it was not until the Second World War brought about a substantial improvement in the strength of the labour movement that the majority were willing to accept a scheme of family allowances, and then only on condition that it was financed by the State, out of general taxation, not by employers.

The most persistent argument against family allowances, however, is based on the assumption, as Eleanor Rathbone wrote,

'that the beauty of the tie between husband and wife, father and child will be impaired, and its strength weakened, if there is anything less than complete financial dependence ... [and] ... the father's motive to industry will be undermined if he no longer feels that he stands between his children and starvation.' (Rathbone 1924:198).

(Anyone doubting the persistence of the latter assumption need only look at the recent debate on benefits to strikers families). Such assumptions were made by people from many parts of the political spectrum. Some members of the Independent Labour Party, including Ramsay MacDonald for example, were totally opposed to family allowances:

'the proposal to endow mothers appears to be an outburst of an insane individualism claiming the right of a man or woman to exercise a selfish will without restraint, and is not the corollary of a rational scheme of social organisation like Socialism ... the mothers' and children's rights to maintenance will be honoured by the family; not by the State.' (MacDonald 1909:150).

Similarly the suffragette movement was by no means unanimously in support of such a scheme. Mrs Pankhurst and Millicent Fawcett were opposed to family allowances because parental responsibility would be weakened. However, as Eleanor Rathbone pointed out,

> 'the prosperous middle and upper class has its own custom of marriage settlements which mitigates to at least as great an extent as family allowances would do, the financial dependency of wives and children on husbands and fathers. Yet I have never heard the custom denounced by well-to-do critics [of family allowances].' (Rathbone 1924:199).

Of course marriage settlements evolved largely to maintain and protect the inheritance of property within a family rather than in recognition of the rights of women. Nevertheless, a comparison of the arguments put forward in support of state recognition of the responsibilities of parenthood among the prosperous, in the income tax system for example, with the arguments used against recognizing those of the poor family, showed quite inconsistent attitudes. More recently, for example in 1963, The Conservative Government's proposals for increasing the child tax allowance were welcomed because this would help 'a great proportion of young professional people ... who are making their way in the world are founding their families and have very great financial responsibility' (*H.C. Debates*: Vol. 675. Col. 530 1963). A year later a Member of the same Party proposed the abolition of the family allowance for the second child on the ground that parents should be told 'you should be capable of bringing up two children without help from anybody' (*H.C. Debates*: Vol. 687. Col. 1121 1964). The poor man needs the greater incentive of totally dependent children to keep him at his unrewarding work; the professional man apparently does not.

On balance, therefore, the family allowances scheme introduced in 1945 only incidentally recognized the needs of mothers and children and then only to a limited extent. By excluding the first child and failing to make the value of the allowance equal to the subsistence cost of a child, the state was only taking a small share in the cost of maintaining its future citizens and workers. However, one small victory was achieved by Eleanor Rathbone during the debate on the Bill which forced some recognition of the status of mothers. Initially the Bill provided that the family allowance should belong to the father and therefore the allowance book would be sent to him. As a result of getting a free vote in the House, Eleanor Rathbone saw this decision reversed and the allowance book belongs to the mother although either parent can cash the allowance. This marked some change in attitudes for in 1911, under the first National Health Insurance Act, a wife entitled to maternity benefit in virtue of her husband's insurance did not own the benefit: it was treated as 'a benefit for the husband' and paid to him! It was two years before that clause was repealed and maternity benefit became the property of the woman.

Working women

The picture of the economic position of women contained in the Beveridge report was only a partial one. It was even more incomplete and out-of-date by the end of the war.

During the war two and a half million more women were mobilized for paid industrial employment either full or part-time. By 1943, for example, over 40 per cent of all married women were in paid employment compared with one in seven in 1939. This included one in five of married women with children.[4] Beveridge regarded this as a temporary and exceptional phenomenon and in 1942, at a time of considerable uncertainty about the military and economic future of the country, perhaps this was reasonable. However by the end of the war those concerned with shaping our social security system had little excuse for making this false assumption.

In the first place, the Government was committed to a policy of full employment (H.M. Government 1944) and the fear amongst the economic policy makers was one of a *shortage* of labour. It was important therefore that women not only be encouraged to stay in employment once the war was over but that more women should be recruited to the labour force. 'The need to increase the working population is not temporary, it is a permanent feature in our national life ... women now form the only large reserve of labour left and to them the government are accordingly making a special appeal' (Ministry of Labour 1947:183).

Second, during the war attitudes towards the employment of married women had become more favourable as indicated, for example, by the removal of the marriage bar in the teaching profession and the civil service. Women wanted, or expected of economic necessity, to combine marriage with paid employment. In a study conducted by the Wartime Social Survey for the Ministry of Reconstruction in 1943, half the married women aged over thirty-five years and almost one-third of those under thirty years of age said when interviewed that they wanted to stay in employment even after the war was over. Altogether 60 per cent of occupied women in 1943 wanted to work after the war (Thomas 1944:29). By the end of 1946 there were still 875,000 more women in the working population (700,000 of them actually employed in industry) than in

1939. The Government Actuary's view expressed in the Beveridge
Report in 1942 that the war-time increase in the employment of
women 'will be in large measure temporary' (Appendix A:194) was
nevertheless incorporated in the 1946 White Paper on Social
Insurance. It was sadly at odds with the Governments' economic
policies and the wishes of women themselves.

*Changes in the economic and legal implications of
marriage and parenthood*

Women in the labour market
The economic relationship of a substantial proportion of married
women was not one of total and permanent dependence on their
husbands even in 1945. Since the end of the Second World War
married women have joined the labour force in steadily increasing
numbers and have acquired an economic status of their own, albeit
an inferior one to men, for a woman's average full-time wage is still
only half that of a man, and discrimination against women in
employment is by no means limited to those with little skill or
education.[5] Those concerned with economic policy realized that
women had an important contribution to make to the economy,
particularly in filling the expanding number of poorly paid,
unskilled jobs. In 1969 the Department of Employment forecast
that 'it seems probable that the employment situation for women
and girls will continue to be a good deal better than that for men
and boys because of the growth in the public sector of "less
skilled" jobs and the decline in the numbers of predominantly male
industries' (Department of Employment 1969:313). By 1972 there
were five and a half million married women in the working
population, two and a half million more than in 1951. There were a
million fewer single women and slightly fewer men (Central
Statistical Office 1973:89). So the post-war expansion in the
working population can be largely attributed to married women
who now comprize nearly a quarter of the working population
compared with 13 per cent in 1951. Although as the Department of
Employment warn 'trends should be interpreted with care because
of changes in the coverage questions and definitions of the censuses
of population', these trends 'are so clear that they cannot be
dismissed on (these) grounds' (Department of Employment
1974:8).
　The latest projections suggest that although the rate of increase
in married women's activity rates slowed down between 1966 and

1971, the trend will continue upwards. By 1986 it is estimated that nearly two out of three married women aged between thirty-five and fifty-nine years will be economically active compared with one in five in 1951 (see *Table 1*).

Table 1 Married women's economic activity rates

proportion of married women economically active in the following years				proportion of men economically active
Age	1951	1961	1971	1986	1971
20-24	36.6	41.4	46.7	48.7	92.5*
25-34	24.4	29.5	38.4	43.3	99.1
35-44	25.7	30.4	54.5	66.4	98.9
45-54	23.7	35.3	57.0	73.2	98.1
55-59	15.6	26.0	45.5	60.5	95.7
60-64	7.2	12.7	25.2	33.2	85.2
65+	2.7	3.4	6.5	9.5	16.8

*Age group is 18-24 years. Students are included as economically active in figures for men and women.
Source: Department of Employment (1974:10) Office of Population Censuses (1973:182).

The proportion of younger married women in the labour force has also increased but less dramatically than among the older married women. The care of young children is still keeping many women at home, although many more are combining motherhood with paid employment and if satisfactory child care facilities were available even more would do so.[6] The younger the children, the more likely the mother is to stay at home. In 1971 less than a fifth of mothers with children under five years old and two-fifths of those with children of primary school age worked either full or part-time whereas half of the mothers with children of secondary school age went to work (Central Statistical Office 1973:88).

Today, the *majority* of women combine marriage with paid employment. More women get married[7] and they marry and have their children younger.

'In the past it was usual for a woman to leave work when she married, but now it is more usual to remain at work until the first child is due. With smaller families and less time between children the period of time while a woman has children under school age is considerably reduced and her total absence from the labour force for bringing up her family is much shorter than in previous generations.' (Department of Employment 1974:8).

Women as economic supporters
Women's earnings are essential to many families. In 1970 the Department of Health and Social Security estimated that the number of poor two-parent families in which the father was in full-time work (poor being defined as having an income at or below the current supplementary benefit scale rates) would have nearly *trebled* if the father's earnings had not been supplemented by the mother's. Altogether an estimated 180,000 two-parent families had an income within £2 of the 'poverty line' and a quarter of a million more families would have been in this position if they had relied solely on the father's wages (Department of Health and Social Security 1971a:14). Results from the one per cent sample of the 1971 census show that nearly two million women under retirement age are the chief economic supporters[8] in their households. The figure includes 300,000 married women under retirement age and 520,000 lone mothers with dependent children, about a half of whom were receiving supplementary benefits (Office of Population Censuses 1972: Table 29). Single women should not be forgotten either, and it has been estimated in 1973 that about 300,000 single women have elderly or infirm dependents, 8,000 of whom receive supplementary benefit (*H.C. Debates*. 1973. Vol. 855. Col. 268, Joyce Butler). Thus altogether, at the very least, one in six of all households, *excluding* pensioner households, are substantially or completely dependent upon a woman's earnings or benefits and the *majority* of these households contain either children or adult dependents. Among pensioner households a woman is the chief economic supporter in just over half the households; and lest it be thought that the vast majority of women in retirement are living on pensions earned by their husbands, it should be noted that at the end of 1970 just over 2 million women were getting retirement pensions on their own insurance compared with 1.4 million wives and 1.4 million widows receiving a pension on their husband's insurance (Department of Health and Social Security 1971b).

Quite clearly then, as the previous Home Secretary said in September 1973 in the introduction to the government's discussion paper *Equal Opportunities for Men and Women*, for women 'work is no longer an extra or subordinate part of life' (1973:5). Their earnings make an essential contribution to the incomes of many households and 'the needs of the economy require the continued employment of large numbers of married women' (H.M. Government 1972:18). Marriage may interrupt but it no longer terminates a woman's employment. One of the major assumptions underlying the social security schemes introduced at the end of the last war is false. Before looking at the extent to which it has therefore been abandoned, particularly in the form of pensions provisions and the proposals for tax-credits, we should first examine the validity of Beveridge's other major assumption that the legal relationship between husband and wife and parent and children justified the special treatment of married women.

Women's legal dependence on men
A man's legal obligation to maintain his wife has never been a guarantee of her financial security, particularly if he is poor. It is an obligation that is difficult to enforce until the marriage breaks down, although until 1971, when under the *Matrimonial Proceedings and Property Act 1970* the 'agency of necessity' was abolished, a wife could pledge her husband's credit for things which she 'reasonably required'. The financial arrangements made between husband and wife will depend on whether the couple appear before the Magistrates' Court for a matrimonial order or obtain a divorce. Matrimonial orders, which are more likely to be used by the poor, are still based on the concept of guilt. A single act of adultery by the wife can prevent her getting a maintenance order and anyway she has to prove her husband has committed a 'matrimonial office' in order to get maintenance for herself not just for her children. Even if she is successful, however, she may get very little. The limits on the amount of a maintenance order for wife and children were abolished under the *Maintenance Orders Act 1968*, but this made little difference to the amount paid by husbands because only a minority were paying the maximum anyway. For example, in a recent study (McGregor *et al.* 1970), 70 per cent of defendants against whom orders were made in 1965 had incomes below average earnings, so not surprisingly only one in five fathers were ordered to pay the maximum. Moreover two-fifths of the men were in arrears with their payment. As the Graham Hall Committee on Statutory Maintenance Limits concluded in 1967, 'however hard magistrates and court officials try to operate the present system sensitively and effectively they cannot provide more than the defendant produces' (Committee on Statutory Maintenance Limits 1968:76). Wives may now be required to pay their husband's maintenance following the *Matrimonial Proceedings (Magistrates Courts) Act 1960*), but only 'where by

reason of the impairment of the husband's earnings capacity through age, illness or disability of mind or body, it appears to the court reasonable in all circumstances so to order'.

If the separated or deserted wife claims supplementary benefit which is almost certain to provide a higher and more regular income than a maintenance order, the Supplementary Benefits Commission has a duty to enforce her husband to maintain her, unless she commits adultery in which case his liability to maintain her ceases. The right and duty to claim from liable relatives goes back via the *Poor Law Act 1834* to the *Elizabethan Poor Law 1601*. The *National Assistance Act 1948* reduced the number of liable relatives to husbands and wives for each other and parents for children, thus relieving children of their statutory duty to support their parents. It is interesting to note that this Act imposed maintenance obligations equally on *both* spouses for the first time. In other words the working wife of a man who becomes dependent upon supplementary benefit can be forced by the Supplementary Benefits Commission to pay him maintenance. The Commission, however, is no more successful in enforcing a man's obligation to maintain his wife and children than the courts, even though a man can still be sent to prison for defaulting on maintenance payments. In 1967, for example, only 16 per cent of the cost of benefits paid to divorced or separated wives and mothers responsible for illegitimate children was reclaimed from the men liable to support them (McGregor *et al.* 1970:162).

More prosperous men are more likely to be able to afford to maintain their ex-wives. They are helped by the fact that they can offset any maintenance order (which to the recipient is regarded as taxable income) against their own income tax. Their marriages are more likely to end in divorce than legal separation and since the *Divorce Reform Act 1969*, divorce is no longer based on the concept of guilty party but on irretrievable breakdown. Under the *Matrimonial Property and Proceedings Act 1970*, the courts can order one spouse to compensate the other out of his or her assets for the consequences of the breakdown of the marriage and alongside an order granting custody to one or other parent, either mother or father may be ordered to make maintenance payments for their children if they have wilfully neglected to provide for them. In the divorce courts now, at least in theory, men and women can be treated less unequally when their marriages end, than was formerly the case. It is no longer assumed automatically that the wife was totally dependent on her husband and that only the 'innocent' party deserves maintenance.

The man's legal obligation to maintain his wife still offers little protection to the poor man's wife, and under the divorce laws now in operation it is recognized that the duty and ability to maintain each other or their children may rest on either spouse. The truth of the assumption in the social insurance system that wives are dependent on husbands and are therefore totally maintained by them is perhaps slightly questionable. The changes in the economic and, to a lesser extent, the legal relationship between husband and wife require a radical review of the treatment of marriage and parenthood in the social security system.

The present social security system and proposals for change

The current situation

The 'special insurance status of married women' has meant in practice that a woman on marrying can 'choose' whether or not to continue paying full national insurance contributions. The wife who elects not to pay full contributions must depend on her husband's contribution record for entitlement to a widow's or old age pension. Any contributions made by her before her marriage are ignored. She therefore receives no sickness or unemployment benefit for herself except as a dependant of her sick or unemployed husband. Nevertheless some employers, universities for example, behave as if all married women in their employ receive national insurance sickness benefit in their own right and deduct it from their pay when they are ill. This makes nonsense both of employer's sick pay schemes and of the national insurance scheme and is a blatant form of discrimination against married women. She cannot receive an old age pension until her husband also reaches retirement age. If, however, the marriage legally ends before she has reached 60 years of age, to avoid losing entitlement to a full national insurance pension she must start to pay full contributions herself until she retires. Legislation in 1970 enabled her to use her husband's contribution record *before* as well as during their marriage if his record is better than hers. Should her husband remarry, she is not now deprived of the pension earned perhaps by many years of unpaid 'vital work' as a housewife. However, a wife has no right even to *know* whether her husband's national insurance contribution record is complete and therefore may not know whether or not she will receive a full pension on his retirement or death.

The wife who pays full contributions will qualify for a maternity benefit as well as a maternity grant provided she leaves work for the required number of weeks before confinement. Between 1948 and 1953 this was paid at a higher rate than unemployment benefit as Beveridge proposed, but since then the rate has been reduced to that of a man's unemployment or sickness benefit. This means a married woman still receives a larger benefit when she is pregnant than when she is ill or unemployed, for a married woman receives a lower rate of sickness and unemployment benefit than a single man or woman. She will qualify for an old age pension at sixty years of age irrespective of whether or not her husband has retired, but she will have to fulfil stricter contribution conditions than her single sister. In order to qualify for a pension at all she must have paid, or been credited with contributions for at least half her married life. Her contributions paid when a worker before her marriage count for nothing in this respect. This means a woman who marries say, at forty-five years of age, and continues to work until she is fifty will not be entitled to any pension ten years later in spite of the fact that she had paid contributions for over thirty years, simply because for over half her *married* life she had ceased to pay contributions. In those circumstances she would still be entitled to a pension as a dependant of her husband's, but only when he retired. There is no way, moreover, in which a man can acquire a right to a pension earned through his wife's contributions. If she dies before he does, even if she has been the sole financial supporter because of his inability to work, he receives nothing. There is no widower's pension even for the sick or disabled. Dependent husbands are given limited recognition in sickness and unemployment benefit, for a woman can claim an additional allowance for a dependant husband if he *cannot* work. It is not sufficient, as in the case when the unemployed or sick man is claiming an allowance for his wife, to show he is not working. In other words the insurance scheme makes no provision for the situation in which a man chooses to stay at home while his wife goes to work.

Therefore in spite of the fewer benefits available to the wife who decides to rely solely on her husband's contributions, there is much to encourage her to do so. Apart from the lower benefits paid to her if she contributes fully, the full flat-rate contribution will represent a considerably higher proportion of her earnings — perhaps seven or eight per cent — than the average male earner, who does not pay more than six per cent of his earnings in insurance contributions even if contracted into the graduated scheme. In 1972, for example, three and a half million of the five and a half million working wives earned between £9 and £13.33 a week, at a time when average male industrial earnings were over

£35 a week, and average full-time female earnings were £18 a week (Select Committee on Tax-credit 1973: Vol. II:409). It is hardly surprising that three-quarters of maried women elected not to pay the full contribution (*H.C. Debates*. Vol. 855: Col. 406).

Under the *Social Security Act 1973*, married women can still choose to rely on their husband's contribution for the basic state pension. The choice of paying full contributions is made less unfavourable because an earnings-related contribution will not be the 'disproportionate contribution burden' on women which flat-rate contributions are (H.M. Government 1971:14). However, unemployment and sickness benefit will continue to be paid at a lower rate to married women contributing fully. As Baroness Seer commented during the Bill's passage through the House of Lords, 'women are still seen, in terms of social security, in their marital status rather than as persons' (*H.C. Debates* 1973: Vol. 342, Col. 1124).

Future intentions

Both the recent developments in the state pension scheme and the proposals for linking the income tax and social security systems provided an opportunity to throw away Beveridge's old-fashioned inegalitarian views about women. The 1970 Conservative Government did not take it, and the 1974 Labour Government, while rejecting the Conservatives' pension scheme had not published proposals when this paper was written.[9]

Pensions
The *Social Security Act 1973* included the pension scheme outlined in the White Paper, *Strategy for Pensions* (1971). The basic state pension was to have been flat-rate and paid for by completely earnings-related contributions (up to the limit of one and a half times a man's average earnings). In addition the scheme gave 'every employee the opportunity to build, on the foundation of the State Scheme, an earnings-related pension for himself, or his wife, through an occupational pension scheme or, failing that, a State reserve scheme' (H.M. Government 1971:3). There was scant recognition of the fact that, in the near future if not already, the majority of married women will be in paid employment for most of their married lives. Indeed the White Paper states 'many wives and widows work for only a part, and often only a small part, of their adult lives' (1971:15). No evidence is given for this statement which is blatantly false. Once again those concerned with social security matters appear to be totally ignorant of the facts and figures collected by those dealing with economic policy.

Women, married or single, would have fared badly in the State Reserve Scheme which, in the words of a previous Minister of State to the Department of Health and Social Security, 'has the character of a fall-back scheme'. Its members would have been those excluded from occupational schemes: the low paid or mobile worker described by the same Minister as 'being little more than birds of passage' (*H.L. Debates* 1973: Vol. 342, Col. 112). In fact about half of its contributors were expected to be women. Married women who took paid employment would have had to contribute on the same basis as men and single women. The scheme was based on actuarial principles, so as women live longer than men and retire earlier (a provision made in 1940 to encourage women back to work and to reduce the need to increase men's pensions), inevitably the pension which their contributions would have earned them would have been lower. Thus the woman who contributed from the age of twenty-two years for all her working life would have received a pension worth 13 per cent of her earnings at retirement (assuming earnings rose at 3 per cent a year), compared with a man who would have received 19 per cent. (*The Times* March 7, 1974). Add to that the fact that many women will have their earnings interrupted for a few years and that we are still a long way from achieving equal pay, in spite of the recent *Equal Pay Act*, a funded scheme of this kind is likely to pay a woman a very inadequate pension indeed, as it is importing the inequalities of the labour market into retirement.

Many women would have had no choice but to join the State Reserve scheme before they marry and have children, for the age of entry of many occupational schemes is twenty-five years for women: an age when a woman is *most* likely to be out of the labour force and at home with small children. In 1971 less than a third of women employees belonged to an occupational pension scheme. Moreover, whereas under the *Social Security Act 1973* employers are under a legal obligation to offer their occupational pension scheme, if they have one, to all male employees, there is no obligation to make it available to the women working for them.

The women who do belong to their employers' scheme will at least get tax relief on their contributions, unlike those made to the Reserve scheme, and they at least have the option to leave their widower's a pension. However, they may still be treated unequally, as the Conservative government explained in 1973 in *Equal Opportunities for Men and Women*

'the Government does not believe that it is necessary to require occupational pension schemes to provide benefits for men and women on the same basis ... many women will not wish to

make the necessary payments ... commonly there is not the same
need for benefit to be payable to a widower on the death of his
wife as to a widow on the death of her husband; and women
might reasonably object to being obliged to contribute towards
widowers' benefits on the same footing as men contribute
towards widowhood cover.' (1973:11).

Thus under the *Social Security Act 1973* widows must
automatically be provided with a pension on the death of their
husbands but under the *Finance Act 1970*, a woman could only
provide a pension for her widower and claim tax relief on her
contributions if he had been financially dependent on her and she
accepted a lower personal pension. Tax relief is available on
contributions towards widows' pensions, for widows, by definition, are dependents in the Board of Inland Revenue's eyes. The
provision was changed under pressure from women's organizations, so now women can make provision for their husbands,
dependent or not, without losing tax relief. It will be interesting to
see whether the same cohabitation rules apply to widowers as they
do to widows. A widow loses her state insurance pension if she
cohabits or re-marries. A similar provision is creeping into
occupational schemes, for example the proposed new scheme for
university teachers has just such a clause. How will cohabitation be
defined by the various schemes (there are about 65,000
occupational schemes) and will they employ an inspectorate? If an
occupational pension is a form of deferred pay then whoever
inherits that pension should be entitled to keep it whatever their
circumstances. If however it is paid in recognition of the *needs* of
the pensioner and his or her spouse, which a cohabitation rule
implies, then actuarial principles are an inappropriate basis on
which to calculate such pensions.

It is clear that under the scheme contained in the *Social Security
Act 1973* many women would not have received the pension they
needed when they retired because of their unequal status in
employment. They still only have an opportunity to build on the
basic state pension when they are in the labour force. Their time
spent at home caring for children or disabled or elderly dependants
earn them no entitlement in their own right to a pension, instead
they can only acquire a pension by virtue of being their husband's
dependant. We have much to learn in this respect from our
Common Market partners, particularly France, where since the
summer of 1972, women who stay at home to look after their
young children are credited with pension contributions in their own
right. In Britain in 1972, 28 per cent of retirement pensioners were

receiving a means tested supplementary pension. Three-quarters of them were women. The pension provisions in the *Social Security Act 1973* were all too likely to have perpetuated this situation.

Tax-credits
Any scheme that attempted to link the social security and income-tax systems would require an examination of the needs and responsibilities arising from marriage and parenthood. Proposals for a tax-credit scheme have been the subject of much discussion and quite properly much attention has been paid to provisions for children. As a result the 1970-74 Conservative Government had already promised that the child tax-credit, which would replace family allowances, the family income supplement, and the tax allowance for children, would be paid to the mother. Like family allowances they would be paid irrespective of the marital and employment status of the child's parents. This would mean that at the time when the scheme came into operation there would be in effect a transfer of income from the father to the mother of the family, as he loses his tax allowance which is worth substantially more than the cash family allowance. Thus mothers would receive directly from the state allowances paid to them in respect of each of their children. This would give them a greater degree of financial independence than that achieved by the present very modest family allowance. Many questions remain unresolved, particularly the actual value of the credit and the age or stage at which a child ceases to be a dependant. Nevertheless the proposal as it stands at present is a method of adjusting family income to family size in a way that recognizes the status of mothers more fully than any of the existing schemes.

The treatment of married women showed no such improvement. The tax-credit scheme as outlined in the Green Paper, *Proposals for a Tax-credit System* (1972) treats married women as dependants who would therefore be excluded from the scheme. Instead a married man would receive a larger tax-credit than a single man or woman and if his wife worked she would continue to receive earned income tax relief. The Select Committee proposed a modification of this which would give a married woman a tax-credit in her own right if she was in employment earning at least a quarter of a man's average wage. Her husband would then receive a single man's credit.

Conclusions

Women then are regarded either as workers or dependants. Their role and contribution to society as mothers caring for young children or looking after elderly or disabled relatives is totally ignored. No distinction is made between the woman without children who works and the working mother. Neither is there a distinction made between the wife who stays at home because she has her children or relatives to care for and the wife without dependants who stays at home by choice. Each situation is different, and the questions which need to be raised and answered are whether or not marriage *per se* should continue to be subsidized by the State and in what ways should the needs of the responsibilities arising from parenthood be met.

Altogether one in four married women without dependants to care for stay at home although they are capable of working. Many of them will belong to the middle or higher income groups. Tax allowances on behalf of such wives cost the state about £750 million annually (Select Committee on Tax-credit 1973: Vol. 1:21) which is nearly double the cost of family allowances. Should that money be spent instead in recognizing the needs of mothers and giving women a real choice about whether they stay at home to look after children or go out to work? Again, looking at France, in addition to making a substantial increase in the single-earner allowance paid to women with young children who stay at home, in 1972 a new child care allowance was introduced to assist mothers to pay for their children to be cared for while they work. While there were strong economic and demographic reasons for making these changes, at least the debate was conducted in terms of giving mothers the *right to choose* whether to work or stay at home.

Social security measures based on the assumption that marriage means total and permanent economic dependence for most women are failing to meet their needs. To develop a social security system that is more appropriate to the variety of women's needs, a man's obligation to maintain his wife *per se* would require re-examination and modification. How far could it be regarded in tax and family law, as well as in social security, as a mutual obligation shared between spouses? The Select Committee on Tax-Credit said 'as long as one spouse in fact has greater opportunities to earn more than the other, differences in treatment are likely to arise in the field of taxation and in the field of social security' (1973:32). However, we have seen that under the present social security system and in the proposals for change the inequalities women face in the labour market are not only reflected but reinforced: the social security system does not compensate for them. Delphy suggests that 'the unjust position of women on the labour market and the discrimination which they suffer are the result — and not the cause ... of the marriage contract' (p.79). If that is so then by supporting inegalitarian relationships within the family, the social security system is assisting the economic exploitation of women.

Such a social security system also supports the economic exploitation of male wage earners. The situation in which the father stays at home by choice while his wife works is persistently ignored in the social security system. For example, the Family Income Supplement introduced only recently to help families in which there is a low wage earner, states quite categorically that 'in the case of a couple it must be the man who is in full-time work'. In most families the father does not stay at home to look after the children, why should it matter if he does? The opponents of the introduction of family allowances, and even school meals, feared that the family would disintegrate if the responsibility of poor fathers for the upkeep of their children was in any way shared by the state. More importantly it was believed that some men, particularly those in low paid jobs, would no longer bother to work as hard or even at all if their dependants were cared for by the state. Is there a similar fear shared by those who refuse to recognize the situation in which the man stays at home and his wife works? Or is the refusal to accept women as economic supporters of some households, particularly those in which there is a male adult, a means of maintaining the belief that women's wages are either for their sole support or are mere supplements to a man's wage? Such a belief is one of the means of justifying women's low wages relative to men's. Also as long as it is expected that women rather than men must stay at home to look after children, thus interrupting their careers, professional women will find it difficult to compete with men. Moreover by allowing women to supplement rather than substitute for a man's wage, low wages for men are perpetuated. As we have seen there would be many more poor families if mothers did not enter the labour market.

However, the ideological underpinnings of the economic system must not be ignored. The inability of those individuals and groups who influence the developments of social policy — and they are largely men — to recognize women as equals, has an ideological as well as an economic basis. As Eleanor Rathbone wrote forty years ago, 'The economic dependency of the married woman is the last stronghold of those who, consciously or unconsciously, prefer woman in subjection, and that perhaps is why the stronghold is proving so hard to force' (Rathbone 1934).

Notes

1 In 1934 a man's weekly contribution to unemployment insurance was 10d, a women 9d. Men received 17s benefit, women 15s.

2 A study in 1932 showed that out of 5,724 weeks of incapacity among married women employed in the industry, 3,625 weeks were due to childbirth (Labour Party's Advisory Committee on Women's Questions 1935:8).

3 In 1942 a single man received 18s sickness benefit, compared with 15s for a single woman and 13s for a married woman.

4 See Thomas (1944). This was a study of 2,609 civilian women aged between 18 and 59 years.

5 In 1971 the earnings distribution of women in full-time work who had achieved higher education or a degree was almost the same as the earnings distribution of men with *no* educational qualifications. See Office of Population Census and Surveys (1973).

6 In 1961 for example, 26 per cent of mothers with dependent children were in paid employment compared with 37.8 per cent in 1971. A third of the latter worked more than 30 hours a week (Office of Population Censuses and Surveys 1972). In 1971, 40 per cent of women who were not in paid employment but intended to return to paid work when their children were older, would return earlier if satisfactory child care facilities were available (Office of Population Censuses and Surveys 1973).

7 In 1971, among women aged 50 years and over, 15 per cent were single, compared with 11 per cent of 30 to 44 year old women. The average age of marriage for women in 1951 was 24.6 years, in 1971 it was 22.6 years (Central Statistical Office 1973).

8 The definition of chief economic supporter gives precedence to full-time over part-time, male over female, and older over younger workers in the household, thus counting the husband as the chief supporter even if his wife earns more than he does.

9 I have subsequently written on the Labour Government's 1975 social security legislation (Land 1975).

References

Beveridge, W. 1942. *Social Insurance and Allied Services* (the Beveridge Report). Cmnd. 6404. London HMSO.

Central Statistical Office. 1973. *Social Trends.* No. 4. London: HMSO.

Department of Employment. 1969. *Gazette 77* (4).

— 1974. *Gazette 82* (1).

Department of Health and Social Security. 1971a. *Annual Report for 1970.* London: HMSO

— 1971b. *Two-parent Families.* London: HMSO.

Gardiner, J. 1976. Political Economy of Domestic Labour in Capitalist Society. In D. Leonard Barker and S. Allen (eds.), *Dependence and Exploitation in Work and Marriage.* Harlow: Longman.

H.M. Government 1944. *Employment Policy.* Cmnd. 6527. London: HMSO.

— 1971. *Strategy for Pensions.* Cmnd. 4755. London: HMSO.

— 1972. *Proposals for a Tax-Credit System.* Cmnd. 5116. London: HMSO.

— 1973a *Equal Opportunities for Men and Women. Government Proposals for Legislation.* London: HMSO.

— 1973b Select Committee on Tax-Credit. Vol. I. *Report and Proceedings.* London: HMSO.

— 1973c. Select Committee on Tax-Credit. Vol. II. *Evidence.* London: HMSO.

House of Commons Debates. 1963. *Hansard.* Vol. 675.

— 1964. *Hansard.* Vol. 687.

— 1973. *Hansard.* Vol. 1.

House of Lords Debates. 1973. *Hansard.* Vol. 342.

Keynes, J.M. 1940. *How to Pay for the War.* London: Macmillan.

Labour Party's Advisory Committee on Women's Questions. 1935. *Women in Industry.* London: Labour Party.

Land, H. (1975). The Myth of the Male Breadwinner. *New Society.* October 9.

Macdonald, R. 1909. *Socialism and Government.* Vol. II. London: International Labour Party.

McGregor, O.R., Blom-Cooper, L., and Gibson, C. 1970. *Separated Spouses.* London: Duckworth.

Ministry of Labour. 1947. *Gazette 45* (6). London: HMSO.

National Labour Conference. 1905. *Report on the State Maintenance of Children.* London.

Office of Population Censuses and Surveys. 1972. *Census 1971, Great Britain. Summary Tables*. London: HMSO.
— 1973. *General Household Survey, 1971. Introduction Report*. London: HMSO.
Rathbone, E. 1924. *Family Allowances* (2nd edition 1947). London: Allen & Unwin.
— 1934. Foreword. In E. Reiss, *Rights and Duties of English Women*. London: Sherratt and Hughes.
The Times. 1974. March 7.
Thomas G. 1944. *Women at Work. Wartime Social Survey*. London: HMSO.
Webb. S. 1907. *The Decline in the Birth-rate. Fabian Tract* no. 131. London.
Women's Family Allowance Campaign. 1973. *Evidence* in Select Committee on Tax-Credit, Vol. II. In H.M. Government 1972.

JENNY SHAW

Finishing School: Some Implications of Sex-segregated Education

A proposition familiar to most sociologists is the claim that in the process of industrialization schools annexed some of the 'functions' of the family, thereby impoverishing the family and creating, amongst other things, conditions of conflict or problematic discontinuities between the home and the school. The nub of this argument lies in the view that specialization in technology and social relations was both increasing and inevitable, and that schools were simply part of the process. However, specialization, like upward mobility, has only ever been the destiny of a minority of those who pass through schools, and only recently has recognition and interest in the experiences of the majority led to a redefinition of the part educational institutions play in industrial societies.

De-schoolers are not alone in doubting the claim that schools uniquely provide children with either necessary or sufficient preparation for living in such societies. The duplication of content between what is learnt at home and at school reinforces the view that much of that is taught in schools could equally well be learnt away from them. Furthermore, looked at from the standpoint of girls, the educational objective of many schools might well be described as insurance *against* specialization.

This paper will examine educational institutions from the point of view of their effects on girls and, whilst this cannot be defended just because it is not the normal approach, it may help us at this moment in time to revise some of our assumptions about the central features of our society. The recognition that many of the models and ideas currently in use in sociology (as elsewhere) have been formulated explicitly or implicitly to account for male behaviour and that they are often inapplicable or misleading when applied to women is proceeding. This is most noticeable in fields such as deviance, occupational sociology and, most importantly, the analysis and measurement of social class but has yet to be accepted, and revised models systematically applied, in the sociology of education.

The choice of whether to stress the social control features of education or its potential for individual growth and mobility has depended largely on whether the life-chances of boys or of both sexes were being considered. The view that schools are opportunity structures for the able is not so strongly adhered to as it once was, but possibly it would never have had much appeal if the fortunes of girls had been considered as thoroughly as those of boys. However, most of the standard literature in the field has been based on studies of boys' schools, which has produced a 'bias', the dimensions of which we are only beginning to discover.[1] In considering some of the implications of the sex typing principle which is still embodied in our educational system — i.e. that the sex of a child should be a determinant of the education he or she receives — I must therefore stress the tentativeness of my thinking and that I rely upon material from scattered sources, having at present limited data of my own that directly bears on the subject.[2]

Schools and the division of labour in society

This paper has two related themes. Both concern the contribution that schools make to the division of labour. It is difficult to demonstrate that educational institutions are simply 'responsive' to or 'reflective' of the occupational structure, although such a view is intuitively attractive — as is the view of schools as major agencies for maintaining the dominant (and sexist) culture. But one central phenomenon does have to be explained: how is it that girls, who begin their school career with what appears to be a flying start over boys, being as much as two years ahead in reading and in physical and psychological maturity, come to leave school with far fewer qualifications (Douglas 1968)? The other side of all selective educational systems is systematic discouragement, but the paradox of the British model is that by its own critera of success its most promising pupils persistently under-achieve. From a difference between the sexes in the girls' favour there follows an extraordinary reversal of fortune.

The argument of the first half of the paper rests on the assumption that divisions of knowledge, in their institutionalized form of curricula, correspond more or less directly to divisions of labour. We can see in the range of choice offered to boys and girls both the means and the expression of economic and social control. The second part of the paper deals with the accommodation made by schools to the demands of our present economy, which requires a minority of skilled specialists and a majority of less skilled, less specialized workers. One means of preparing children to enter the labour force (on terms set by the prevailing economic structure) has been to rely on skill-labels or educational certificates as a condition of entry to jobs, and to allow educational institutions a near monopoly of issuing them.

Streaming by sex

Although this paper bears a title referring to the consequences of sex-segregated education, it is not intended to present the issue as one of mixed versus single sex schooling, despite the growing volume of work addressed to that subject. In part this is because I am not entirely happy with the available material, for, although Dale (1969, 1971, 1974) has dedicated his professional career to championing the cause of co-education and especially to showing that mixed schools are superior to single sex ones on social grounds, the evidence is far from consistent, and in fact the differences in performance between the two sexes show greater disparities than the differences between the two types of school.[3] Over the country as a whole there is one single sex school for every two mixed (Benn and Simon 1972) but an individual's chances of attending a single sex or mixed school vary regionally and to some extent reflect parental aspirations, for middle-class children are slightly more likely to go to a single sex school, which may be a real or 'disguised' grammar school (as Benn and Simon (1972) call some of the comprehensives). In rural areas the possibility of going to a mixed school is less, as there are fewer such schools, and in some urban areas (like London) the class variable is less noticeable, as sixty per cent of all secondary schools in the ILEA are single sex.

The question of sex segregation in education is not, however, simply a matter of physical location — of whether there be one or two sexes in the particular building; it is essentially one of curricula differences. Both single sex and mixed schools restrict certain subjects to children of each sex. The use of sex as a salient criterion in the provision of learning facilities occurs almost wholly amongst the directly vocational subjects, which can represent a considerable porportion of school time; and less formally as between science and the humanities, where boys take the former and girls the latter. Benn and Simon (1972) were obviously surprised when they asked the 587 mixed schools in their survey if any subjects were closed to pupils on the grounds of sex and discovered that 50 per cent restricted some subjects to boys and 49 per cent of schools did the same for girls. In Scotland the figures were even higher, with 70 per cent limiting some subjects to boys and 68 per cent to girls. The commonest reason for this was that the teachers of boys' subjects refused to include girls in their classes. The subjects frequently proscribed for girls included: engineering, gardening, woodwork, metalwork, technical drawing, building, navigation, physics with chemistry, rural science, pottery, and surveying. For boys, catering, needlework, clothes design, dancing, human biology, jewelry, and mothercraft were amongst the forbidden subjects. Occasionally it was said that a pupil of the 'wrong sex' was admitted on demand and some schools pointed out that the options were open in theory but that in practice no-one ever took them.

The use of sex as an organizational principle is close in effect, if not design, to the institution of streaming, with all its sociological concomitants. Streaming, however it is known, invariably implies differences in course content and is likely to have an attendant ideology in the form of the 'psychology' of cognitive differences, or administrative ease, which, as Simon (1971) shows, is itself an effect of curriculum differences. The manner in which differences in performance accommodate to levels of provision and expectations and are then reinforced as grounds for discrimination is well documented (Rosenthal and Jacobson 1968). Lacey (1970) has indeed suggested that under-achievement is the product of streaming and the sub-culture of opposition or commitment that accompany it. His material, however, relates only to a boys' grammar school and there are grounds for thinking the same conditions would not apply in girls' schools. In a replication of Hargreaves's study, conducted in a girls' school, one of the striking differences was that the lower streams were actually *more* committed to the school norms than the higher streams and had less of a non-academic 'counter-culture', as expressed in distinctive forms of dress and values (Brown 1972). In the replication study's school it is quite likely that criteria other than intelligence had been used as a basis for streaming, which may account for the differences, but if this is the case, the chances are that such practices are quite common in girls' schools. In the Lacey and Hargreaves studies of boys' schools, ability and commitment to school norms went together, as did sexual precocity, trendiness, opposition, and low performance; while in the girls' school and in Douglas's study, early maturity, extreme fashion consciousness, and high ability were associated.[4] In girls' schools the absence of the inverse polarization that has been noted in studies of boys' schools supports the view of female communities as being both less differentiated and less concerned with academic success.[5] A woman no longer has to repudiate her sex and enter a convent to get an education at all, but in so far as educational institutions are themselves seen as prizes for competing groups and ideologies, they will inevitably reinforce the values of whichever groups have gained control.

It is hardly surprising that mixed schools are actually more like boys schools rather than being somewhere midway between all-male and all-female schools. The chances of the head of a mixed school being a woman are much smaller than of its being a man. Dale has gone to great lengths to promote co-education and he concludes that, despite the deterioration in girls performance in mixed schools as compared to girls in single sex schools, 'the question of comparative progress in academic work should never again be raised as an obstacle to a policy of co-education' (Dale 1974). But his grounds for supporting co-education rest entirely on the substantial improvement in *boys* performance and the overall greater happiness, maturity, and adjustment of pupils of both sexes in mixed schools, which he considers to be a result of some mutually moderating process.

Boys and girls educated together certainly do have an effect upon each other, but whether, under our prevailing culture, it is one of *mutual* benefit is questionable. Despite the possibility that mixed schools may offer a wider range of subjects than a single sex one, and that in this respect they compare favourably with girls' schools which often have poorer facilities for science and mathematics, the social structure of mixed schools may drive children to make even more sex-stereotyped subject choices, precisely because of the constant presence of the other sex and the pressure to maintain boundaries, distinctiveness, and identity. In all-girls' schools, being both clever and attractive is a compatible, but not necessary, combination. Such a combination may be less viable in a mixed school where, in a climate of overall anxiety about appropriate sex behaviour, dichotomies are presented and choices have to be made. Little protection from, or alternatives to, failure (or success) in romantic competition are afforded. In some areas, such as sport and games, a double-bind situation may arise, whereby success in physical terms means failure in social ones (Willis and Critcher 1974).

In a discussion of different types of streaming, Young and Brandis (1967) consider that, under certain conditions, one of the functions of a system based on a combination of ability and moral

qualities would be to create tension between the streams and to use
the threat of possible descent into the lower stream as a lever to
keep the higher stream at work. Young and Brandis were concerned
that where low IQ and moral evaluation were confounded in a
comprehensive school, working-class children would lose the chance
of a coherent and occupationally relevant course, albeit second
class, and the chance of belonging to a fee-saving sub-culture.
Further, they would suffer downward mobility more often than
upward in those schools where movement between streams took
place.

A version of this process may be becoming established via the
sex-based subject boundaries and may describe the relations
between the sexes in co-educational schools. From the little
evidence that we have, girls' schools would seem to approach their
second type of comprehensive, where children of mixed ability find
themselves in the same stream; but there is one important difference:
failure is not so 'personalized'. The sharpness of these processes
described by Young may be modified in the girls' schools as
occupational selection is regarded as less critical.

The social construction of girls failure
The use of sex as a basis for organizational and curricular decisions
is irrational in educational terms, for children usually have had no
prior experience of the subjects to which they are assigned. It
makes 'sense' only in the wider perspective of schools as agencies
maintaining and reproducing accepted social divisions. The effect
of these decisions amount to what Goode (1967) calls 'the
protection of the inept', as lower overall levels of skill may be
produced both among those insulated from competition and those
whose competition is feared. Furthermore, by using ascribed
characteristics such as sex to 'legitimize' either the boundaries
within education or between primary and secondary labour sectors,
the chances of economically based forms of identification and
solidarity are weakened.

Turner (1964), who addressed himself to the problem of
women's ambition, thought, rather traditionally, that girls were
more concerned with status than class and that they pursued their
ambitions (especially material ones) indirectly through their
menfolk. The reason he gave for the different meanings that his
measures of ambition produced for the two sexes was, exactly, that
educational and occupational aspirations were related to material
ends for men but not for women, whose overall ambition was both
'lower' and more 'differentiated'. This really amounts, yet again,

to the 'over-socialized conception of woman'. Implicitly this account is based on a version of the 'achievement motivation' thesis, for we are told that the values that distinguish ambitious from non-ambitious men also distinguished men from women. Only secondary importance was given to the constraints placed on the *direction* of ambition and, therefore, of motivation too. Turner found that his sample of women chose to add the role of career to that of traditional home-maker rather than choose between them (so much for cognitive dissonance) and certainly recent British material bears this out (Young and Willmott 1973).

But the puzzle remains and for me is two-fold. First, do girls really believe that marriage and a family are going to provide a life-long activity when, even as long ago as 1950, the average age of first marriage was twenty-two and women's age at the time of the birth of their last child was twenty-six? With 42 per cent of all married women working, and more in the working class, is it likely that girls are totally unaware of this, especially if they take their own mothers as models? Or is it more likely that marriage and the expectations that accompany it function to interrupt girls' views of their future and to discourage long-term planning? Unqualified women and other low-paid workers probably get skilled at marginal analysis pretty quickly, so that the difference between working or not is a rational assessment of the situation, possibly learnt long before leaving school. A comment made to me by a 13-year-old pupil of an all-girls comprehensive on the relevance of compulsory subjects illustrates this: 'I can see the point of English as I might have to write to the Council or Social Services, but Art, I can't give my husband a painting for his dinner can I?'

One thing that is certain is that the distinctions that are embodied in school timetables are persistent. As long ago as 1923 the Consultative Committee of the Board of Education recommended that specialization of the curriculum by sex be discouraged. But the messages about the right and proper distribution of knowledge are also messages about power. This is illustrated by the study of Nailsea comprehensive (Richardson 1973), for here, when concessions were made and each sex was allowed to take the subject traditionally reserved for the other, they could do so only by being organized into single sex groups in an otherwise mixed school. Further, although some loosening of the boundaries does seem to be taking place, it tends (as in the occupational structure at large) to be more in the direction of boys taking up girls' subjects, such as cookery, rather than the other way round. When boys take 'girls' subjects, the meanings swiftly change; thus cookery becomes a prelude to a career in catering for boys, whilst as taught to girls it is still intended as a general domestic skill, and not primarily a saleable one.

Bernstein (1973) has introduced the categories of classification to refer to the strength and degree of boundary maintenance between the contents of a curriculum, and framing to describe the context or relationship within which teaching and learning takes place. From these concepts he derives two basic types of curricula: a collection one, where subjects may be quite disparate but have very strong boundaries around them (consider the 'timetabling' restrictions that permit certain combinations of subjects and not others); and an integrated one, where few such prohibitions occur and subjects (or knowledge) are seen essentially as part of a piece. He argues that socialization into existing social structures is aided by a collection code which usually displays clear principles both in terms of what is taught and how it is taught (classification and frame).

In discussing the overt and covert ideological bases of the different types of curricula, Bernstein makes use of Durkheim's concepts of mechanical and organic solidarity. He suggests that the underlying structure of collection codes is one of mechanical solidarity, although it produces specialists who contribute to organic solidarity. Such a view corresponds well both with the style of girls' schools and their more rigid social structures (i.e. described as more centralized, rulebound, and bureaucratized than boys schools) and with their pupils' probable occupational futures as members of a sector of the labour market which functions in the economy by providing a supply of necessary, low-cost labour. Whilst we cannot conclude that boys' education has necessarily adopted the 'integrated' type of curriculum, it becomes clear that the strongly hierarchical and sexist social structure in which we live has favoured the collection model for girls education, with all its consequences. For example, if girls stay on to take 'A' levels they are more likely to follow a collection type curriculum; if they take a science subject at all it is likely they will take only one and not three, and this is obviously inevitable in schools where biology is the only science available.

There are of course other areas marginal to the curriculum, where sex is treated as pertinent, such as games and welfare. A physical education teacher explained to me that he did not know any of the girls in his form as he had never taught them. The reasons given for this were that the risk of misinterpretation or of accusations of improper behaviour were too great. Despite the virtual impossibility of guaranteed privacy in schools, this belief is widespread and male post-graduate certificate in education students are warned on entering schools never to be left alone with a girl pupil. Welfare is frequently seen as something women are innately well equipped to do because they are innately equipped to be mothers; so the job is often thrust upon women teachers. Moreover, the idea that there are specifically 'girls' problems' leads to further institutionalisation of dual standards.

At present we can only speculate on the meanings of these boundaries. Quite why it is possible to have boys and girls doing the same subjects on different occasions but not both together, or what the deeper meanings are of the allocation to male and female of physical space such as playgrounds and places in assemblies, we are not yet in a position to say. But their survival indicates an importance attached to these boundaries, especially in a society where the public rhetoric has for so long supported co-education.

II Sex-based educational differences and the labour market

This part of the paper returns to the question of the steady and uninterrupted falling off of girls' attainments throughout secondary education which all the longitudinal studies document, and suggests that this can be linked to the construction of a differentiated work force. Girls eventual over-representation in the part-time and unskilled sectors is due in part to having lower and fewer qualifications; which in turn has to be understood as a product of their schooling. The practice of segregating education, whether within schools by curricula means, or between schools physically, makes an unique contribution to the maintenance of spearate labour forces.

The fact that the social structure maintains a low level of differentiation for women is expressed in one way by the lower levels of skill that they are expected to, and do, attain. But there are other expressions — for instance, in the organization of the schools themselves. Female organizations, including girls' schools, have been described as tending towards centralization, bureaucratization, and 'petty' rulefulness. One explanation of this has been offered in terms of their having either a weak 'knowledge base', or their being staffed by semi-professionals (Simpson and Simpson 1969). With the possible exception of mathematics and science teaching, this view cannot be substantiated, because girls' schools are not notably less professionally staffed than boys' schools — although in the past there was a grain of truth in this judgement, especially for ex-secondary modern schools. An alternative view might be that women, like other subordinated groups deprived of adequate representation in positions of power and authority, are bound by social relationships of mechanical solidarity which imply both less differentiation and a greater reliance on rules and external control (Durkheim 1947). Authority relations in girls' schools may be more bureaucratic, petty, and rule-bound precisely because of the difficulty women face in occupying positions of authority in a culture that associates masculinity with such positions, and with the consequent lack of female models, other than maternal ones.[6] Certainly the position of a senior woman teacher is a lonely one, especially in a mixed school, and it is a state that is perpetuated by the Burnham Committee's insistence that if, in a mixed school, the deputy head is a man, then a woman on the staff must be made 'senior' mistress (and vice versa if the deputy head is a woman). The consequence of this is not only to reinforce marriage but its implied division of labour as a model of cross-sex relations, but for women in particular it often has the effect of blocking career routes because one is not of the 'right' sex for the job.

Whilst on the subject of role and sex segregation, the possible links with what has come to be called conjugal segregation can be considered. The 'density' of kinship networks as a condition for great conjugal segregation may be questioned, but the question of what leads to various divisions of labour remains (Bott 1971). As Bott's critics have urged, a sharp division of labour in the marital home is a function of the values of the community: it is likely to occur if the community supports such arrangements. We might note though, that where schools treat sex as a basis for educational organization, they do nothing to counteract the marked tendency towards role-segregation based on sex in the home and elsewhere.

In the recent and otherwise comprehensive survey of the available material on inequality by Jencks (1973) there is little mention of inequality as applied to women (although there is an interesting footnote referring to the greater difficulties that upper middle-class families face in trying to ensure a good marriage for their daughters as compared to their attempts to secure a decent education (Jencks 1973:216)). While Jencks's preference for explanation in terms of initial class position and a measure of luck as determinants of the eventual distribution of income, may be acceptable, it is harder to agree with his view that the educational process is only marginal in establishing inequalities of opportunity, particularly when considering groups like women. For women, whatever their class origins and educational level, are likely to receive less pay than men of equivalent class position. As his critics have pointed out, inequality is not confined only to the rewards attached to certain jobs, but concerns how people are recruited into these, or any, jobs. Inequalities based on class position may reinforce those based on sex or vice versa, but neither can be clearly explained in terms of the other. The common tendency to treat a woman's class as derived from her husband if she is married and from her father if she is not, may have been reasonable when large numbers of women were not permanent members of the labour force (an anomalous situation of the inter-war years; see Parkin 1971). Unfortunately, however, it has encouraged sociologists to locate women socially in terms of status, to discount housework as work, and to ignore its place amongst the forces of production, or to confine their economic understanding of women to hived-off comsumption activities. These are, of course, not unimportant, but they only make sense when understood as part of a woman's total market situation. We have to look at her position within the whole mesh of relations of production and not just at whether she owns the means of production or sells her labour. Galbraith (1974) has recently indicated the complexity of the problem by suggesting the different functions that women play as 'consumer specialists' in an economy dominated by planning or in one governed by the market.

Although we know rather little about the processes of occupational choice, we do know that there is an extraordinary adjustment of ambition and aspiration to socio-economic realities and that as children pass through school they tailor and trim their expectations (Williams 1974). Quite how they manage this is more of a mystery for, as Hill (1962) points out, it is precisely at the juncture of leaving school that children are given minimal formal assistance and direction, least of all by teachers. Their direct exposure to the dictates of the market is significant not only because of the schools' effective abdication, but because it suggests that if there is a correspondence between the organizational principles and values of the school and those of the labour market, it is a structural one unmediated by professional guidance 'experts'. I think there are some striking similarities between the patterns of education and those of the work force such that the two systems are mutually determining and release us from the search for theories of decision-making and choice, be they conscious or unconscious.

Sex differences and skill-labelling

Sex must not be ignored as a critical variable in education for, as one of the authors of the National Child Development Survey shows (Davie 1973), it accounts for an even bigger difference in measured ability than those other well tried indicators, class and overcrowding. Possibly the clearest difference of all is that girls leave school less well qualified than boys, although nowadays they do not leave all that much sooner. In 1971-2, 33.5 per cent of boys left school aged 15 compared to 33.7 per cent of girls. But it is worth noting that, unlike boys, a larger proportion of the girls remaining at school after the official leaving age do not prepare for examinations — which might indicate the different values that sex confers on education. In 1971-2 girls got slightly more 'O' levels (23 per cent had more than five subjects) than boys (22.5 per cent), but at 'A' level there was a considerable reversal, with 9.1 per cent of boys getting three or more but only 6.6 per cent of girls managing to do so; an outcome that is only partially explained by differential aims and relative length of schooling. When we look at curricular differences, the pupil who takes science is likely to remain longer in full-time education at every stage than is the arts student, who is more likely to be a girl (Phillips 1969). Overall, the numbers of school leavers who go on to full-time higher education is pitifully small for both sexes. In 1970 only 7.6 per cent of boys and 4.4 per cent of girls went on to university. (Department of Education and Science 1974) Among the under 18s entitled to be released from employment to take part-time courses during working house, only 10.1 per cent of the girls as compared with 38.8 per cent of the boys did so.

One may doubt the importance of all this if, like Leibenstein (1969), one believes that it is rare for the labels thus acquired really to indicate the degree of skill held, especially given the wide range of skill possessed by those bearing similar labels. But, as he has succinctly argued, although the sort of education that one receives is only marginally related to the type of work that individuals eventually do, the labels that they bear are much more important. One of the consequences of not being suitably labelled is that in so far as the 'higher standards' lobby is successful, the chances of occupational mobility once in the labour market are shortened and the barriers between job classifications consolidated, and not only at the professional level. This near impossibility of movement between jobs is part of the trap that the lower paid workers suffer and it may be precisely as 'skill-labelling' institutions that schools feed into what has recently been called the dual labour market (Doeringer and Bosanquet 1973; Barron and Norris 1975). This formulation holds that there are two relatively autonomous sectors in the labour market, one characterized by high earnings, high skill levels, low staff turnover, career structures, and/or prospects for on-the-job training, and the other displaying the reverse features of low pay, high turnover rates, low skill levels, and no training on the job, nor career prospects. In analysing the labour market it is noted that women and coloured workers are grossly over-represented in the second sector. Further, the above characteristics really belong to the *sectors* and not to those working in them, although the attribution is often transferred.

Firms appear to have a choice of whether to be high or low wage employers as wide differences in pay have been shown to co-exist within the same job category, industry and region (Mackay *et al.* 1971). This suggests that something other than the market is determining wage rates and firms' ability to act in this fashion. Most probably this is the cumulative result of their own discriminatory practices and of the acquired and rational responses of employees forced to remain in the unrewarding sector. But it is also a function of the use of educational qualifications to prevent mobility between jobs. Writers on the dual labour market have noted the near impossibility of moving out of the secondary sector once within it and that this amounts to an almost irreversible handicap for older, immigrant, or female workers — all the groups who left school early and without qualifications. Unfortunately it is a characteristic of low-paid jobs and of skill-labelling that workers' positions are not redeemed by value being placed on experience or by the chances of being upgraded. Sponsored mobility offers a slim chance in view of the fact that in the UK apprenticeship is preferred to upgrading the semi-skilled, but not for girls. At this point we must note that whilst nearly 39 per cent of boys leaving school in 1972 entered apprenticeships or their equivalent leading to skilled occupations, less than 8 per cent of the girls did so (a rate of 1.5 (Department of Employment 1973)). Most of the girls who did were destined for hairdressing. Furthermore, in the electrical engineering industry, where women made up half the labour force in 1970, there were only fifty girl apprentices compared with 4,466 boys. If it were possible to obtain regional data on employment opportunities and first placements by sex, it might provide a way of testing whether there are sharper and more rigid curricula divisions in schools in areas where there is both high overall unemployment and distinct sectors within the labour market.

In the most general sense all schools are obviously mediators of the opportunity structure for both sexes, but it may be that schools, especially those in poorer areas, take a rather broad view of those 'opportunities' for their girl pupils and implicitly see themselves as preparing girls for the marriage market as well as for the labour market. The prospect of marriage as an alternative 'success' may account for the lower levels of ambition and the disaffection that girls display, though this should not necessarily be seen as a device for 'cooling out' the less able girls in particular. What schools may rather opportunistically be concerned with is the convenient distraction that the girls romantic hopes provide, which reduces the schools' responsibility for their future (i.e. they can attribute the lack of scholastic success to the girls themselves). Certainly, by failing to present girls with futures in terms of careers, schools create the possibilities of later 'role-conflict', which may further 'qualify' women as especially suitable for the secondary labour market; for here, if anything is prized, it is precisely such dispensability or willingness to be separated from their jobs.

Conclusion

In this paper I have concentrated on secondary education because I consider it no accident that sex is most evident and debated as an organizing principle within this part of the education system, for this is the sector most responsive to the demands of the labour market. Sexual division has virtually disappeared as an issue in primary education where 'job choice' is five to ten years away. In higher education, however, there are other, still unresolved, divisions by sex.

The argument has centred on the mutual interdependence between certain features of the labour market and those aspects of education, especially curricular ones, that distinguish the sexes. The issuing of certificates and labels by schools makes a central contribution to that process and to the significant differences in educational outcome that the sexes achieve. The meanings and consequences of sexual divisions in our society are translated into educational terms so that the different sub-cultures of boys' and girls' schools are but specialized versions of a wider culture, in which female futures are still defined in essentially domestic terms — a stereotyping which our educational system does little to undermine.

Notes

1   Popular and important books in the sociology of education like Jackson and Marsden (1962), Lacey (1970), Banks (1955), Banks and Finlayson (1973), and Hargreaves (1967) are all based on data from boys schools.

2 In some exploratory work I have made into the social context of truancy and non-attendance, the most striking variable was in fact that of sex. In one area the lowest rate was for the boys' school, the highest for the girls, and the mixed school fell between the two.

3 The data on whether mixed or single sex schools are better for boys or girls in terms of academic achievement is not conclusive. Some of the differences in rates of achievement for either type of school may be a function of other characteristics associated with the school, for example mixed schools tend to be larger than single sex ones, are more likely to be rural, and to have lower proportions of children from middle-class backgrounds. Douglas (1968) lists these and other differences in his Supplementary Tables. To some extent Douglas's and Dales's findings differ but from the recent publication of Dales's final volume (1974) the evidence points more strongly to there being a distinct improvement in boys' performances, especially as measured by certificates gained (a finding earlier reported by Sutherland in N. Ireland (1961:158-69)) in mixed schools, whilst girls seem to do better in single sex schools.

4 While protective anti-school sub-cultures are not formed by low-stream girls in the same manner as by boys, this does not mean that girls do not participate in some form of 'youth culture'. Rather, as Murdock and Phelps (1973) suggest, youth culture can be differentiated into 'street' and 'pop' culture, the former being more open to boys and the latter equally available but more subscribed to by girls.

5 There is an interesting parallel to this argument in the finding that the spread of girls' measured abilities is narrower than that of boys (Davie 1973).

6 A careful analysis of this situation can be found in Richardson (1973) which might be compared with a much older study by Milner (1938) on a girls' school and with Holmes's (1965) discussion of the difficulties inherent in establishing authority relations under initial conditions of mechanical solidarity.

References

Banks, O. 1955. *Parity and Prestige in English Secondary Education*: London: Routledge.

Banks, O. and Finlayson, D. 1973. *Success and Failure in the*

Secondary School. London: Methuen.

Barron, R. and Norris, G. 1976. Sexual Divisions and the Dual Labour Market. In D. Leonard Barker and S. Allen (eds.), *Dependence and Exploitation in Work and Marriage*. Harlow: Longman.

Benn, C. and Simon, B. 1972. *Half-way There*. Harmondsworth: Penguin.

Bernstein, B. 1973. *Class, Codes and Control*. London: Routledge and Kegan Paul.

Bott, E. 1971. *Family and Social Network*. London: Tavistock.

Brown, V. 1972. *Social Relations in a Girls Secondary School*. Dissertation for B.Ed. Birmingham (unpublished).

Dale, R. 1969. *Mixed or Single Sex School*. vol. I. London: Routledge and Kegan Paul.

— 1971. *Mixed or Single Sex School*. vol. II. London: Routledge and Kegan Paul.

— 1974. *Mixed or Single Sex School*. vol. III. London: Routledge and Kegan Paul.

Davie, R. 1973. Eleven Years of Childhood. *Statistical News* no. 22. August, 1973.

Department of Education and Science. 1974. *Statistics of Education*. vol. 2. London: HMSO.

Department of Employment 1973. *Gazette*. London: HMSO.

Doeringer, P.B. and Bosanquet, N. 1973. Is There a Dual Labour Market in Great Britain? *The Economic Journal*. June.

Douglas, J.W.B., Ross, J.M., and Simpson, S.R. 1968. *All Our Future*. London: Davies.

Durkheim, E. 1947. *On the Division of Labour in Society*. Glencoe, Illinois: Free Press.

Galbraith, J.K. 1974. *Economics and the Public Purpose*. London: Deutsch.

Goode, W. 1967. The Protection of the Inept. *American Sociological Review*, February.

Hargreaves, D. 1967. *Social Relations in a Secondary School*. London: Routledge.

Hill, J.M. 1962. *From School to Work*. London: Tavistock.

Holmes, R. 1965. Freud, Piaget and democratic leadership. *British Journal of Sociology 16* (2):123-39.

Jackson, B. and Marsden, D. 1962. *Education and the Working Class*. London: Routledge and Kegan Paul.

Jencks, C., 1973. *Inequality*. London: Allen Lane.

Lacey, C. 1970. *Hightown Grammar*. Manchester: Manchester U.P.

Leibenstein, H. 1969. The Economics of Skill-Labelling. In J.A. Lawreys and D.G. Scanlon (eds.), *World Year Book of Education*. London: Evans.

Mackay, D.I., Boddy, D., Brack, J., Diack, J.A., and Jones, N. 1971. *Labour Markets under Different Employment*. London: Allen and Unwin.

Milner, M. 1938. *The Human Problem in Schools*. London: Methuen.

Murdock, G., and Phelps, G. 1973. *Mass Media and the Secondary School*. London: MacMillan.

Parkin, F. 1971. *Class, Inequality and Political Order*. London: MacGibbon and Kee.

Phillips, C. 1969. *Changes in Subject Choice at School and University*. London: Weidenfeld.

Richardson, E. 1973. *The Teacher, the School and the Task of Management*. London: Heinemann.

Rosenthal, R. and Jacobson, L. 1968. *Pygmalion in the Classroom: Teacher Expectations and Pupils' Intellectual Development*. New York: Holt, Rinehart and Winston.

Simon, B. 1971. *Intelligence, Psychology and Education*. London: Lawrence and Wishart.

Simpson, R.L., and Simpson, I.H. 1969. Women in Bureaucracy. In A. Etzioni (ed.), *The Semi-Professions and their Organisation*. New York: Free Press.

Sutherland, M. 1961. Coeducation and School Attainment. *British Journal of Educational Psychology 31:* 158-169.

Turner, R. 1964. Some Aspects of Women's Ambition. *American Journal of Sociology*.

Williams, W.M. 1974. *Occupation Choices*. London: George Allen and Unwin.

Willis, P. and Critcher, C. 1974. Women in Sport. In *Cultural Studies 5*. Birmingham: Centre for Contemporary Cultural Studies.

Young, D.A. and Brandis, W. 1967. Two Types of Streaming. *University of London Institute of Education Bulletin*.

Young, M., and Willmott, P. 1973. *The Symmetrical Family*. London: Routledge.

SALLY MACINTYRE

'Who Wants Babies?'
The Social Construction
of 'Instincts'*

Introduction

My concern in this paper is to draw attention to 'normal reproduction' as a socially constructed phenomenon and a sociologically interesting topic of study. I am particularly interested in the 'vocabularies of motives' (Mills 1940) surrounding reproduction and the differential attribution of motives to certain categories of persons.

My contention is that reproduction and the everyday theories surrounding it have been neglected as sociological topics of enquiry. Readers may protest the converse — that there is an extensive literature on reproduction. I am suggesting, however, that sociologists have taken normal reproduction, and the meanings attached to it, for granted as part of the natural order. Attention has thus been focussed on unwed mothers (Roberts 1966; Rains 1971), illegitimacy (Thompson 1956; Pinchbeck 1954), abortion (Callahan 1970; Horobin 1973), unwanted pregnancy (Sloane 1969), or on the number of children that people want (Woolf 1971). That is, the topics studied refer to *deviations* from what is perceived as normal, phenomena regarded as socially *problematic*, or to the *details* of reproduction.[1]

By studying apparent deviations from cultural norms we may clarify and highlight the 'normal', but we may also fail to recognize the social construction of the normal as well as of the deviation, and provide sociological explanations for deviation but not for non-deviation. Further, we may fail to take cognisance of variations, by time and by situation, in definitions of the normal and in the avowed and imputed motives for normal action.

*I would like to thank my colleagues at the M.R.C. Medical Sociology Research Unit for their comments on earlier drafts of this paper, and to acknowledge the financial support of the Social Science Research Council for the research project on which it is based.

I am suggesting that our knowledge concerning some central events and phenomena in our social world, such as sex, marriage, and reproduction, is of the 'thinking as usual' type described by Schutz (1964).[2] We have not attended to the question 'what is normal reproduction like', because we have deemed it to be part of the natural order and therefore as not in need of theoretical attention. We may also assume that 'accounts' (Scott and Lyman 1968) or 'vocabularies of motives' (Mills 1940) are not available or amenable to study because they are not called for by such taken-for-granted behaviour as reproduction.[3]

However, in the everyday world of our society there do exist some explanatory theories for reproduction to which appeal may be made. One such account is based on the concept of a 'maternal instinct'. This concept is often taken to imply that humans (and especially women) want to have babies, or have instinctual drives towards reproduction; that this drive has individual and species survival value; that pregnancy is normal; and that childbearing is woman's highest, yet most basic, function.

Probably few sociologists would accept the existence of such an instinct. However, some would claim that given the ubiquity and universality (both historically and cross-culturally) of a belief in the maternal instinct, then the question 'who wants babies? And why?' is not a pertinent one. Following Thomas's dictum that 'if men define situations as real, they are real in their consequences' (1928: 584), they would argue that if reproduction is regarded as normal, and a concept such as the maternal instinct incorporated into everyday life, then reproduction does not need to be explained, nor will there be any vocabularies of motives to be examined. Given this position, what requires explanation is not individuals' acceptance of the taken-for-granted world and its normative order, but the social determinants of the construction of 'the maternal instinct'.

I would claim, however, that we do need to enquire whether, and what, accounts for having babies are imputed or avowed in a society at any point in time.

Without making some attempt to specify: (a) what accounts are proffered and accepted; (b) by whom are they proffered; (c) to whom are they attributed; we run the danger of erecting what may be an unwarrantably monolithic and universal model of normal reproduction, and of assuming a homogeneity and consensus of motives and beliefs not found empirically. This is particularly necessary to counterbalance grand level theories of the Parsonian type, which tend to describe the meaning of sex, marriage, and reproduction, and their relationships to the family and other social institutions, but without taking seriously actors' definitions of the situation (despite lip service being paid to the importance of subjective meanings). As Maher points out elsewhere in this volume informants who are old, male, and of high status have been particularly trusted in sociology and anthropology. Their statements may, however, represent a dominant value system rather than actual behaviour, and stem from the exercise of a certain cultural hegemony; hence the need to specify the three points noted above.

Sylvia Clavan points out that:

'Analysis of the research done shows that almost all definitions of sex behaviour as conforming, normative, deviant or changing, are based on social expectations of the male and female fulfilling their roles as part of a nuclear family unit or in anticipation of creating such a unit.' (1972:296)

Similarly, in studies of reproduction, the yardstick of the nuclear family unit is used as the basis of research classifications, and sex, marriage and reproduction are often linked together in such a way as to imply that each explains the other. This bracketing together may be unfruitful, however, in that it collapses into one what should be separate and interesting questions — about the meanings attributed to sexual activities, to marriage, and to reproduction, and the perceived relationships between the three. We have tended to avoid asking whether differentially situated actors or groups bracket these three phenomena together and define 'normal reproduction' only in terms of a nuclear marital unit.

Though sex, marriage, and reproduction may be linked empirically in a particular society and its dominant ideology, we still need to enquire into the processes leading to them and the meanings attributed to them. We cannot assume *a priori* that people have babies because they are married, or marry in order to have babies; nor that people have babies because they have had sex, or that they have sex in order to produce babies.[4]

The division between 'married' and 'unmarried'
One crucial social/sexual division in our society is that between married and unmarried persons. This division thrusts deeply into assumptions about behaviour, motivation, and feelings in the whole arena of sexual and reproductive life. It is this distinction between 'married' and 'unmarried', and some of the perceived correlates of these statuses, to which I wish to address the question,

'Who wants babies — and who says so?'.

My current research is concerned with 'decision-making' following conception in single women. I have recently come to regard some of the research questions in their original formulation as potentially doing violence to the experiences of such women. This is because the research problem was defined in a way that incorporated certain assumptions from some prevailing social ideologies.

The original research question was: 'How do single women who become pregnant resolve their situation?' and certain choices were posited. These included marrying the father of the baby, termination of pregnancy, surrendering the child for adoption, and becoming an unmarried mother. Some of the underlying assumptions were, that being pregnant while single is problematic, a situation that needs to be resolved; that marriage is one resolution of the problem; that single women basically do not want babies and that they may, therefore, seek termination or adoption; and that the choices posed above (e.g. marriage and termination) are mutually exclusive.[5]

These questions relate to empirically common outcomes and as such are appropriate areas of research concern. However, some of the assumptions underlying such research may vitiate any analysis of the processes and mechanisms involved in single women reaching these outcomes of pregnancy. That is, certain questions (e.g. about the problematic nature of pregnancy for a single woman, or the linkage between sex, marriage, and reproduction) may not be asked, because 'everyone knows' the answers, and this neglect of the important issues may lead to the perpetuation of these assumptions.

Thus, we need to ask women whether they define unmarried childbearing as problematic (and, if so, in what ways), and whether they perceive options such as termination of pregnancy and marriage as mutually exclusive. We also need to ask those helping professions whose decisions may affect 'outcome rates' about their definitions of the situation and their imputations of motives and feelings. It may be important to ask *whose* definitions of 'what it is like to be pregnant and unmarried' most influence rates of, for example, marriage and termination.

Where acceptable vocabularies of motives or definitions of the situation vary between differentially situated groups, [6] we may find empirically common outcomes to events such as pregnancy in single women perceived very differently by these groups. In this situation 'outcomes' may be as much due to rate-producing processes as to behaviour producing processes (Kitsuse and Cicourel 1963).

Ideologies linking marriage and reproduction

The following sections present a discussion of some ideologies of reproduction. This is oriented around the differential attribution to married and unmarried women of motives for, and responses to, motherhood, and disjunctions between avowed and attributed definitions of the situation. Note that I am not here imputing 'real' motives or feelings, but presenting accounts provided to me. Thus, I am treating these ideologies as topics of enquiry, rather than as taken-for-granted resources for the enquiry (Zimmerman and Pollner 1970).

Having indicated some of the background to the ideologies espoused by three helping professions (doctors, nurses, and social workers) I shall present a summary of these ideologies as they pertain to married and unmarried women, and then document the operation of these ideologies in practice.

Though in the introduction I have referred to 'persons', hereafter I refer to women. The omission of men from the discussion is due to a lack of empirical data on avowed or attributed feelings concerning fatherhood. I have been as remiss as most other sociologists in assuming that marriage and childbearing are primarily of importance to women rather than to men, and hence neglecting men in the research design.

The study from which the material was derived adopted two main research strategies. The first involved following up a small number of women from an early stage of pregnancy. Interviews were conducted with each woman throughout her pregnancy and with all official agents with whom she came into contact (e.g. consultant gynaecologists re termination of pregnancy, social workers re adoption, etc.). Access to medical case notes was granted. Twenty-eight such women were followed through their 'pregnancy careers' in this manner — fourteen were derived from their first contact with a general practitioner, nine from their first contact with an ante-natal clinic, and five from a hospital gynaecological ward. 'Outcomes of pregnancy' for these women comprised ten terminations, six spontaneous abortions, six legitimate births (including one neonatal death), and six illegitimate births (including one surrender for adoption).

The second strategy was to examine those agencies or locales through which such pregnant women might typically pass: their staffing, operational philosophies, organizational routines, and modes of interacting with clients/patients. This involved observing the work of health visitors, nurses, and clinicians in an ante-natal clinic, that of nurses and doctors in a gynaecological out-patient clinic, and that of a hospital medical social work department. Supplementary material was gathered by attending medical and social work meetings, by general interviews with doctors, nurses, and social workers, and by conversations with women who had passed through the maternity care system at various times.

In using case history or interview material for this paper pseudonyms have been used and identifying detail altered throughout.

Background — the theories of professionals

Hern discusses the ways in which most doctors accept 'the widely shared teleological definition of the female as essentially a reproductive machine' (Hern 1971:5). The physician's view implicitly assumes not only that pregnancy is normal but that it is:

'... an especially desirable event from the viewpoint of woman's physiological, psychological and social functioning and that failure (or worse, refusal) to become or remain pregnant is, therefore, pathological. In this context it is not surprising that even the major text books of obstetrics pay little or no attention to how a *woman* feels when she is pregnant, how *she* feels after an abortion, whether *she* regarded the pregnancy as normal or desirable.' (1971:5)

That is, from theories that pregnancy and childbearing are normal and desirable, it is *assumed* that all women will define them as such. Various consequences follow. Hern points out: '... it follows that every woman who wants an abortion must need to have her head examined, and this is exactly what has happened'. (1971:7)

Thus, the desire not to have babies must be explained. One sort of explanation proffered is that rapid hormone changes in early pregnancy may produce emotional responses (mis-)interpreted by the woman as distress. As an epiphenomenon of hormonal changes, this response can be defined by clinicians as transitory and as less 'real' than the basic desire to have a baby. Women are, therefore, informed: 'But you'll be thrilled when the baby is born.'[7]

One report (I.P.P.F. 1972) notes that in Scandinavia for many years the policy was to try and convince abortion-seeking women to change their minds and continue with pregnancy, on the grounds that it was the physiological changes of early pregnancy that were causing depression and the desire to terminate pregnancy. This policy created delays between abortion applications and the operation, a late gestational age at abortion, and distress among those women granted the operation. In pointing out that this distress might be as plausibly attributed to the delays, to anxieties due to uncertainty, and to more complex operative procedures, as to inevitable trauma at the destruction of the foetus, the authors commented: 'The bulk of the literature is perhaps best interpreted as an example of doctrinal compliance in which both the investigator and those being investigated produce data which supports the initial hypothesis' (I.P.P.F. 1972:32).

Women may, of course, become overtly more accepting of their pregnancies or babies than they appeared initially. This may be less an inevitable resurgence of the maternal instinct, however, than a response to the massive pressure exerted by the expectations of significant others (and particularly medical experts — cf. Zemlick and Watson 1953) in a culture which employs 'good motherhood' as a central defining characteristic of female identity.

Clinicians' theories may, therefore, be somewhat self-validating in that the routine practices and expectations based on the theories may themselves help to produce the predicted responses. Once a construct of a normal drive towards, and desire for, motherhood has developed, it may be difficult for it to be capable of disproof by its proponents.[8] In addition, a crucial point in relation to medical theories about motherhood is that the overwhelming majority of obstetricians and gynaecologists are male. That is, a specialism relating solely to the functioning of women is staffed mainly by men, who then have the socially legitimated authority to determine 'what women are really like'. In this context Thomas's aphorism, suitably accented, is particularly pertinent: 'If *men* define situations as real ... etc.'

The majority of nurses are female. However, partly because of its sex composition as well as its occupational tradition of service to 'the doctor', the nursing profession may give more credence to the theories of doctors than to those of women patients, and it may enhance its professional standing by allying itself to the medical profession and its body of knowledge. Nurses' theories about motherhood may, therefore, be informed more by those of clinicians than by their own experience or that of their female patients.

The psycho-dynamic theories of motherhood that developed in

the 1940s (Deutsch 1947) stressed the existence of unconscious urges towards motherhood. Given this formulation, desires for motherhood could be attributed irrespective of women's stated feelings, and deviations from predicted responses could be incorporated into the theories by concepts such as defence mechanism, reaction formation, or pathology, leaving its central premises untouched by the evidence from women's conscious subjective responses. Like those of the clinicians, the models of the psycho-dynamic theorists of motherhood tended to be unchallengeable for its proponents.

Young dealt extensively with the idea of unconscious urges in her work on unmarried mothers: 'There can be no doubt that the drive which propels an unmarried mother results in compulsive action. To say that her behaviour is the result of immorality or of free choice is to ignore all the evidence' (Young 1954:36). She seems to imply that every pregnant woman must have wanted (albeit unconsciously) to have become pregnant, whatever the woman's definition of the situation. Like many 'drive' theories, however, the evidence for the existence of maternal drives is the phenomenon that the 'drive' is used to explain, for example, pregnancy.

An interesting feature of Young's work (and other work in this tradition) is that this drive is seen as in need of explanation for unmarried women, though not for married women. It is assumed that the factors 'causing' unmarried motherhood are different from those 'causing' married motherhood: indeed some of the factors used to explain unmarried motherhood are often similar to those used to explain why married women might *not* have babies (e.g. 'lack of personality structure and love').

The assumption of unconscious motivation towards motherhood, differing between married and unmarried women, was extremely pervasive in the literature on unmarried mothers in the 1950s and 1960s; e.g. 'Whether illegitimacy is seen as the result of an unconscious wish to punish one's parents, a desire for adult status, or simply adherence to subcultural practices, it is taken for granted that the unwed mother becomes pregnant because motivated to do so' (Furstenberg 1971:192).

The psycho-dynamic literature is worth examining for two important reasons. First, it provided a more acceptable vocabulary of motives than was previously available for unmarried pregnant women — pregnancies could be attributed to 'forces beyond the woman's control' rather than to immoral conduct. Appeal could thus be made to biological urges in a way that absolved the individual of responsibility for her actions and, therefore, from blame or stigma, viz. Scott and Lyman's discussion of biological urges as acceptable accounts (1968:4)[9] Second, these theories have informed the operational philosophies of many branches of one helping profession — social work. The assumptions drawn from the psycho-dynamic theories underpin the social workers' body of knowledge and are reflected in their routine practices in relation to, and their responses to, unmarried pregnant women or mothers.

The professional views sketched above are also informed by, and reciprocally interact with, the more general belief systems and everyday knowledge of the culture in which the professions are embedded. As Busfield (1974) points out, in modern British society there is an especially strong socialization of women into the desirability of marriage and motherhood. In the prevailing ideologies of reproduction there is an inextricable link between marriage and motherhood: 'On the one hand it is expected and regarded as desirable that those who marry will have children; and on the other it is expected that those who want to have children will marry' (Busfield 1974:14).

Married couples with children are regarded as constituting the 'proper, natural and complete family', the church marriage service enjoins childbearing, and there is an explicit norm against childlessness within marriage (viz. Peck 1973). Thus: 'Childbearing is encouraged not only directly by the high value placed on children, but also indirectly by the value attached to marriage, since once married, for whatever reason, couples are subject to strong expectations that they will have children' (Busfield 1974:33).

The use of strictures against selfishness in attempts to encourage couples to have children is particularly significant: if childbearing is normal, a natural instinct, and the ultimate fulfilment for every woman and couple, how can desisting from such a pleasure-producing instinct be selfish? This attribution of selfishness implicitly recognizes that motherhood may not be a universal instinct, and the existence of normative pressures towards childbearing renders more necessary the view of 'the maternal instinct' as a social construction that is employed as induced motivation within certain social contexts.

It is within this general cultural framework of beliefs about reproduction, and its relation to social institutions such as marriage, that the theories of the medical, nursing, and social work professions have developed and are operationalized.

Professional theories relating to married and unmarried women
We are now in a position to spell out some of the components of
professional theories about reproduction in relation to the
distinction between married and unmarried women. The following
schematized summary may appear over-simplified, provocative,
and based on little evidence. Given that the intention is to highlight
and draw attention to some basic everyday lay and professional
assumptions, this is an approach deliberately selected.

The equation of marriage with motherhood, and non-marriage
with non-motherhood, is extremely pervasive even among those,
for example clinicians, who claim to be concerned with biological
universals. There is an underlying contradiction between the view
of all women as essentially similar and endowed with strong
maternal instincts, and the view that differentiates between women
by marital status. At its crudest, this leads to the position that the
maternal instinct only operates in married women, and not in
unmarried women.

This co-existence of two versions of reality leads to the following
assumptions:

For married women:
(i) pregnancy and childbearing are normal and desirable, and
conversely a desire not to have children is aberrant and in need of
explanation.

(ii) pregnancy and childbearing are not problematic, and to treat
them as such indicates that something is wrong.

(iii) legitimate children with a living parent should not be
surrendered for adoption or taken from the mother, as this would
occasion too much distress for the mother. (Indeed the concept of
such children being surrendered permanently, for adoption by
strangers, is almost unknown in Britain). A married woman who
wants to give up her children is by definition aberrant and is seen as
trying to 'get rid of' her children.

(iv) If a couple is childless it is clinically advisable that they
receive diagnostic attention and, if necessary, treatment, for
infertility.

(v) It is clinically advisable on occasion to advise a woman to
have a child.

(vi) The loss of a baby by miscarriage, stillbirth, or neonatal
death occasions instinctive deep distress and grief.

For single women:
(i) Pregnancy and childbearing are abnormal and undesirable

and conversely the desire to have a baby is aberrant, selfish, and in need of explanation.

(ii)   Pregnancy and childbearing are problematic, and not to treat them as such indicates that something is wrong.

(iii)   Illegitimate children should be surrendered for adoption and a mother who wants to keep her child is unrealistic and selfish.

(iv)   Diagnostic attention and treatment for infertility is not clinically advisable or relevant — unless the woman is about to get married. It is not proper for her to adopt a child.

(v)   It would be most inadvisable and inappropriate clinically to advise a single woman to have a child.

(vi)   The loss of a baby by miscarriage, stillbirth, or neonatal death should not occasion too much grief or distress, and may even produce relief.

In summary: one solution for the problems of a single, pregnant woman is to get married. If she is going to get married, she will want the baby: if not, she will not want it.

The theories in operation — doctors, nurses and social workers
The classic waiting room joke —

> Doctor: 'I've got good news for you, Mrs. Brown.'
> Patient: 'It's Miss Brown, actually.'
> Doctor: 'I've got bad news for you, Miss Brown'.

epitomizes the crucial effect that information about civil status may have on a doctor's perceptions of the meaning and implications of a biological event — pregnancy.

Through detailed interviewing of a small series of pregnant women and their general practitioners, suggestive evidence emerged as to the typifications of patients used by general practitioners (Macintyre 1973).

For one series of fourteen single women, I was able to construct, from the descriptions provided by both women and their doctors, a list, in order of frequency, of the questions general practitioners asked the women at their first consultation regarding the pregnancy (i.e. for pregnancy confirmation). According to both the women and the doctors, the four most frequent and earliest questions were:

(a)   possibility of marriage to the putative father
(b)   previous contraceptive usage
(c)   relationship with the putative father at consultation
(d)   relationship with the putative father at conception

This is consistent with statements made by general practitioners in general interviews (i.e. not concerning specific patients) about their routine management of pregnancy in single women. All the general practitioners spontaneously mentioned that they would, in the words of one: '... ascertain whether matrimony is contemplated — and proceed from there'.

Note that while topics (a) and (c) above relate to current and future plans on the woman's part, topics (b) and (d) relate to the past. Many of the women expressed surprise at the number of *past* oriented questions — the number of boyfriends they had had, intercourse pattern with the putative father, past contraceptive usage, etc. Some saw this as voyeurism on the part of the general practitioner, and as irrelevant for future management and current concerns — put most cogently by one woman, who said: '... What does it matter what form of contraception we was usin' — it didna' work, did it?'.

On the general practitioner's part, these past-oriented questions would appear to be directed towards establishing a general typification of the patient — of the order of 'the type of girl who ...' from which various deductions can be made. These questions are not considered pertinent for married women, because 'everyone knows' (and particularly doctors) what marital relationships, including sexual relationships, are like. But it is problematic what sorts of relationships single women have, and their patterns of sexual behaviour.

Thus, it would appear unlikely that married pregnant women are routinely asked such questions as:

'Who is the father of your baby?'
'What was your relationship with him at the time of conception?'
'Are you still seeing him?'
'When did you start sleeping with your husband?'

Of course, such questions may occasionally be asked, but only when there is evidence that the patient is not a 'normal' married woman.

Some of the women anticipated such questions. In making the decision to consult a doctor, one feature of the consultation anticipated with some apprehension was close questioning about intimate aspects of life style, sexual behaviour, relationships, and motivation. This apprehension was related to a concern that from the evidence 'single and pregnant' would be imputed or deduced a characterisation as 'promiscuous'.

For some patients this concern was justified, as general practitioners appeared to operate with the model of single women being radically different from married women in their sexual relationships. That is, the general practitioners deemed single women to have sexual relations qualitatively and quantitatively different from those of married women. For example, one general practitioner commented on a single pregnant patient who had a trichomonal infection:

'I mean, it was a simple trichomonal vaginitis which is a common infection anyway in pairs who have sexual intercourse, married or unmarried. But the fact that she's got it … it's really a function of intercourse and she's unmarried so she's obviously being promiscuous.'

Questions are asked about marriage intentions because if the patient is going to get married, 'management' is simplified. If the patient does not intend marriage, this is the signal that something is wrong, that the pregnancy is unwanted. Several general practitioners said that they discussed marriage, adoption, keeping the child, and termination, in that order and with a positive response to an earlier topic precluding discussion of later topics. The question of marriage was raised first: if the patient was going to get married, the general practitioner would not raise the other possibilities or the question of the 'wantedness' of the pregnancy, but would proceed with physical checks, making arrangements for antenatal care, etc. If she did not intend marriage, he would raise the further possibilities on the assumption that the pregnancy was 'problematic'.

Patients are aware that the alternatives are perceived by the medical profession as mutually exclusive. This may lead to a variety of situations in which the patient has to present a distorted version of her situation in order to attain the solution she desires. An example of this is where the woman is in a steady supportive relationship with her boyfriend and intends marriage, but does not want the baby. If she wants a termination of pregnancy she may mislead doctors as to her relationship with the putative father, e.g.:

Pat: 'Well, he (i.e. the g.p.) said to me — well, John and I have decided we're going to get engaged on the 1st June. He says, well, in so many words, he says to me, if you go and see the gynaecologist you can't very well go and say, "we're getting engaged" because obviously you'll be getting married. And I says, "well, no, right enough" — 'cos he would say why do you want it terminated when you're getting married anyway?'

The gynaecologist did ask her about marriage plans and she told him she would not be marrying the putative father because they were too young, etc. The termination was agreed to, and a week after the termination she formally became engaged to her boyfriend.

The reverse situation can be illustrated by Jenny, who wanted to keep the baby but not to marry the putative father. She was offered a termination referral by her general practitioner, which she refused, and during her pregnancy found a lot of pressure on her either to get married or to surrender the baby for adoption. In order to cope with this she let people believe that she would be marrying the putative father, only after the baby was born stressing that she had no intention of so doing. She found it difficult to convince people that, although fond of the putative father (who wanted to marry her), she had no desire to get married. 'I said this, but they still don't believe it, you know. It's like bashing your head against a brick wall'.

Both Pat and Jenny in their own accounts of their lives 'de-bracket' sex, marriage, and motherhood. Pat was in a stable relationship, was going to get married with parental approval from both sides, she and her boyfriend deemed themselves well off materially and emotionally, and they had been sexually active for some time. But she did not want a baby: for her, sex, marriage, and motherhood were not necessarily connected. But in order to convince the gynaecologist that she 'really' did not want the baby, she had to claim that she was not getting married.

Jenny, similarly, saw no necessary personal connection between sex, marriage, and motherhood. She enjoyed sex and she enjoyed motherhood; but she did not want to get married, and saw marriage as requiring completely different motivation from motherhood.

In looking at consultant gynaecologists' case notes and letters to general practitioners, where termination is at issue, it is clear that the question of marriage is perceived as crucial. Thus:

Ann: 'I saw this 16-year-old schoolgirl who is pregnant to a young mechanic. There is no physical abnormality and there is no history of serious illness.

I think she should seriously consider marrying this young man as a solution to her difficulties.'

Janet: 'It was felt that this girl and her boyfriend should get married and that termination should not be done. Seemingly the boyfriend is keen to get married to her and she intends continuing the relationship in any case.'

Here the physicians are portraying termination and marriage as alternatives, and marriage as a 'solution' to the problem of pregnancy.

The concern with marital status is also manifest for those who are continuing with the pregnancy. At one main antenatal clinic, unmarried women are asterixed on the daily clinic list, and singled out for special attention. All unmarried women are routinely asked whether they wish to see a social worker, and if they say 'No', are given a card with the social worker's name and telephone number on it. For married women, it is only those patients who themselves ask to see a social worker, or who are adjudged by clinic personnel to have social problems, who are put in touch with a social worker. Post-natally, unmarried women fall into the category of 'at risk' patients towards whom special attention regarding contraception is directed, e.g. a health visitor sees every unmarried woman on the ward for contraceptive advice before discharge. During a period of observation in the clinic, I noted also that consultants averaged 4.1 minutes with married women and 5.7 minutes with unmarried women for their routine physical check-ups.

Jenny described with some amusement how a consultant at the clinic had spent twenty minutes commiserating with her for her mild depression and mood change. When she had said that she thought that these symptoms were normal at her stage of pregnancy and due to hormonal changes, the consultant brushed this aside and appeared to attribute her feelings to ambivalence about the baby and the approach of unmarried motherhood.

In contrast, a married woman, Valerie, attempted to initiate a discussion with her consultant about her ambivalence and depression concerning her pregnancy and impending motherhood. The consultant's response was to normalize these feelings as intrinsic to her stage of pregnancy, and to disregard the issue of the validity of her not wanting motherhood.

One is not here criticising the clinic for its systematized concern with potential problems on the part of single pregnant women. It can be argued that a responsible clinic will take note of research findings or empirical experience regarding 'at risk' groups and focus attention on them. However, theories about differential motivations and 'problematic-ness' may be rendered self-validating by the routine practices at a clinic. If one asks unmarried women about ambivalence towards motherhood and about problems associated with motherhood, one will probably find ambivalence and problems. If at the same time one normalizes, and treats as desirable and unproblematic, pregnancy in married women, one is less likely to unearth ambivalence and problems among married women.

The stress placed on marriage as problem-solving is most clearly demonstrated by the intermediate category of women who have conceived while single but who attend the clinic as married women. These women are treated as unproblematic and placed into the normal married category. However, these prenuptial conceivers may define their situations more in terms of uncertainty, fears, and problems than do 'routine' unmarried mothers define their situations. Some of the women who had conceived while single, married before attending the clinic, some during attendance, and others remained single throughout their ante-natal career. What most differentiated these three groups was not their own perceptions of their situation, relations with family or putative father, or social/financial situations, but the responses of the helping professions to them.

Elizabeth, for example, was sixteen when she became pregnant. She delayed attending a doctor until four months pregnant, married very quickly after pregnancy confirmation, and lived with her husband in her parents' three-bedroom house, the rest of the family consisting of her parents, younger brother, and grandmother. She recounted her anxieties about the need for rapid adjustment to marriage and impending motherhood, fears about whether she wanted a baby, strained family relationships, and financial problems. She was married, however, at her first visit to the clinic, and as such was treated as a 'normal' married woman, delighted at the pregnancy, and for whom it was not appropriate to enquire into possible pregnancy-related problems.

Barbara, on the other hand, was a twenty-eight-year-old university graduate and ex-social worker, who lived with supportive parents in a large suburban house, having decided that she wanted a child and did not want to marry. The response to her at the clinic was one of concern and anxiety about her problems — which she defined as non-existent. Much of the concern was focussed around exactly that point — it was felt that she lacked insight in insisting 'that everything's perfectly o.k., thankyou — I'm delighted with the thought of the baby'.

In these situations, women's own definitions of the situation are relegated to secondary importance in comparison with what the medical profession imputes to be their real situation or feelings, based on the single/married distinction. Interviews with patients who had aborted spontaneously also highlighted variations in attributed desires for motherhood, and the low status given to the woman's subjective experiences.

Thus, Joanna was interviewed on the ward just after she had miscarried:

Q: 'How did you feel when you first thought you were pregnant?'

A: 'I was glad. I really wanted a baby ... it was when I missed two months. But I didna' go to the doctor. I was quite happy about it.'

Q: 'And what about your boyfriend?'

A: 'Oh, I told him. He was pleased — he was wanting a baby as well.'

A: 'Well, I realized — I thought I'd lost the baby — I was real upset. When the doctor told me I'd lost the baby — we'll be trying again — for another one — I wanted the baby.'

Joanna's account was, therefore, that she and her boyfriend had been pleased about the pregnancy and looking forward to the baby: she had been very upset when she lost the baby, and planned to try again for another one as soon as possible.

A nurse on the ward expressed a very different view. She described Joanna as being very immature and rather 'strange'. She said that the previous day Joanna had 'had had a little bleeding and had to go down to theatre to have it cleared up' (i.e. had a D & C operation to complete a spontaneous abortion) and had then been very upset and had broken down completely and cried all day. The nurse described this distress as *ipso facto* demonstrating that Joanna should not have had the baby anyway, and that it was just as well that she had lost the baby given her obvious immaturity. The nurse then said: 'I give up with these women.' She had offered Joanna the Pill, a routine practice for single women, and Joanna had refused because she wanted to try again for another baby. This was taken as further illustration of Joanna's 'madness'. Later in the conversation with me the nurse said she thought sociologists studying abortion ignored the guilt and distress following induced abortion — 'no woman being able to tolerate the loss of a foetus with equanimity'.

The account by a married woman who also aborted spontaneously forms an instructive contrast:

'I can remember how very good they were to me in hospital. I thought they were marvellous at the time. They were very understanding. They treated me as if they knew that I was very upset. They expected me to be upset.'

Q. 'And it was assumed that you wanted children?'
A: 'Oh, yes.'
Q: 'And that you would want to try again?'
A: 'Oh, yes, definitely. Yes, it was ... In there they were very understanding and assumed that I would want to get pregnant again — they told me to wait 6 weeks and then try again.'

This, though no more than suggestive, highlights the way in which responses to motherhood or loss of a child are predicted or expected on the basis of civil status — a social, not biological distinction. It is plausible to assume that a married woman who did *not* express distress at the loss of a baby, nor discuss the possibility of becoming pregnant again, would be regarded as 'odd' or as having underdeveloped maternal instincts by the hospital staff. Married women, quite simply, are supposed to want children as part of their biological and psychological make-up.

This can be illustrated by the experience of a twenty-nine year old married working woman who had been attending a family planning clinic for some six years for the Pill. She reported the clinic staff as becoming increasingly uneasy with her avowed intention not to have children. After a period of cues and hints she was finally directly informed that she ought to have a baby, and that help was available to overcome her problem of thinking she did not want one. Despite her protestations that she was quite happy with her husband and her job, she was informed that perhaps she might be covering up her own inadequacies by her refusal to contemplate motherhood.

A twenty-six year old single woman attended the same clinic asking for a diaphragm, stressing that she knew that this was less reliable for contraceptive purposes than the Pill, but that she was prepared to take this risk as she had previously had uncomfortable side-effects from it. She left the clinic in tears with a prescription for the Pill, having been told that she had been irresponsible and that it had no side-effects of the sort described. By contrast, a gynaecologist addressing a medical audience on the topic of in- or sub-fertility and its relationship with the Pill, suggested that a childless woman in her mid-twenties should be discouraged from going on the Pill and should use less reliable methods instead, as 'if she gets pregnant it doesn't matter very much, if she's married'.

The point here is not that the medical profession disagree among themselves or are inconsistent, but that their theories as to psychological and biological universals *systematically* vary according to social or civil status, the main distinction being between married and unmarried persons. To the question — 'Who wants babies'? — their response on the one hand is that 'all women want babies', but on the other, that 'only married women want babies'.

Social workers also claim to be concerned with psychological universals of the order, 'all women have an urge towards motherhood'. Currently, the ethos among many social workers is that unmarried mothers should surrender their children for adoption in the best interests of all concerned. The whole phenomenon of adoption does, of course, raise issues that are normally outside the cultural repertoire — issues such as giving away a child or vetting people's suitability to have children. However, concepts applicable to unmarried mothers vis-a-vis adoption are not deemed applicable, in social work practice, to married mothers.

Here there may be appeals to different vocabularies of motives: one, appropriate to single women, concerned with the rights and welfare of the *child*; and another, appropriate to married women, concerned with the blood tie and the maternal instinct. It may be that appeals couched in terms of the child's welfare and rights may become more acceptable for *all* mothers and children in the future as questions concerning rights in children become opened to debate. Currently, however, two competing vocabularies of motives co-exist, one for the unmarried and one for the married, and a married woman may not find 'I gave my child away for its own good' an acceptable account.

This can be illustrated by statements made by a speaker at a social work conference on 'The Unmarried Mother and her Decision' (my comments follow the speakers' statements):

> 'A girl may decide to keep her baby for reasons other than the best interest of the child.'

How many married couples orient their fertility behaviour to the best interests of their children?

> 'The girl may be emotionally disturbed and feel needed for the first time. All mothers want what is best for their child in the long run but not all mothers have the ability, strength and restraint to make any decisions let alone the right one: the social worker must point out the situation as it really is.'

How many married women have babies in order to be needed? How many married persons have the ability, strength, and restraint to make actual 'decisions' concerning fertility, let alone decisions that a social worker would deem the right ones?

In response to a question as to whether the child's interests are identical with those of the mother:

'At the end of the day their interests are coterminous. All mothers if able to look at it objectively would feel better by surrendering.'

But she was not referring to a population of all mothers — only to a subset of that population, which happens to be unmarried. When asked about unsupported married women in unsatisfactory living conditions surrendering their children for adoption, she replied that social workers do not agree with that approach and that surrendering a child would be too great an emotional trauma for married women.

The rhetorical question asked by a social worker in another public meeting — 'Why is adoption considered as an option only for illegitimate children — why not adoption for legitimate children in various circumstances?' — and the ramifications of the issues raised by that question illustrate the concerns discussed in this paper.

Conclusion

I have been addressing here the issue of the attribution and avowal of motives, instincts, and responses towards pregnancy and motherhood. My concern has been to indicate that among three helping professions — doctors, nurses, and social workers — reproduction is regarded as 'natural, normal, and instinctive' but that different sorts of accounts are provided for the responses and motivations of unmarried as compared with married women. The accounts proffered by women, and their definitions of the situation, may depart from those imputed by these professions or by other members of society, and may not neatly fall into separate definitions for unmarried and married.

The accounts here provided are, of course, historically and culturally rooted, and I am not claiming that such accounts would have been proffered at previous points in time. However, in a situation of secular changes and appeals to new vocabularies of motive, we may find competing vocabularies among different groups. The helping professions here described may be appealing to an older and previously universally accepted set of accounts couched in terms of the maternal instincts and the bracketing of sex, marriage, and reproduction. It may be that at an earlier point in time these accounts and definitions would also be accepted by women. Partly because of the self-validating nature of these theories, they can be maintained by these professions while women are now prepared to proffer different sorts of accounts which de-bracket sex, marriage, and reproduction.

I have been unable here to provide any analysis of the social determinants of ideologies of reproduction or the derivation of vocabularies of motive. All I have been able to indicate is that the assumption that we know what 'normal reproduction' is, or is perceived to be like, is perhaps untenable at this historical time. This leads me to conclude that rather than accepting the idea of a universal set of motives, both attributed and avowed towards motherhood, sociologists should ask persons — male and female — about the accounts they provide for having or not having children, their decision-making processes regarding parenthood, and their ideologies of parenthood. We should thus treat these accounts as topics of enquiry. An equally important and complementary research strategy should be to treat as a topic of enquiry the nature of definitions of 'married' and 'single', the social sources of these definitions, and their concomitants.

Notes

1 Similarly, most sociological studies of sexual behaviour focus on deviations or details, e.g. the processes and problems of becoming a homosexual (Dank 1971), prostitution (Bryan 1965), premarital sex (Reiss 1970) etc. Little attention has been directed towards becoming or being a married heterosexual.

2 'The knowledge correlated to the cultural pattern carries its evidence in itself — or rather, it is taken for granted in the absence of evidence to the contrary' (Schutz 1964:95).

3 Thus Scott and Lyman point out: 'An account is not called for when people engage in routine, commonsense behaviour in a cultural environment that recognises that behaviour as such' (1968:47).

4 Thus while accepting that coition is necessary (but not sufficient) for reproduction, we need not assume any purposive connection in actors' minds. Further, given that almost all societies have known about or practised some form of contraception, abortion, or infanticide, one cannot assume that reproduction is simply a function of sexual activity, nor that

it is always accepted as part of the natural order. As Kingsley Davis points out:

> 'Ever since the development of culture some millions of years ago, human societies have not relied simply on biological urges to provide children. They have also relied upon induced motivation within a social context — upon definition of the situation, upon custom and mores, upon institutions such as marriage and religion.' (1948:556)

5   This last assumption is explicit in Gill's work, e.g.: 'In neither case are many women likely to proceed to termination who might have resolved their status of single and pregnant by marriage' (1973:89).

6   As Mills points out:

> 'In secondary, secular and urban structures, varying and competing vocabularies of motives operate co-terminally and the situations in which they are appropriate are not clearly demarcated. Motives once unquestioned for defined situations are now questioned.' (1971:116)

7   As described by Doris Lessing in *A Proper Marriage*:

> 'Then he said with a tired, humorous smile that if she knew the number of women patients who came, as she did, when they found they were pregnant, not wanting the baby, only to be delighted when they got used to the idea, she would be surprised.' (1966:117)

8   Note that post-partum 'blues' can also be explained in terms of rapid hormone changes. Hospital gynaecologists and obstetricians do not have contact with patients after discharge back into the community. The clinicians and nurses who attribute post-partum 'blues' to hormonal changes rather than to dislike of the baby and of motherhood, are not the people who may later have to deal with battered babies, given the system of hospital specialism. They are not, therefore, necessarily faced with the evidence that might require their theories to be altered.

9   An unmarried mother told me how she had been visited by a Catholic priest who asked her whether she wished to confess. She told him that she had nothing to confess: he replied that she had 'borne a child out of holy wedlock'. Her reported response to that was, 'That's not a sin, that's just Nature'.

References

Bryan, J.H. 1965. Apprenticeships in Prostitution. *Social Problems, 12* (3):287-97. Winter.

Busfield, J. 1974. Ideologies and Reproduction. In Richards, (ed.), *Integration of the Child into a Social World*. Cambridge: Cambridge University Press.

Callahan, D. 1970. *Abortion: Law, Choice and Morality*. London: Collier Macmillan.

Clavan, S. 1972. Changing Female Sexual Behaviour and Future Family Structure. *Pacific Sociological Review, 15* (3): 295-308. July.

Dank, B. 1971. Coming out in the Gay Community. *Psychiatry 34* (2): 180-97. May.

Davis, K. 1948. *Human Society*. New York: Macmillan.

Deutsch, H. 1947. Psychology of Women — a Psychoanalytic Interpretation. Vol. 2 *Motherhood*. London: Research Books.

Furstenberg, F.F. 1971. Birth Control Experience among Pregnant Adolescents: the process of unplanned parenthood. *Social Problems 19* (2). Fall.

Gill, D.G. 1973. *The Social Aetiology of Illegitimacy: its relationship to adoption and the status of women*. Unpublished Ph.D. thesis. Aberdeen University.

Hern, W.M. 1971. Is Pregnancy Really Normal? *Family Planning Perspectives 3* (1) Journal of Planned Parenthood Federation of America. January.

Horobin. (ed.) 1973. *Experience with Abortion: a case study of North-East Scotland*. Cambridge: Cambridge University Press.

International Planned Parenthood Federation 1972. *Induced Abortion*. A report of the meeting of the I.P.P.F. Panel of Experts on Abortion, held in Novi Sad, Yugoslavia, 24-29 June 1971 and approved by the I.P.P.F. Central Medical Committee in February 1972.

Kitsuse, J.I., and Cicourel, A.V. 1963. A Note on the Uses of Official Statistics. *Social Problems II* :131-39. Fall.

Lessing, D. 1966. *A Proper Marriage*. St. Albans: Panther Books.

Macintyre, S. 1973. *Classification of Social Factors by G.Ps*. Unpublished Paper. August.

Mills, C.W. 1940. Situated Actions and Vocabularies of Motive *American Sociological Review 5* (6): 439-52. Reprinted in *School and Society*. 1971. London: Routledge and Kegan Paul, in Association with the Open University Press.

Peck, E. 1973. *The Baby Trap*. London: Heinrich Hanau Ltd.

Pinchbeck, I. 1954. Social Attitudes to the Problem of Illegitimacy. *British Journal of Sociology 5* : 309-323. December.

Rains, P.M. 1971. *Becoming an Unwed Mother — a sociological account.* Chicago and New York: Aldine-Atherton.

Reiss, I. 1970. Premarital Sex as Deviant Behaviour: an application of current approaches to deviance. *American Sociological Review 35* (1): 78-87.

Roberts, W. 1966. A Theoretical Overview of the Unwed Mother. Introduction to Roberts, R.W. (ed.), *The Unwed Mother.* New York: Harper and Row.

Schutz, A. 1964. The Stranger: an essay in social psychology. In *Collected Papers.* Vol. 2. The Hague: Martinus Nyhoff.

Scott, M.B. and Lyman, S.M. 1968. Accounts. *American Sociological Review 33* (1): 46-62. February.

Sloane, R. 1969. The Unwanted Pregnancy. *New England Journal of Medicine 280* : 1206-1213.

Thomas, W.I. 1928. *The Child in America.* New York: Knopf.

Thompson, B. 1956. Social Study of Illegitimate Maternities. *British Journal of Preventive and Social Medicine 10* (2): 75-87.

Woolf, M. 1971. *Family Intentions.* London: Office of Population Censuses and Surveys and HMSO.

Young, L. 1954. *Out of Wedlock: a study of the problems of the unmarried mother and her child.* New York: McGraw Hill.

Zemlick, M.H. and Watson, R.I. 1953. Maternal Attitudes of Acceptance and Rejection during and after Pregnancy. *American Journal of Orthopsychiatry 23* : 576-84.

Zimmerman, D.H. and Pollner, M. 1970. The Everyday World as a Phenomenon. In Douglas, J. (ed.), *Understanding Everyday Life.* London: Routledge & Kegan Paul.

MIKE BRAKE

I May Be a Queer, But At Least I am a Man:

Male hegemony and ascribed versus achieved gender

If sociology is to avoid falling into the trap of merely reiterating the dominant ideology of a social structure, sceptical examination of the basic assumptions at the base of that social system is required. In considering sexuality too often its political and human aspects have been ignored in favour of descriptions of the bizarre sexual behaviour of exotic deviants. This approach has merely served to treat as unproblematic the nature of new interpretations of sexuality and their political potential. Sexual liberation, like any other form of freedom, is political by definition.[1]

The world of sexuality is too often taken for granted as possessing definite forms and patterns, which have become reified into something which is defined as 'normal'. The human authorship of sexuality has been forgotten, and the influence of the social structure and its parochialism concerning sexuality has been overlooked by those positivists who prefer to ignore that man has produced his world (usually to the detriment of women).

I propose to argue against this position by examining some of the evidence about sex and gender; by considering new forms of consciousness arising among sexual minority groups in our society that are oppressed by the dominant heterosexual male hegemony; and by discussing the problems posed by those who refuse to act in ways considered appropriate to their gender — that is transexuals, transvestites, and homosexuals.[2] In this way I hope to consider the influence that male hegemony has, not only upon the heterosexual, but also on the homosexual world.

For purposes of clarification I propose to consider sex as a biological classification, indicated by primary (genital) sexual characteristics.[3] Gender will be used to refer to those characteristics learned from the culture of the actor, which, as we shall see, are not necessarily related to sex along any universalistic lines. For, 'To be a man, or a woman, a boy or a girl, is as much a function of dress, gesture, occupation, social network and personality as it is of possessing a particular set of genitals' (Oakley 1972:158).

Indeed, it is more than this; to belong to a social set of phenomena such as gender role, is to belong to a status location dictated by the heterosexual division of labour, which may in no sense reflect what the actor feels he or she is. In this sense a particular set of genitals is irrelevant to one's gender, and may merely confuse the actor further.

This rather surprising contention is supported by several pieces of evidence that attack the positivism conception of sexuality. First, the argument for 'natural' behaviour between the sexes appeals to a form of biological social Darwinism, which rests on dubious presuppositions. Primates, for example, do not exhibit the simple behaviour that many social scientists attribute to them. Their sexual life is not an idyllic epic of the Noble Savage, but tends to manifest itself as group sex, often incestuous and bisexual, rather than parallel to the nuclear family. These are the 'natural' forms of sexual behaviour, rather than our own narrow inclinations. Humans, unlike primates, have transcended sexuality as a mere function of species reproduction, into a celebration of human pleasure. Physiologically this is aided by the replacement of the oestrus cycle by the menstrual cycle in women, and by the comparatively large penis of men, the bigger breasts of women, and in both sexes, lack of hair and large lips with corresponding sensory areas in the cortex (Stonier forthcoming).

In addition, sexuality can only be conceived among humans in any sociological sense as a social construct (Nobile 1970; Gagnon and Simon 1973: Plummer 1975) — an action whose social meanings are fashioned through social historical contexts. Thus society defines the nature of sexuality, and sexual meanings are constructed and altered by the actors themselves. People shape their own sexual history, and sexual meanings can be seen not as absolutes, but as ambiguous and problematic categories. Sexual behaviour among humans is rarely performed merely to reproduce; the situation is far more subtle and complex than this.

Gender as an ascribed category

The cultural relativism of gender

If consideration is made of the anthropological evidence, one finds that whilst there is a variety of material showing that all cultures use sex as a differentiating category, the interpretation of gender is far from universal. Margaret Mead has drawn our attention to societies where the modal personality type for both sexes would be seen as 'feminine' in our society (both sexes, for example, are said to 'bear children'), and where both sexes are 'masculine' in our terms, or reversed from our society (Mead 1935).[4] Whatever the methodological shortcomings of these observations, the fact that they noticeably challenge our parochial view of appropriate gender conduct is important.

Other societies consider homosexuality as part of general normal sexual behaviour. Ford and Beach (1951) found in their study of 190 societies, that for those seventy-six for which data was available concerning homosexuality, forty-nine perceived it as normal. In addition, seventeen of these specifically responded to lesbianism as normal sexual behaviour.

Data concerning some of the American Plains Indians suggests that here sexual division is used in an interesting way. The Mohave have developed the notion of a third gender role. These are socially recognized and accepted cross-gender actors. A biological male can become a social female, or vice versa, by entering a third gender category. Their partners are recognized as sexually normal; female husbands, for example, are recognized as the social fathers of their children and male wives simulate menstruation and labour.

Thus, whilst there is usually an attempt to contain transvestites, transexuals, and homosexuals within the categories of male and female gender roles, social recognition can allow a third gender role to develop. Transvestites are often mentioned in creation myths, and among the Navaho they are honourable folk heroes celebrated in these myths.[5] The status of transvestites varies from culture to culture, but the Navaho, for example, traditionally considered them to be attractors of luck and money, and they were given positions of authority over money matters.

We begin to see, therefore, that gender as such is a learned role, whose behavioural content differs from society to society. Further evidence can be found in the material concerning gender identity and hermaphroditism (Stoller 1968; Hampson and Hampson 1961; Hampson 1965; Money 1961 and 1965), where the evidence suggests that gender identity in hermaphrodites relates to their socialized role, rather than to their primary sexual characteristics. This includes their choice of sexual partner, their erotic inclinations, and their sexual phantasies — this last being a good indicator of sexual preference. This would seem to suggest that where society has only heterosexuality as the permitted mode of sexual relationship, with only two gender roles, the actor is forced to conform to one or other of these two categories. Out of this he or she constructs his or her sexual and social identity.

Anomaly in sexual categorization

Social systems and cultures assist actors to resist ambiguity. Men have to make sense of their world at a perceptual and a cognitive level.[6] This is particularly the case at the abstract level of social reality. In this they are assisted by their culture. Jack Douglas (1972) has suggested that morality has an object-like characteristic in Western Society, which makes rules appear independent of apparent free choice. Their essential properties make them necessary to all individuals, giving them an unproblematic nature that resists questioning. This invests them with an eternal, universal absolutism that suggests that they are part of social reality itself. Any failure of this absolutism is dealt with as being insignificant, or by the reassertion of the 'real meaning' of the absolutism, or by somehow bridging or accommodating failures of the absolutism. Absolutism may be challenged by an appeal to justice, or to the absurd, thus allowing the suggestion that the application of the rules may be problematic or by pointing to the existence of anomalies. Thus objects or actors that cross the lines of classification of a culture, or which counter the social reality of rules, are resisted.

In an early work, Mary Douglas suggests that

'Culture, in the sense of the public, standardised values of a community, mediates the experience of individuals. It provides in advance some basic categories, a positive pattern in which ideas and values are tidily ordered. And above all it has authority since each is induced to assent because of the assent of others. But its public character makes its categories more rigid.' (Douglas 1970:51)

She suggests that social systems defend against anomalies by:
  (a) reducing ambiguity by settling for one or another interpretation, so as to restore the original defining categories;
  (b) physically controlling them so that defining categories are not disturbed;
  (c) avoiding the anomaly, so the defining categories to which it does not conform are strengthened; they become the negative side of the approved categories;
  (d) labelling them as dangerous, thus enforcing conformity and putting the defining categories above dispute.
In this way, the world is kept stable with a permanent, recognizable shape. She argues in a later work that she was in error in assuming that all cultures reject any and all anomalies. Indeed some do abhor them, but some ignore them, others respect, or even venerate some

of them (Douglas 1972).[7]

Thus, as has been shown earlier, some cultures abhor homosexuality, transvestism, or transexuality; some ignore it; others respect or venerate it. However, rejection of anomalies has been the traditional response of Hebraic cultures (Douglas 1970) and Judaeo-Christian cultures have been intolerant of sexual anomalies.

What Douglas has failed to develop is the thesis that the stigmatized (or venerated?) can themselves redefine their situation if they act collectively and gain sufficient power to change their cultural definition. Judaeo-Christian morality has laid the foundations of a gut reaction to sexual outsiders, but the outsiders are not passive classificatory categories in the outside world, they are human beings engaged in a dialectic with the political forces of their own society.

Gender as social reality

Our society constructs a situation of ascribed rather than achieved gender. Any ambiguity such as transvestism, hermaphrodism, transexuality, or homosexuality is moulded into 'normal' appropriate gender behaviour, or is relegated to the categories of sick, dangerous, or pathological. The actor is forced to slot into patterns of behaviour appropriate to heterosexual gender roles.[8] In no sense is an actor allowed to choose to become a social male or female; he or she is forced into it on the classification of his or her genitals. Ruth Hartley (1971) has gone so far as to argue that men are socialized into their gender role by being persuaded and coerced into being not-women, that is not being passive, or expressive, or 'feminine'. She reveals to us the roots of male hegemony. Culturally the liberal attitude towards homosexuals and transvestites is to persuade them that they are trapped somehow in the opposite gender, rather than to say that they have separate roles with equal status. The complexities are hinted at by D'Andrade, who argues:

> 'Maleness and femaleness are institutionalised as statuses in all cultures. Such statuses become psychological entities for most individuals. Usually individuals learn to want to occupy the sex status they are assigned. However special cultural conditions can affect the degree to which one sex envies the status of another.' (D'Andrade 1966:202)

Ordinarily then, an actor is socialized into the appropriate behaviour of a gender role which is in itself seen as non problematic. Berger and Luckmann correctly argue that primary socialization takes place in a highly charged emotive atmosphere, where the child possesses virtually no power. The child soon comes up against the confidence trick of cultural relativity.

'In primary socialisation there is not a problem of identification. There is no choice of significant others. Society presents the candidate for socialisation with a predefined set of significant others whom he must accept as such with no possibility of opting for another arrangement. *Hic Rhodus, hic salta* ... it is the adults who set the rules of the game. The child can play the game with enthusiasm or sullen resistance. But, alas, there is no other game around. This has an important corollary. Since the child has no choice in the selection of his significant others, his identification with them is quasi automatic. For the same reason, his internalisation of their particular reality is quasi inevitable. The child does not internalise the world of his significant others as one of many possible worlds. He internalises it as the world, the only existent and conceivable world, the world tout court.' (Berger and Luckmann 1966:154)

Accordingly, any actor who voluntaristically seeks to change his or her sexual fate is responded to as perverted or sick. Bisexuals, homosexuals, transvestites, and transexuals are not seen as the urban guerillas of everyday life, or as the revolutionary activists of role. They are instead controlled by reassignation to the ranks of the pathologically disturbed. Like women, they are oppressed, at best patronized, and constantly reminded of their inferior status should they dare to question the status quo.

Opposition to traditional sexual hegemony is dealt with by being contained by the 'objective reality' dictated by heterosexual, male ideology. Just as women are offered imitations of the roles and functions of men in their demands for feminist liberation, so 'gay' people are offered imitations of the roles and functions of the heterosexual world.[9] Just as men do not attempt to imitate or occupy the roles of women, heterosexuals never attempt to occupy or understand the roles and problems of homosexual people. Any move is uni-directional. Sexual hegemony remains heterosexual, male dominated, and ideologically monogamous.

Gender roles appear to have their roots in the sexual division between men and women. Homosexuality may be institutionalized in pre-literate societies, but it is not allowed any relation of equivalence with heterosexuality in industrial societies. Cross gender is even less tolerated. A major contribution to the

development of gender has been the frequent pregnancies of
women. Women have little choice in structuring 'feminine'
behaviour themselves because of this and the dysfunctional
possibility of pregnancy has strengthened the parameters in which
womens' roles are set. In this way there developed the appertaining
to genders of appropriate ways of acting upon the world. The most
common were aggression for men, and passivity for women.
D'Andrade describes how:

> 'The cross cultural mode is that males are more sexually active,
> more dominant, more deferred to, more aggressive, less respon-
> sible, less nurturant, and less emotionally expressive than
> females. The extent of these differences vary by culture. And in
> some cultures, some of these differences do not exist (and
> occasionally the trend is actually reversed). These differences are
> related to and presumably influenced by which sex controls
> economic capital, the extent and kind of division of labour by sex,
> the degree of political 'authoritarianism', and family composi-
> tion.' (D'Andrade 1966:201)

The politics of sexuality

Structurally, gender appropriate behaviour has developed as an
organized collection of roles whose parameters are created by the
social structure. In Britain sexual intercourse has been contained
within marriage which has then been presented as the ultimate form
of sexual 'maturity'. Historically various puritan traditions have
seen sex as a weakness to be indulged in only when irresistible
(Pearce and Roberts 1973), maintaining sex as primarily a
functional mode of reproduction. The heterosexual nuclear family
assists a system like capitalism because it produces, and socializes
the young in, certain values. These help propagate a docile and
healthy work force, which can also be called upon in times of crisis
to defend ruling class interests (usually disguised as the 'national
good'). The maintenance of the nuclear family with its role-specific
behaviour creates an apparent consensus concerning sexual
'normalcy'. Even contemporary changes can be seen as still
contained within the dominant hegemony. The young are socialized
into regarding being married as having attained sexual and social
maturity. The mass media assist this, at the same time directing
people's consumption patterns to illustrate symbolically their
concern for their family. Early marriage and monogamy socialize
the young to become seduced into having a stake in capitalism
through the purchase of expensive commodities such as a home and

its furnishings.[10] In this way, although they may have little to gain from capitalism, they have a great deal to lose if it is destroyed. A stable social order appears to be in their interests. Any generalized eroticism in our society gets displaced into specific permitted channels (Marcuse 1955: Chapter 5), predominantly privatized and during leisure time, and contained in the nomos-building structure of the social micro-reality of marriage (Berger and Kellner 1964). In order to be able to maintain a modest standard of minimal luxury, a situation develops where both marital partners have to work (see H. Land in this volume). It appears in the interests of both young workers and the owners of the means of production to maintain the social order, and relegate sexuality to a specific secondary place to work; a sort of democratization of capitalism. Any challenge to male hegemony is a challenge not only to the social order, but to the economic mode of production. Any progress of the Womens' Liberation Movement is still hampered by the fact that, should working-class women be given equal pay, a drastic alteration in the economy would have to occur, with consequent radical changes in the social relations created by the economic mode of production. These structural conditions lie at the heart of the resistance to any real equality for women. The liberation of women threatens male hegemony and domination, not only at the level of human relationships but also at the economic level. The threat of militance by women is dealt with by relegation to the ranks of the absurd or the disturbed. It is explained away as emotional and unrealistic — its radical heart is scarred by contempt.

Achieved gender — out of the prison

Our society has laid down fairly rigid gender roles partly to assist us in making sense of our world and partly to maintain through the family legitimacy of inherited property. The emphasis has traditionally been heterosexual, with the roles of women dictated historically by men. Our gender behaviour is a socio-cultural product:

> 'Men and women who are totally lacking in any conscious homo-sexual leanings are as much a product of cultural conditioning as are the exclusive homosexuals who find heterosexual relations distasteful and unsatisfying' (Ford and Beach 1951:14).

There are, obviously, limits to human voluntarism, and these are set by the restrictions of the social structure. We become male or female, homosexual or heterosexual because these are the main approved choices open to us in the social structure we inhabit. In our society we socialize actors to be unable to respond erotically to their own gender. Whilst there may be exclusive homosexuals and heterosexuals at each end of the sexual poles, most of us are probably in the androgynous middle. We are given no choice because either we are oppressively socialized into heterosexuality or we react into non heterosexuality. The total homosexual of our own culture, Mary McIntosh suggests (1968), was an innovation at the beginning of the nineteenth century. Heterosexuality has strengthened the male hegemony that has generated the rigid gender roles our society has ascribed according to genitals. We have no concept of gender as a dialectic between that ascribed and that we wish to achieve. The choices we see as open, become *the* choices. A humanistic sociology must look beyond the massive objectifications of the social world, to enquire whom these objectifications serve. Otherwise dubious ideological appeals can be made to Human Nature. Programming into heterosexuality has obscured any real sexual openness we may possess. Even the profoundly human Sartre (1962) found Hell to be the triangle of heterosexual man, heterosexual woman, and a lesbian, locked irretrievably in combat.[11]

In order to combat the essentially positivistic notion of nature's unchangeable patterns we must clarify our directions,

> ' "We know what we are", said Ophelia, "but we know not what we may be". The gentle and naive Ophelia was wrong; we do not know in fact, what we are, unless we are fully aware of what we may be. Only the beams of the future, when shining through the obfuscate husk of the dull present, can give lie to its alleged monotonous stability, and bring light to its contours ...' (Baumann 1972:9)

An analysis of a manifestation of objectified reality such as sexuality must clearly understand the injustice of the prevailing situation and the possible directions of the future. Humans dialectically create their own history (though not always on their terms), and if they are to make a more just and humane world, they must analyse the oppression of the present in order to create blueprints for the thrust of the future. In this way they understand their collective history and its impact on their own present and individual life.

Androgyny

> 'When a subject is highly controversial, and any question of sex is that, one cannot hope to tell the truth. One can only show how one came to hold whatever opinion one does hold.' (Woolf 1929: 45)

I would state my own position with a further quotation:

> 'My opinion is easily enough expressed; I believe that our future salvation lies in a movement away from sexual polarisation, and the prison of gender toward a world in which individual roles, and the modes of personal behaviour can be freely chosen. The ideal toward which I believe we should move is best described by the term "androgyny". This ancient Greek word — from andro (male) and gyn (female) — defines a condition under which the characteristics of the sexes and human impulses expressed by men and women are not rigidly assigned. Androgyny seeks to liberate the individual from the confines of the appropriate.' (Heilbrun 1973:cx)

It seems that this could be brought about by an alliance among some of the new life-style sexual politics. I am not so naive as to suggest that these are the main political means of radically changing a society, but as the collective expressions of an alternative sexual ideology, they offer a richer quality to life than the restricted sexual expressions we have at present.

Human beings seem to be capable of (and perhaps once expressed) androgynous sexuality. Homosexuality and bisexuality are certainly more common than usually supposed. Palson and Palson (1972) found that in group sex less than 1 per cent of men carried out homosexual acts, but something like 85 per cent of women did. Despite the male heterosexual sexist context of these acts, it would seem nevertheless that men in our society are heavily socialized into not responding erotically to their own gender. Indeed they are taught not to relate to the world through their emotions, as women are. Women have also expressed homosexuality and bisexuality politically through their affiliations with the Womens Liberation Movement. To free themselves from the dominant hegemony, many women have turned sexually to their fellow women. This is noticeably absent in movements such as Men against Sexism.

Our society, despite these explorations, still presents its actors with no choice as regards gender. We are tyrannously ascribed our gender with no choice as to how we may define the situation

ourselves. Achieved gender is totally alien to our society, which
remains rigidly welded to the male-female dichotomy. It is
extremely difficult to step out of these roles relativistically without
an overwhelming sense of alienation, and almost impossible to step
out of them in any absolute sense. There is no third gender role of
an androgynous nature, dialectically created. There is no
recognition of the possibility that men may be socially women (or
vice versa) and detest everything that masculinity or feminity
means.

The new consciousness
The first movement to challenge male hegemony was obviously
Womens Liberation. Basically all sexual politics have sprung from
a search for identity and a demand for the end of the oppression
that prevents the actor defining that identity. The movement
started in the United States, where it was structurally possible
because the amorphous class divisions in that country mystify the
working class into believing that the proletariat are ethnic
minorities. Consciousness then may develop along forms of
oppression other than class oppression. The progress from the Civil
Rights Movement to demands for Black Power has greatly affected
the black minorities in taking pride in their ethnic origins. Women
also began to become conscious of their oppression and to demand
an end to it. Simultaneously they sought a new feminist identity for
the liberated woman. A woman identified woman developed as had
a black identified black. Sexism became equated with racism;
blacks no longer allowed themselves to be insulted and patronized,
and neither did women.

Divisions in the women's movement have occurred between
socialist women, professional women's pressure groups, and
separatist women (see Rose and Hanmer in this volume). However
their analysis of their position all rests on the same basis: their
common consciousness concerning sexism. Their relationships to
men, and to each other, are vigorously analysed in consciousness-
raising groups which explore feminist identity. Collective political
action is planned on the basis of this.

As part of the fight against sexist oppression, and analytically
therefore part of the womens movement, the Gay Liberation Front
was formed. Equating traditional homophile organizations with
the old Civil Rights passive resistance, the G.L.F. embarked on a
programme of activist militance. It advocated 'coming out'
(publicly declaring one's homosexuality) and gay pride; it offered
legal and political support against sexist legislation; and it used the

consciousness-raising group to promote a new identity based on gay pride. Originally an organization for both men and women, it was attacked by the Radicalesbians in America, who accused it of sexism and who left to join the W.L.M. Radicalesbians felt their literature and criticisms were not taken seriously — sexism was not just confined to heterosexual or 'masculine' men. The W.L.M. in this country has made the same accusations and gay women are leaving the G.L.F. (Galman 1973; Teal 1971; Humphreys 1972; Abbott and Love 1972).

Gender as a dialectic

Male hegemony, then, dominates not only the heterosexual but also the gay world. The fashionable myth of unisex in the Glamrock image of the rock subculture is not a dramaturgical statement about twenty-first century man, but a reinforcement of 'machismo'.[12] The image is that of Superstud; not only does he make it with women, but even with men. Righteous feminine men are attempting to give up their power as men, not to extend it into the gay world. For most gay people, role models have had to be sought traditionally in parodies of the heterosexual world. This is because there are no clear categories for those who wish to be outside of traditional roles. Male hegemony not only dictates the traditional roles of women, but even those of gay men and women. The result in the traditional homosexual (or straight gay) world is emulation of the heterosexual world, with pressure for gay weddings and respectable acceptance. If homosexuals act out visibly opposite gender roles, they are accused of lacking dignity — itself a male concept with echoes of a correct and respectful demeanour. Homosexuals are attacked for acting out roles superimposed by the straight world. The G.L.F. slogan

'Are we a bunch of screaming faggots — yes.
Are we a load of butch dykes — right on'.

is quite correct in its unashamed defense of roles that upset heterosexuals. New sexual roles, whether traditional, gay, or androgynous cannot be created until the homosexual/heterosexual, male/female divisions are eroded. Gay activists have sought to move away from guilt and self-hatred, with its self-oppression and apologetic secrecy; from a position of asking for legal and social acceptance to aggressive redefinition of their situation in the context of revolution. One of the most incisive criticisms has come from the Radicalesbians who have, in the United States, crystallized for women the contradictions in the feminist cause.

Jill Johnston argues that, 'Passivity is *the* dragon that every woman has to murder in her quest for independance ... lesbian chauvinism ... is the aggressive assertion of your sexual and sensual needs' (1973:154). She goes on to suggest that in the lesbian butch/femme dichotomy there is an imitation of the heterosexual traditional role. There are

> 'Strict monogamous expectations and a terrifying dependency common to both butch and femme. The elimination of butch and femme as we realise our true androgynous nature must inevitably mean the collapse of the heterosexual institution with its role playing dualities which are defined as domination of one sex over another' (Johnston 1973:155).[13]

Altman (1973) argues that the lesbian is doubly oppressed as she has to repress not only homosexual but to an extent heterosexual urges.

The logical extension of the extreme feminist and Radicalesbian position is to take up feminist separatism. Separatism argues that male, as opposed to class, exploitation is the real oppression. It is the only alternative for a feminist who lacks a Marxist perspective. There is just enough truth in the separatist analysis, and enough male chauvinism in the Left, for this to sound convincing. Until Marxist men erode their chauvinism, give up their power, and indicate to the W.L.M. that they will insist on full equality for women, especially gay women, will socialism be seen for what it is, a way of life. The vilification of sisters who, as a result of sexist oppression have withdrawn totally from men, by Left men, is like white racists explaining to black 'under-achievers' that the reason they fail white, culture-oriented, meritocratic education tests is because they are stupid.

Because of the nature of their oppression, women and gays (men and women) react emotionally, falling back on stereotyped behaviour. They behave badly, create public scenes, and blatantly rock the boat. They remain undignified in a situation where dignity is false consciousness. This can only be understood in terms of their relationship to sexist oppression. The infiltration of false consciousness is to be found in gay men and women's imitation of the straight world. One member of a respectable homophile organization (notoriously anti-drag), for example, puffed furiously at his pipe whilst complaining of being barred from a public house which had banned gays and complained, 'They said I was effeminately dressed. I was furious. I may be queer, but at least I am a man.' Another example can be found in the attitudes of extreme separatist women who imitate the worst elements of machismo, behave sexistly to other women, and fight with broken bottles. These are reflections of the worst elements of male hegemony, but society with its present dichotomous roles leaves them little choice.

Crossing over
Some of the worst sufferers from this form of oppression are the transvestite and transexual groups. They polarize the opposition to ascribed gender, and their attempts at achieved gender are ridiculed, vilified, and often met with physical force. Transvestites, or 'TVs', are people who cross dress in the clothes of the opposite gender. Stylistically they are making articulate statements about the absence of achieved gender in contemporary society.[14] Transvestites and transexuals are often heterosexual. The English Beaumont Society, a pioneer organization assisting transvestites, in fact bans homosexuals, claiming most of its members are married. It excludes itself from sexual politics, and has been summed up by one G.L.F. transvestite as, 'a tea and lace curtains society, composed of men puffing pipes and calling themselves Sandra and Alice'. Its members remain politely cloistered within the confines of heterosexual respectability.

Transvestites and transexuals polarize the problems of gay activism. At one level they are accused of sexism because of their concern with traditional femininity, but it must be remembered that the masters are not supposed to dress as slaves, and men who dress as women are giving up their power as men. Their oppression is similar to that experienced by gay men and all women, but they feel the need for a separate organization to analyse their position. In America radical transvestite groups have demanded free hormone and surgical treatment for transexuals and the abolishment of cross-dressing laws for transvestites, with full legal membership of the chosen gender. They are opposed by radical gay activist groups, such as Red Butterfly, who argue one's true gender is what one feels it to be, but that to alter the physical characteristics of one's body is to miss the point. One can create a gender socially, that is, men can give up their power as men by appearing dressed in a 'feminine manner'; women can dress as men, thus rejecting programmed appropriate clothing and style. To undergo surgical changes is to accept that sex and gender are the same. We must recreate the old gender roles without giving up genitals.

Transvestites

Transvestites can be perceived, with transexuals, as revolutionaries who publicly challenge the notion of ascribed gender. Many attempt to retreat into heterosexual respectability and emphasize their non homosexuality. In the only radical sociological analysis of transexuality and transvestism, Carol Riddell argues, 'In no way is the transvestite encouraged to develop his or her inclinations, to express them publicly, to politicise them into a rejection of the system which produced the need for them' (Riddell forthcoming).

Transvestites, despite the difficulties of analysis, due to our poverty of knowledge in this field, can be roughly classified as follows:

1 *theatrical drag artistes* — 'Mother camp'. Here drag is used as a professional costume, in the sense that a performance takes place at specific times in front of a specific audience, formalized in a theatrical public performance. Newton (1972) has indicated that they are professional performers, who carefully do not try to totally pass as women. This is seen as too 'tranny' (transvestite) and possibly offending an audience. Mainly they are males dressed as females (although the Edwardian music hall sported quite a few cross-dressed females). They minstrelize women, and often merely voice their audience's sexism. Their self-image is that of professional entertainer and they are as relevant to the gay struggle as the Black and White Minstrels are to Black Power. They are Auntie Toms who assist in self-hatred by refusing to take feminism seriously.

2 *'closet' transvestites*. This is an atomized group, dressing up individually in secret. They desperately attempt to conceal from public knowledge their private desires and inclinations. They have greatly internalized the dominant ideology and suffer considerable shame over their cross dressing. Their desperation can lead to traumatic breakdown and they may be treated clinically as 'fetishistic perverts'.

3 *conventional transvestities* — 'straight TVs'. This group has 'come out', in so far as their members appear in drag in public, but only in certain structured situations. They lead a double life, which is firmly contained within the framework of mainstream, bourgeois, sexual morality. They are found in organizations such as the Beaumont Society. They emphasize their normality, drawing attention to their non homosexuality and their freedom from 'perversion'.

'The Beaumont Society exists to serve the interests of the "true transvestite", and to some extent transexuals of the gender motivated type. It does not admit persons seeking partners for homosexual or similar reasons.' (Beaumont Society 1973)

The Beaumont Society goes to great lengths to point out that they will not recruit members with sexual motivations, as 'this will offend wives and girl friends'. There seem to be very few members who are females cross dressing ('butch drag'). The statement: 'We feel that we have little or nothing to offer homosexuals and their presence within the Beaumont Society could prove both embarrassing and detrimental ...'[15] is typical of public statements made by it.

'I would rather have one understanding female on my side, than one hundred homosexuals ... bring homosexuals into the picture — the scene changes, and you are heading for disaster — the shadowy figure of homosexual influence, patiently waiting in the wings ... I don't see why we should give homosexuals en masse the key to our fortunes.' [16]

The conventional transvestite image is that of the suburban matron at a Masonic dinner, or the conservative middle-class woman so dreaded by the W.L.M. Their feminity is that of the passive, programmed woman dominated by male hegemony. Demure and ladylike, they follow Virginia Price's advice — if you have to be a woman be a lady.[17] Like the young teenage girl unsure of her poise, they study hints on deportment and grooming. They take care to avoid sexual politics of any kind.

4 *'drag queens'*. This group is usually homosexual, unlike most of the previous transvestites, and are intrinsically part of the gay scene. They represent an unrespectable deviant element in the gay world at the opposite pole to the respectable straight gay. The drag queen uses her appearance in an ironic and mocking way, distinctly identifying with the opposite gender. She makes no secret of her interest in sex, and her homosexuality. She operates by behaving in a highly flamboyant camp manner — a 'screaming nelly' queen. Witty and aggressively humourous, she is found as an intrinsic part of the gay ghetto.

5 *'radical queens'*. Radical queens are 'street transvestites' (they appear in public in drag), but far from trying to pass as women, they in fact take care to look like men dressed as women. Dramaturgically they present a piece of street theatre aimed at attacking

fixed gender roles. A kind of Agit-Prop guerilla attack is made on the straight world. Usually gay, they deny they are transvestites, but claim to be destroyers of male-female stereotypes. They despise the highly stylized drag of drag queens, who see radical queens as 'naff drag' (straight drag) who are frightened of 'glam drag'. Radical queens argue that transvestites are clothes fetishists, confined within traditional feminity, who fail to see the importance of challenging traditional roles. Transvestites, especially those trying to pass, feel that radical drag is easy, and that radical queens are evading their own transvestism.[18]

6 *'street transvestities'*. This group can be divided into those who are conservative street transvestites, passing as women, but refusing to leave bourgeois feminity, and those radical street transvestites who align themselves to gay activism. They are not necessarily homosexual, which may create more problems. They feel that G.L.F. does not appreciate their problems, especially if they are heterosexual. They are excluded from most womens groups, and banned by radical lesbians (the New York Radicalesbians banned transvestites with a curt 'No pricks'). They feel that they are women, and now many have formed their own groups. There are groups in New York such as S.T.A.R. (Street Transvestite Action Revolutionaries) and the Femmes Against Sexism, and even one group who live as women, relate to women and see themselves as male lesbians. The latter are naturally resented by lesbians because they have not suffered as lesbians. Trapped in a mass of contradictions these groups are not women certainly, but neither are they men. They have suffered not so much for what they are, but what they are not. They have given up their power as men to dress as women, and whether they are homosexual or heterosexual any hope of an unoppressed future must be developed within the structure of gay activism.

Transexuals
Transexuals feel themselves to be trapped in the body of the wrong gender, they are the wrong sex. Their genitals are not a joyous expression of sexuality, as with homosexuals, but a sign of their oppression. They live as the opposite sex, passing by posing as the opposite gender, finally hoping to cross over to the opposite sex by the use of surgery. Usually they are men seeking to become women.[19] and with this group surgery is less difficult and hence more publicized. (With a penis graft, usually the penis can only be used as a urinary tract.) Often they are obsessed with the operation

which will give them a new lease of life, even where the possibility of this remains a phantasy. They are often excluded from feminist groups until the post-operational stage, and are attacked by radical queens for the same reason as drag queens — their failure to challenge traditional roles. Radical gays also criticize them on the grounds that surgery is opting out. The reactions of most groups to transexuals is comparable to the experiences of lesbians addressing the local Womens Institute.

Transexuals seeking National Health surgery find themselves severely oppressed by establishment medicine. A rejection obstacle race has to be undergone in order to prove sincerity. The transexual may have to apply several times for surgery in order to show that she is serious. It may be insisted that she lives and works as a woman for a year before surgery. Married transexuals are refused help until they divorce. At first hormonal treatment is offered, but as fear of discovery increases, surgery is sought. Any neurotic or psychotic manifestation may mean termination of treatment, as does coming out, involvement in sexual politics, or statements to the mass media. Criminal convictions may also terminate treatment, and this increases the hazards of using a public toilet. Everyday episodes become major traumas. In addition clinics may lay down rules concerning demeanour and appearance, and supervize grooming. The transexual is coerced into passing as a programmed woman, with the dignity befitting a lady. As her future lies in the hands of establishment medicine — unless she has a very expensive foreign operation — she has no choice but to follow these dictates. The fear of termination of treatment obsesses the transexual, and great difficulty is experienced in interviewing them, though some have published interesting autobiographies (Morris 1974; Bogdan 1974).

The new eroticism

The only way that the tyrannous dictates of ascribed gender can be challenged is for the women's movement and Gay Liberation to recruit and demystify their oppressed transvestite and transexual brothers and sisters, whilst developing sensitivity to each other's problems. The disagreements between them rests in turn on the confusion over the interpretation of sexual roles. This is reflected in the confusion of the straight world which mixes up sexual role with sexual preference. To prefer erotically one's own gender can be a completely different phenomenon from cross dressing or identifying with the opposite gender. Where transvestites and transexuals are heterosexual, they can be even more alienated than homosexual transvestites and transexuals. The latter feel even the gay movement has failed to understand their problems. Nevertheless all share the sexual oppression experienced by those outside of heterosexual male hegemony, and any solution will come from an alliance with a politically activist gay movement which is part of the feminist struggle.

Gender confusion is carried on into the gay world from the straight — for ultra masculine/feminine stereotypes still exist in the gay world. As Johnston remarks (1973) the butch/femme roles reflect straight ideas about masculinity and feminity. Her lesberated woman not only relates to her own gender erotically, but also transcends the aggressive/passive butch/femme roles which are extensions of male hegemony concerning feminine passivity. Continuance of these roles leaves sexism unchallenged and unchanged. Gay men also often reflect sexism, even opposing the admittance of gay women to homophile organizations. There are few gay femme men, radical effeminists, i.e. gay men with feminist ideas. Just as the straight Left needs honestly to face its own sexism and to realize that socialism is not just the economic redistribution of material needs but also new styles of living and relating, so the gay movement has to face up to its own contradictions and realize that the oppression of gays is part of sexist oppression, and this extends to transvestites, transexuals, and bisexuals. Gay men, of all men, must not be sexist.

Bi-sexuality may be an intermediate solution for those on their way to relating to their own gender, but it may also be the ultimate aim in a world where concepts such as butch/femme, male/female, homosexual/heterosexual no longer exist because they no longer have any meaning. However, whilst bisexuality may involve the problems of both worlds, it can operate from the safety of a heterosexual pair bonding and lack the social isolation felt by the total gay. Wendy Wonderful sums up the political position,

> 'I'm bisexual, and when I say I'm having an affair with a man, its groovy, but when I'm having an affair with a woman not only is it not so groovy, but its not acceptable, thus the oppressed part of me is the lesbian and therefore I say I am a lesbian.' (Johnston 1973:179)

Many however refuse to stand up with their gay brothers and sisters on the false consciousness grounds that they are not really gay. Bisexuality has its own specific problems, but bisexuals cannot play safe by claiming allegiance to heterosexuality. Because it is commonly assumed one is heterosexual, a statement of bisexuality means one is seen as a heterosexual who has gay affairs, not the other way round. Gay people are not just like heterosexuals with the exception that they relate to their own gender, anymore than black people are just like white, but with a different skin pigmentation. We are who we sleep with. To be gay is an intimate part of one's identity. Being gay means one needs to develop consciousness with all sexually oppressed groups. It means being involved with the war against sexism, by promoting groups like the Men against Sexism among straight men, but without trying to equate the problems of the powerful with those of the powerless as many straight men try to. Sexism has to be constantly challenged among all groups. Jill Tweedie's criticism of the transexual Jan Morris, for example, points out,

'And once able to pass for a woman, she proceeds to reinforce the bar of the woman's cage. Though she mentions her growing awareness of women as second class citizens, by her behaviour she bolsters that discrimination, acting helpless, coy with waiters, passive with male friends, finding luggage to heavy for suddenly weak arms, crying easily, making frivolous remarks on cue, even saying (unforgiveably) "Occasionally I regret my manhood when it comes to getting a job done properly".' (Tweedie 1974).

Morris retains too much of her previous gender's stereotype of women to be a right-on sister. Being a woman is more than crossing over. To continue male sexism is merely wasting a unique opportunity. Involvement in the gay struggle is understanding and opposing sexism and supporting those who are sexually oppressed. If being anti-gay is the last legitimate prejudice of Left and Right, then being anti-transvestite and transexual is the last permitted genocide — many kill themselves in desperation. The suffering of gay people is the result of the oppression of ascribed gender with its appropriate behaviour and psychology. It is not the fault of the oppressed — the screaming queens, butch dykes, transvestites, and transexuals. Women and gays need mutual support against gender tyranny.

'It's the man in the woman in the man
in me,
that loves
the woman in the man in the woman
in you,
Christ — its getting crowded,
There's room for you in the Gay Liberation Front' (GLF poster)

Acknowledgement

I would like to thank my brothers and sisters in the women's movement and in Gay Liberation for their criticism and advice, and in particular Don Milligan whose assistance was invaluable.

Notes

1 With a few notable exceptions, something as human as the nature of sexuality has been structured in the mainstream of sexual conformity. The dangers of approaching something as human as sex and gender are suggested by Lichtmann's attack on other forms of positivistic approach

   'For positivism, the social world is a given fact, and knowledge consists of describing it as it is. The objective of enquiry is not understood as a purposive moral being engaged in a struggle for its self realisation, but as a finished thing. At each moment of existence, it is as real or final as at the next. In fact it would be more accurate simply to say that these categories do not apply. Human beings are given to the inquirer, they are facts in the world. That is all. We do not attempt to create their moral struggle, for we do not know of it.' (Lichtmann 1970:75)

2 Homosexual in this paper applies, of course, to male and female homosexuals.

3 However even the objective definition of the Oxford Dictionary reads '... e.g. The fair sex (female), or the stern sex (male) ...'

4 Even though Mead's general categories of 'masculine' and 'feminine' are crude, nevertheless the societies are sufficiently different to have attracted the attention of a Western female anthropologist.

5 Of particular interest are two early papers: Devereux's (1937) account of homosexuality among the Mohave, and Hill's (1935) study of transexuality in Navaho culture. Interestingly enough, in the Navaho creation myths the transvestites threw in their lot with men to help them overcome the women.

6 The way in which cognitive and sensory input is 'made sense of' can be found in the work of the early Gestalt psychologists, especially Heider (1944), and in Festinger's theory of cognitive dissonance in attitude formation (1957).

7 She argues (Douglas 1972) that the cultural response depends
   inter alia on the relation of the society to other societies, and the
   importance of the classificatory system which the particular
   anomaly crosses.

8 The challenge that stigmatized activities such as homosexuality
   make to the reification of sexual behaviour is analysed in Frank
   Pearce 'How to be immoral, ill, pathetic and dangerous — all at
   the same time' (1973). For the relationship between this and
   capitalism see Pearce and Roberts (1973) and also Don Milligan
   (1973), who offers a clear analysis of the relationship between
   the traditional nuclear family, capitalism, and the threat of out-
   cast sexual activities. A Marxist analysis of the phenomology,
   ideology, and politics of sexual hegemony will be found in a
   collection of readings by Brake and Pearce (forthcoming).

9 By gay people, I refer to the constellation of actors whose life
   style and sexuality differs from traditional monogamous
   heterosexuality, to include inappropriate gender behaviour or
   sexuality. This obviously includes homosexuals, bisexuals,
   transvestites, and transexuals.

10 I have discussed this in an article (1973). Capitalism by no
   means invented sexism, and other social systems are of course
   guilty of it, but sexism is intrinsically a part of capitalism, and
   not a residue of it as in state capitalist countries. This is
   discussed in Brake and Pearce (forthcoming).

11 Happily in our society there are households where such domesticity is seen as the Gates of Paradise, rather than the Doors of
   Hell. This can only occur when the inhabitants are prepared to
   challenge sexual hegemony and to guard carefully against
   sexual exploitation.

12 Machismo, or macho, is used to designate very butch masculine
   values, involving the domination of women as sexual property
   and the glorification of violence.

13 Johnston conceptualizes lesbian chauvinists as a group of
   sexually active women who mutually act as aggressors. Because
   they do not possess the inherent power of men they become
   equals through their loss of passivity and decorum. For her the
   liberated woman can only be a lesbian — the lesberated woman.

14 By style, I mean the dress, demeanour, perceptions, and cogni-
   tions that are dramaturgically organized to make visible statements about ways of acting upon the world.

15 Leaflet distributed at the first national Transvestite and Trans-
   sexual Conference Leeds, March 20, 1974, quoting the
   Northern Division Representative of the Beaumont Society.

16 Discussion document from the Leeds Transvestite and Transexual Conference which quotes a Beaumont Society Bulletin sent out to its members.
17 Virginia Price is a transexual who produces works on grooming and deportment for the well behaved transvestite and transexual (see Price 1967 and 1971).
18 One of the problems of passing is whether to use a male or female public lavatory. Under English law, the former if used in cross dress leaves one open to a charge of importuning, whilst the latter is only a breach of the peace. Importuning is punishable by prison, so the 'Ladies' is safer.
19 For the purposes of clarity I have described the fate of born males dressed as females (M-F TV) or born males living as females (M-F TS). Born females dressed as males (F-M TV) or living as males (F-M TS) have been clinically, at least, seen as rare. In fact, they are now increasing, due to the Movement. Because of fashion, butch drag is less obvious than it was, and because of its very nature is less flamboyant. However F-M TVs and F-M TSs are very vulnerable to physical assaults because they directly threaten macho values, and because they are seen as easy game in a fight. My omission of any detailed discussion was to clarity points concerning gender roles which are applicable to both groups, not to minimize their suffering, nor to subject them to even more sexism.

References

Abbott, S. and Love, B. 1972. *Sappho was a Right On Woman*. New York: Stein and Day.
Altman, D. 1973. *Homosexuality — Oppression or Liberation*. New York: Discus Avon.
D'Andrade, R. 1966. Sexual Differences and Cultural Institutions. In E. Maccoby, *The Development of Sex Differences*. Stanford: Stanford U.P.
Bailey, R. and Young, J. 1973. *Contemporary Social Problems in Britain*. London: D.C. Heath.
Bauman, Z. 1972. Culture, Values and the Science of Society. *University of Leeds Review 15* (2) Oct. Leeds: Leeds U.P.
Beaumont Society. 1973. *Transvestism and the Beaumont Society*. London: Beaumont Society.
Berger, P. and Killner, H. 1964. *The Social Construction of Reality — a treatise in the sociology of knowledge*. New York: Doubleday.

Berger, P. and Kellner, H. 1964. Marriage and Construction of Reality. *Diogenes xlvi*: 1-23.

Brake, M. 1973. Cultural Revolution or Alternative Delinquency — an examination of deviant youth as a social problem. In Bailey and Young.

Brake, M. and Pearce. F. forthcoming. *Circles and Arrows — Critical Perspectives of Human Sexuality*. Palo Alto, California: Mayfield Press.

Bogdan, R. 1974. *Being Different — the Autobiography of Jane Fry*. New York: J. Wiley.

Devereux, G. 1937. Institutionalised Homosexuality of the Mohave Indians. *Human Biology 9*: 508-27.

Douglas, J. 1972. The Absurd and the Problem of Social Order. In J. Douglas and R. Scott (eds.), *Theoretical Perspectives in Deviance*. New York: Basic Books.

Douglas, M. 1970. *Purity and Danger*. Harmondsworth: Penguin.

— 1972. Self Evidence. *Proceedings of the Royal Anthropological Institute*. London.

Festinger, L. 1957. *A Theory of Cognitive Dissonance*. New York: Row Peterson.

Ford, C.S. and Beach, F. 1951. *Patterns of Sexual Behaviour*. New York: Harper.

Gagnon, J. and Simon, W.X. 1973. *Sexual Conduct — the Social Sources of Human Sexuality*. Chicago: Aldine.

Hampson, J.L. 1965. Determinants of Psychosexual Orientation. In F.A. Beach (ed.), *Sex and Behaviour*. New York: J. Wiley.

Hampson, J.L. and Hampson, M. 1961. The Ontogenesis of Sexual Behaviour in Man. In W.C. Young (ed.), *Sex and Internal Secretions*. New York: Balliere, Tindall and Cox.

Heider, F. and Simmel, M. 1944. An Experimental Study of Apparent Behaviour. *American Journal of Psychology 57*: 243-59.

Heilbrun, C. 1973. *Towards a Recognition of Androgyny*. New York: Knopf.

Hill, W.W. 1935. The study of the Hermaphrodite and the Transvestite in Havaho Culture. *American Anthopologist 37* April-June.

Humphreys, L. 1972. *Out of the Closets*. New Jersey: Prentice Hall.

Johnston, J. 1973. *Lesbian Nation*. New York: Simon & Schuster.

Lichtman, R. 1970. Symbolic Interactionism and Social Reality — some Marxist queries. *Berkeley Journal of Sociology*, January. University of California.

McIntosh, M. 1968. The Homosexual Role. *Social Problems xvi* (2) Fall.

Marcuse, H. 1955. *Eros and Civilisation*. Boston: Beacon Press.

Mead, M. 1935. *Sex and Temperament in Three Societies*. London: Gollancz.

Milligan, D.N. 1973. *The Politics of Homosexuality*. London: Pluto Press.

Money, J. 1961. Sex Hormones and other Variables in Human Eroticism. In W.C. Young (ed.), *Sex and Internal Secretions*. New York: Balliere, Tindall & Cox.

— 1965. *Sex Research - new developments*. California: Holt Rinehart and Winston.

Morris, J. 1974. *Conundrum*. London: Faber.

Newton, E. 1972. *Mother Camp: female impersonators in America*. New Jersey: Prentice Hall.

Nobile, P. (ed.) 1970. *The New Eroticism*. Maryland: Random House.

Oakley, 1972. *Sex, Gender and Society*. London: Temple Smith.

Palson, R. and Palson, C. 1972. Swinging in Wedlock. *Transaction 19* (4) February.

Pearce, F. 1973. How to be Immoral, Ill, Pathetic and Dangerous all at the same time. In S. Cohen and J. Young, (eds.), *Mass Media and Social Problems*. London: Constable.

Pearce, F. and Roberts, A. 1973. The Social REgulation of Sexual Behaviour and the Development of Industrial Capitalism. In Bailey and Young.

Plummer, K. 1975. *Sexual Stigma — an interactionist perspective*. London: Routledge and Kegan Paul.

Price, V. 1967. *The Transvestite and his Wife*. Los Angeles: Argylle.

— 1971. *How to be a Woman though Male*. Los Angeles: Chevalier.

Riddell, C. forthcoming. The Tyranny of Gender. In Brake and Pearce.

Sartre, J-P. 1962. *Huis clos*. London: Appleyard.

Stoller, R. 1968. *Sex and Gender*. New York: Science House.

Stonier, T. *From War to Peace — the evolution of society*. Unpublished paper. Dept. of Sciences and Society. University of Bradford.

Teal, D. 1971. *The Gay Militants*. New York: Stein and Day.

Tweedie, J. 1974. Stereotypes of Man and Woman. *Sunday Times*, May 5.

Woolf, V. 1929. *A Room of Ones Own*. London: Hogarth.

HILARY ROSE AND JALNA HANMER

Women's Liberation, Reproduction, and the Technological Fix

We wrote this paper for three very simple reasons: that human reproduction is necessary for the continuance of the species; that a significant section of the women's movement sees reproduction as the source of female oppression; and that science and technology are continuing to make rapid advances in the regulation and modification of reproduction. Our particular concern is whether these advances, given that science and technology are part of the culture and institutions of a class bound and patriarchal society, are likely to add to women's liberation or to their oppression.

Advances over the past one hundred years in the science and technology of regulating reproduction have created the possibility that women, without limiting their sexual activity, can choose if and when to bear children. This 'choice' is at the level of technical feasibility; choice in actuality is limited by religion, class, race, husbands, knowledge, state action, or inaction — to name but a few key factors. However, science and technology do not stand still, advances in knowledge continue to be made at an ever increasing rate, and, most importantly for the purposes of this paper, the gap between new knowledge and its implementation is shortening.

Yet despite the relevance to women of much of the new work in, for example, developmental biology, science and technology have been either little or relatively uncritically discussed within the women's movement. To a considerable extent the exclusion of science and technology from the movement's agenda is explained by the exclusion of women themselves from the hard (i.e. masculine) sciences. Apart therefore from a certain amount of descriptive work showing how women are hindered from entering the institutions of science, and are at a status and financial disadvantage even where they manage to gain entry (Lewin and Duchan 1971; Grunchow 1970), the movement has not extended its analysis of the male dominated culture to consider the culture of science. In what follows we critically analyse those strands within the movement which discuss reproduction, point to the implications in this area of the theoretically unresolved question of the relationship between the women's struggle and class struggle, and set the whole in the context of the science and technology of regulating reproduction both presently being developed and also being planned.

Women's liberation on reproduction

Within the women's movement there are two major theoretical wings: the radical feminists and the feminist marxists. The former see sex as the primary contradiction; the latter see some combination of sex and class. Each wing is faced with its own central theoretical problem. For the radical feminists, who advocate political lesbianism, the central problem is that of the continued reproduction of the species. For the feminist marxist the problem is to articulate a necessary relationship between the liberation of the class and the liberation of women. Consequently within radical feminism there is occasionally expressed a belief that science and technology can be used positively to re-organize and eventually eliminate natural reproduction; whereas for the most part the feminine marxists accept natural reproduction, but seek to alter the social forms and ideology surrounding it.

Radical feminism and the technological fix

One main thesis of radical feminism asserts the biological basis of women's social inferiority, and has been most forcefully developed by Shulamith Firestone (1971). Her book, the *Dialectic of Sex*, has precipitated an important debate on artificial reproduction both within and outside the movement. Her view is that it is because women bear children that it has been possible for men to gain ascendancy over them, for the subjugation of women is rooted in the division of labour which begins with the differing roles males and females have in the reproduction of the species.[1] This division of labour is institutionalized in the family.[2] Therefore, to free women it is necessary to eradicate the family, at first by developing alternative life styles and social institutions and eventually by reproducing people artificially, eliminating the female reproductive function. Equality for women is to be accomplished through scientific discoveries that progress from the artificial reproduction of babies to the elimination of childhood, ageing, and eventually death itself. The technological fix ensures the new utopia.

Firestone argues that certain current social, economic, and technological trends support the changes she is advocating. The family is under a death sentence from two sources. First, there is no longer a need for universal reproduction; and, second, the coming cybernetic mode of production will make the family as a unit of reproduction and production obsolete. Cybernetics alters human beings' relations to work and even the need to work, and this change in production will eventually 'strip the division of labour at the root of the family of any remaining practical value'. Thus, the woman will no longer be needed to service the paid male worker (and his children) as in present day assembly line technology.

Firestone points out that there is no image of the perfect society created by feminist women, nor even any utopian feminist literature. She suggests that the perfect society for women would involve flexibility, multiple role options that exist simultaneously and also can be chosen serially. One option during the transitional phase towards the ideal society would be the opening up of professions that satisfy the individual's social and emotional needs, so that the pressure on women to establish family units is not so great. Another transitional solution is to encourage 'deviant life styles' which imply non-fertility, such as relationships between two or more people, of the same or different sex, living together in groups. She thinks that after several generations of non-family living 'our psychosexual structures may become so radically altered that the monogamous couple ... would become obsolescent'.

To some extent her solutions are shared by other theorists of the family as diverse in ideological orientation as Mitchell (1966; 1971) and Packard (1968). It is also the case, as reported by Skolnick and Skolnick (1971), and Abrams and McCulloch (see their paper in this volume), that people are living in more diverse households or 'family' structures. As we shall argue later concerning various reproduction technologies, the liberatory or repressive character of these forms is ambiguous, to be determined not only by who holds the power but also by the ideology embedded in and surrounding them.[3]

Marxism and women
Firestone's thesis stressing the primacy of the sexual division thus stands in direct opposition to the Marxist tradition, which (with the possible exception of the Chinese revolution) has followed the Bolsheviks and stresses the primacy of class. For Marxist women in contemporary Britain the choice is sharply posed. Either they can join one of the various male-dominated Marxist groups or, eschewing this dominance, they can become active within the women's movement but as non-aligned Marxists. By male dominance we mean more than the obvious aspects, such as exclusively or nearly exclusively male leadership (particularly as theoreticians, while the

women's contribution is limited to administrative tasks); we mean also the male ideological hegemony. Consequently the act of choosing to join appears to place the interest of the male industrial worker — which is seen as synonymous with the class — above and separate from the interests of women. The alternative, of remaining non-aligned but active in the women's movement, is in effect to work in a movement which by its class composition is to a great extent divorced from working-class experience and struggle.

Orthodox Marxism thus sees the class struggle as primary, a concern for the position of women as secondary: an issue which will be resolved — and depending on the faction, possibly only thought about — after the revolution. This is no recent development, it arose prior to the degeneration in Marxist thinking associated with Stalin (although with his medals for fecund Stakhanovite mothers Stalin played his part). It is, for example, expressed quite unambiguously in Lenin's exchanges with Zetkin and Kollontai during the early years of the revolution. (Zetkin 1925:52-53). Whether it was the practical issue of famine and civil war or a more profoundly embedded view of Lenin's is not material to the argument. Lenin clearly put to one side the ideas of free love and the withering away of the family as expressed in the Communist Manifesto as a bourgeois preoccupation. Instead, like Engels, he saw the solution in terms of women entering the productive process as workers; liberation would, in some unspecified way, flow from this. The nature of this 'solution' is illustrated by the present situation whereby women in the Soviet Union, despite some necessary assistance with child care in nurseries and creches, merely carry out double work — in the workplace *and* in the home.[4]

What other disagreements developed between Stalin and Trotsky, both were the heirs (note the sex) of Engels and Lenin in their adherence to this economist solution, and neither the orthodox communist parties in or out of the Soviet Union nor the various Trotskyite groupings differ sharply from this view.

The theory and experience of the Chinese revolution was different. At a theoretical level the question of sexual (and generational) repression within the family and the need for the struggle to be anti-patriarchal is discussed within Mao's early writings (1927:23-25). In addition, within the history of the revolution itself the part played by the profoundly oppressed peasant women was crucial, as documented for example in Jack Belden's *China Shakes the World* (1949):367-421), or to a lesser extent Hinton's *Fanshen* (1966:538-546). Against the prostitution and slavery of women in both Imperial and Chiang Kai Shek's

China, the puritanical monogamy of post-revolutionary China represents a major advance; however there is little diversity tolerated in either sexual expression or social forms. Because women are in theory 'half the sky', the Chinese communist party does not see the struggle against sexism as a class struggle. In practice they are reticent in articulating their analysis of the nature of the issue; sexism seems to be seen as a contradiction among the people rather than between the people.[5] This, as we shall discuss later, has had profound implications for the planning of reproduction.

With the exception of the Maoists the revolutionary Left takes little theoretical interest in this discussion. However, while in Europe many countries have experienced considerable growth in Maoist groups and movements, in Britain they have remained trapped in a multitude of groupuscules, each too small to make a significant contribution to this debate. The challenge of the radical feminists, who argue that women are the class, is thus in practice for the most part ignored. Their analysis is felt to be of such little theoretical interest that it is only worth the attention of the women's section, certainly within the bigger Marxist groups.[6] Consequently for any systematic discussion of Firestone's and other radical feminists' theses and their relationship to a class analysis, it is necessary to consider the contribution of the feminist Marxists.

Feminist marxists
For the feminist Marxists there is considerable difficulty in linking the two concepts of sex and class; either they are opposed or they operate on different planes. However, despite the problem of specifying the relationship between feminism and the class struggle, for the women Marxists the attempt, and belief in its success, is an essential credo:

> 'Within the women's movement therefore, we reject both class struggle as subordinate to feminism and feminism as subordinate to class struggle. Class struggle and feminism are for us one and the same thing, feminism expressing the rebellion of that section of the class without whom the class struggle cannot be generalised, broadened and deepened.' (Michel and Southwick 1972).

The position of the feminist Marxists is in this respect not totally different from that which Lenin found himself in. Far from indifferent to the question of women's liberation, he was unable to articulate the relationship between the liberation of the oppressed sex to that of the oppressed class. Thus, like Lenin, the Marxist feminists all too often have to invoke an invisible hand of socialism which will ensure that at the revolution both the women and the class are liberated.

Juliet Mitchell's (1966) work, which draws extensively on Althusser, points to a possible method of analysis and action. Instead of discussing the women's condition as a monolithic entity, Mitchell seeks to specify the separate structures that together form the complex whole. Each separate sector is to some considerable extent autonomous, and each has its own momentum; therefore the complexity created by the synthesis of all the structures is itself continuously shifting. Mitchell then distinguishes the four basic structures as: production, reproduction, sex, and socialization. Each is autonomous and therefore requires discrete analysis, yet at the same time all four are linked in the complex continuously changing totality that is the woman's situation. Sometimes the movements in the separate structures cancels each other out, but at the moment when the separate structures reinforce one another and intensify the contradictions, the conditions for revolutionary change exist.

Two other writers working within the Marxist framework are Selma James and Maria Rosa Dalla Costa (1972). Their critique of the inadequacies of past and existing Marxist theory and practice is particularly sharp. Dalla Costa, for example, points out that Gramsci denies that working-class women are part of the class, and speaks of the need to 'neutralize' them, seeing the male industrial workers as *the* class. Dalla Costa rejects the view that women are not engaged in social production; housework, including childbearing, creates labour power and thereby value. It does not seem to be so because a woman does not receive a wage and is trapped in pre-capitalist forms of production.[7] What is also peculiar to women's work, as Dalla Costa, James, Rowbotham (1973) and countless other women writers have observed, is the social isolation that stems from housework. However, to compress the separate structures of reproduction and production seems to us to be theoretically disadvantageous. This is particularly clear in a non-Italian context, for where women are increasingly engaged in production (in the conventional sense) and decreasingly engaged in reproduction, the need for a conceptual distinction between the two activities increases rather than decreases.

None the less, despite this merging of production and reproduction, Dalla Costa makes in one brief footnote an important point concerning the need for women to control reproduction science and technology. Although the argument is quite undeveloped by her, the point is significant and we shall return to it.

Radical feminism's 'consort to conceive'

Carla Lonzi of Rivolta Feminile (1972) writes as a radical feminist, but one whose theoretical stance is profoundly influenced by a Marxist analysis — quite unlike that of Firestone who regards aspects of the superstructure such as science and technology as free and independent — a mistake none of the feminist Marxists make. Like Mitchell she separates reproduction from sexuality in an analytical sense, but unlike Mitchell she does not regard the split between them as an anathema to bourgeois ideology. This may be explained at least partly in that Mitchell's original article was pioneering work published in 1966 whereas *We Spit on Hegel* was published in 1970, when both the situation and women's consciousness of the situation were different.

Rivolta Feminile's documents (some are collective and anonymous) argue that a male world is able to turn the separation of reproduction and sexuality to a male and bourgeois advantage. They speak of men 'colonizing women through the penis culture', and certainly, despite the efforts to develop an alternative and egalitarian ideology of heterosexual relationships, in practice a sharp imbalance remains. This is particularly evident in the age differences between men and women in both marriage and 'love affairs'. The advantage men gain from feeling and being able to draw on a potential pool of all women younger than themselves (their decrease in male physical attractiveness being compensated for by high status, money, etc.) while in practice most women feel, and are, unable similarly to consort with men twenty or thirty years younger than themselves, loads the dice against women. In affairs the age difference and therefore the power status element is often even more marked than in marriage so that the split between sexuality and reproduction made possible by contraception and abortion tends at present both to aid women but also to increase male hegemony. Men obtain sexual satisfaction, their dominant status being amplified by permissiveness and, because affairs are predominantly infertile, the population is limited.

Rivolta Feminile's recognition of this is expressed in their thesis that women should only consort with men sexually for the purpose of reproduction. Thus in the interests of the liberation of women, assessing the present relationships of the structures of reproduction and sexuality, they argue a position on heterosexual contact remarkably like that of St Paul. Real sexuality and tenderness, it should perhaps be added, is seen as something to be shared with women; men's utility is to be limited to the act of fertilization. Biological necessity is recognized but the social forms are to be completely re-fashioned.

The question of reproduction is thus set constantly against the position of women and their struggle for liberation. Within the movement, whatever the tendency, the need for women to be able to control their own bodies (ie. reproductive function) is seen as a primary and crucial step towards their freedom. They see discussions of the control of population, whether to increase, to stabilize, or to decrease it, as a societal abstraction, managed and dominated by male others.

Thus while the women's movement all over the world seeks in some general sense to increase women's control over their own bodies as part of their wish to control their own lives, within the writings we have discussed theoretical positions are adopted that would lead to three differing demands over and above this general demand:

1. that women should, with the aid of science and technology, abandon natural reproduction — essentially a theory of the technological fix (Firestone 1971);

2. that women should seek to control the management of birth control technology including its research and development (Dalla Costa 1972);

3. that women should only consort with men to conceive (Rivolta Feminile in Lonzi 1970).

Science for liberation or subjugation
Firestone, having analysed the core of women's oppression as residing in her biological destiny, invokes the aid of science and tehcnology to liberate her. For the social problems that confront woman (albeit with biological parameters) a technological fix is prescribed. Her conception of science is almost nineteenth century in its confidence in the inherently progressive nature of science and technology. While there has been a long history of scepticism — not least the savage irony of Jonathan Swift's attack on the pretensions of the Royal Society disguised as the 'Academy of Laputa' — certainly since Nagasaki and Hiroshima science has lost this innocence. As Oppenheimer said, 'the physicists have known sin'. Whereas in the writing of Left and Right scientists up to the late 30s, science was portrayed either as neutral or as progressive, contributing to human liberation; following 1945 the previous naive juxtaposition of science and progress settled down to a more cautious view of science as a two-edged sword, either cutting for or against humanity (Rose 1972). Eventually a third attitude arose, highly critical of science and of the inhumanity of its methodology;

this view, whether promulgated by the social theorists of the neo-Marxist Frankfurt school (Habermas 1971; Marcuse 1964; Schmidt 1971), the conservative Ellul (1965) or the anarchist writings of Roszak (1970), contributed towards a view of science as repressive.

For that matter if we examine the social structure of science, it is difficult to understand why science and technology should appear to be the allies of women. They are historically a stronghold of men, and, since the end of the First World War, increasingly locked into the state and industry. Whereas the pursuit of scientific knowledge in the past was the activity of disinterested amateurs, scientists are now increasingly controlled by the state and industry. The major items of the scientific research and development budget continue to be directed towards the needs of military, space, atomic and economic goals, with 'welfare' occupying a very residual role (Rose and Rose 1969). The contrast betwen the Haldane Report of 1918 on the Machinery of Government, which defended the principle of autonomy for science, and the recent Rothschild Report (1972) which seeks to strengthen the customer/contractor relationship in scientific research, epitomizes this trend. In a situation where not only the allocation of research funds between research areas substantially determines the structure of knowledge, but when within this overall funding pattern Rothschild seeks even greater control, where can Firestone's expectations of science seriously be placed?

Our view is not only that such hopes are unrealistic but also that their naivete about science may make it more difficult for women to see the dangers flowing from some new technologies of reproduction.

The ideologies of regulating reproduction
The conflicting ideologies of birth control over the last century reflect the struggle over who shall control the technology and at the same time reveal the nature of the technology itself. These issues, as we shall argue, are intensified by the proposed reproductive technologies of the future.

Regulating reproduction through late marriage, infanticide, abortion, some forms of circumcision, rudimentary chemical and physical intervention (vinegar on a sponge in the uterus, linen condoms, etc.) are, as Himes's (1936) classical text points out, not new in medical history. However, over the last one hundred years science and technology have dramatically increased the efficacy of the means of regulating reproduction. Beginning with the advance in rubber technology in the 1870s which produced more effective condoms and eventually the cap, research moved from physical methods of regulation to chemical methods. The triumph of the pill in the late 1950s marked a dramatic step forward for women, particularly in the industrialized societies. A return to physical means was evinced by the introduction of the coil, a technique which has been widely employed in developing societies.

Once the efficacy of scientific birth control was established, the ideological debate over its employment was also enjoined. The eugenicist movement, partly as an ideological expression of imperialism abroad and ruling-class interests at home, had long argued that population control of inferior people as defined by class and race was a necessary and desirable goal. Naturally it saw in scientific birth control a more acceptable way of securing its ends. The most brutal forms of eugenic control saw their apotheosis in Nazi Germany, beginning with sterilization and marriage laws, but leading finally to the gas chamber. There were ripples in Britain in the proposals canvassed in the 1930s that the unemployed should be sterilized, and in the practice of shutting away in subnormal institutions young girls who had evinced their feeble mindedness by having a baby without securing a husband first. Some such women were released only in 1973, having been shut away for thirty years for their 'crime'. In the United States too, compulsory sterilization was practised, particularly against poor blacks. In 1930, twenty-four states had sterilization laws for the 'feebleminded, criminals and paupers' (Pickens 1968). Even in the 1970s there have been a continuing number of cases of the involuntary sterilization of black women. In 1973 the American Civil Liberties Union took up the case of two young black sisters who at twelve and fourteen had been surgically sterilized in Montgomery Alabama in 1964 (National Welfare Rights Organization 1974). It is also the situation that in some states free Medicare for women giving birth to a baby is dependent upon her agreeing to subsequent sterilization. A similar situation seems in certain cities to be developing as hospital policy on abortions in the National Health Service.

Not surprisingly the eugenicist nature, both of internal programmes of birth control and also of those in developing countries (particularly when sponsored by imperialist countries), has been widely recognized. Birth control is seen as genocidic by a number of black and Third World movements. However, some of the debates that have taken place concerning population control programmes show signs of acknowledging both the eugenicist element and also the liberatory element for women themselves. Increasingly it seems that it is women who are recognizing the positive aspect of birth control technology even while sharing with men an agreement as to its societal function.

Eco-eugenicists
To this traditional eugenicist argument has come a new ally, the ecological movement, preaching zero population growth. Starting from an unimpeachable position concerning the finite nature of the earth and its resources, it deftly moves into an argument for retaining the developing world as a natural wilderness and restraining economic growth within the industrialized world. As little redistribution is proposed, zero population and the provision of wilderness seem to be little more than the claims of the haves to preserve their advantages. Indeed the ecologists' interest in population control has mobilized a good deal of enthusiastic support from the middle classes, but ruling-class allies are drawn from groupings such as the Council for the Preservation of Rural England, itself representative of old landed and new business/landed interests — that is, the great bourgeoisie itself. In so far as women are made to feel guilty for polluting the earth with their children, the ecology movement merely adds sexism to the traditional racism and class dominance of the eugenicists' movement.

Social engineering and population control
While at present no society has the knowledge of the social and psychological factors and the level of technological competence needed to control population growth in any precise way, either to increase, stabilize, or decrease it, there is a long history of state intervention. In feudal Japan, for example, the Samurai in certain rural areas where infanticide had been carried out to such a level that the economic activity was threatened, provided family allowances to encourage the peasants to preserve their young. However, while the case for intervention was for this society a matter of survival, intervention and estimates of a desired population level are rarely so straightforwardly rational. Exhortation, financial inducements and enlarging or restricting birth control facilities have all been used. France, for example, has had for many years a generous family allowance programme and limited birth control facilities, but is still unable to increase her population to the levels deemed attractive by politicians.

Increasing the population through financial incentive is less efficient than the technique of first providing an extensive abortion service and then withdrawing it. The Soviet Union in the 1930s,

Rumania in 1966, and Bulgaria, Czechoslovakia, and Hungary in 1973 have all used this with some success. A decision, which previously belonged to the women, is withdrawn — via the medical profession — to become the decision of the state.

Various social techniques are being used to reduce population. Negative family allowances, for example, where the mother receives family allowances only if she produces the right number of children, were discussed for Mauritius by Titmuss, Abel-Smith, and Lynes (1961), and have recently been adopted by Hong Kong. This, as studies of family budgeting under duress show, affects the fathers least, because as the bread winners they have to have food; the children most sharply, because of a young child's response to poor nutrition; together with the mothers, because they typically deny themselves food in order to feed their children. Few administrative proposals for regulating population through economic incentives and disincentives have been so draconian, and it is not without significance that such a proposal was carried out in the context of a colony. Other techniques dependent on the provision of services to limit population are a mixture of social and technological engineering — epitomized perhaps by the highly publicized and not very successful transistor radio/male sterilization programme in India.

In Britain, although the birth rate is in fact slowing down — to some extent slackened by the increased provision of birth control services and the liberalization of the abortion law — there is a sustained attempt to generate an ideology of zero population growth. One recent conference of natural and social scientists held by the Institute of Biology went further, advocating a population for Britain of some 40 million (Taylor 1973). A paper produced within the British women's movement suggests that there are three possible ways of looking at the role and image of women in this situation, whereby women are no longer forced to produce children but are to be actively discouraged (Halperin, Kenrick, and Segal 1973). The first is a continuation and intensification of the traditional view of women as the most flexible part of the industrial reserve army (last hired, first fired). The second relates to women not in the paid labour force, or in the unpaid as producers of children, who need to learn to accept themselves as 'super consumers' in the 'none is fun' image. The third is to encourage women to take on wider social roles in order to encourage them to have fewer children, a view that echoes the Ross report which noted that zero population growth would be likely to result in 'increasing demands by married women for employment and other opportunities for social participation outside the immediate family circle' (Ross Report 1973). In setting out these three roles the contradiction is revealed between the first two and the third, which would entail a very different kind of society. If a society, despite its zero population growth goal, is unwilling to make significant social concessions to women, it must resort to more repressive measures against them. But before we discuss how this might be done we will look at the liberatory potential in developments in birth technology.

Population control in women's hands
The area of folk medicine that related to childbirth, contraception and abortion was traditionally, as Ehrenreich and English (1973) point out, in women's hands. The history of the professionalization of medicine, which occurred prior to the advent of scientific medicine was therefore not primarily concerned with the replacement of superstition and quackery, also the history of the replacement of women healers by male doctors. The attack on the 'witches' is interpreted by Ehrenreich and English in a similar vein. They argue that the 'witches' were practitioners of folk medicine who experienced civil repression at the hands of the male-dominated Catholic Church precisely because their work enabled women to control their reproductive functions. One way, for example, of infallibly detecting a witch, cited by the *Malleus Maleficarum*, was that the woman had been instrumental in securing an abortion. Interference with the natural process of unlimited reproduction was thus the major reason for the Church's persecution of the 'witches'.

The significance of women medical workers is seen too in the twentieth century, when the potentiality of scientific birth control had been realized.[8] The deep affection by women, particularly poor women, for Marie Stopes and the other women doctors of the pioneering birth control clinics of the twenties and thirties stood in sharp contrast to the feelings inspired by the eugenicist movement.[9] For that matter the self-help centres springing up first in the United States in the late sixties and now in Britain, for pregnancy testing, internal examination, etc. and abortion clinics run by women for women reflect this growing conviction that the care of women's bodies should be in women's hands.

Yet both Marie Stopes and today's collectivist self-help centres are deviant strands within the general norms of a patriarchal and capitalist society, and we have to turn elsewhere, notably China, for a society which, having made some false starts on the planning of reproduction, has now established a line that both gives the control to women and is extremely successful. With the rapid popoulation growth experienced since liberation China has had to develop a clear policy on planning reproduction as much as on planning production. Thus while some groups, like the national minorities, after decades of population decline, are encouraged through the introduction of fertility clinics to have larger families, most, especially those in the economically abundant areas, are encouraged to limit their family size.

As Hawthorne (1970) points out, fertility depends on seemingly small things such as the age people decide to get maried. In China one key method of controlling births is through encouraging relatively late marriage: in the towns the desired age is twenty-five for women and twenty-seven for men, in the country twenty-three for women and twenty-five for men. After two children, spaced with the aid of the coil or pill, some women agree to be sterilized, a very final step for a woman who may be only twenty-six. As Han Suyin (1974) points out, this programme of birth planning, the most efficient in the developing world, is carried out primarily by the women themselves by word of mouth education and exemplary action. Even the bare foot doctors, like the more highly trained, play a relatively minor role, as 'women do not wish to be advised on these matters by young unmarried persons'. Scientific education and any display of posters is eschewed, as when it was tried the peasants felt that they were being invited to commit infanticide once more. Instead the women are encouraged through collective discussion to emulate the confident action of the women cadres who, having had two children, have had themselves sterilized. The immense mobilization of the women, themselves discussing and deciding 'whose turn it is to have a baby', means that the interests of the whole society and those of the individual women are seen are harmonious.

Biological engineering and the managed society

However, for Western democracy committed to individualism, given the intractability of human beings, the immense complexity of the social engineering strategy (albeit with biological elements) leads, if the state requires more population control, to one that is primarily biological engineering. It is therefore to some of the new technologies at least partially under development to which we now turn our attention.

(1) *Choosing boys with Etzioni*
One of the possibilities, which is well advanced technically, concerns the choice of the sex of the unborn child. Despite Ogburn's (1964)

cultural lag hypothesis of the time gap between technological change and societal adaptation, only Amitai Etzioni (1971) seems as a sociologist to have given any thought to the kind of society this intervention in reproduction will produce. Sharing the assumption that Western civilization proceeds by adjusting to new technologies, Etzioni considers the implication of choosing boy babies. People he notes, have measurable preferences about the sex of their children. More families stop having children after a boy is born than a girl, and men, in particular, state a preference for boys. He predicts that if it were actually possible to choose, many more than those who stated a preference when there was no means of definitely acquiring it, would choose boys, 'even if it were taboo or unpopular at first ... could become quite widely practised once it became fashionable'; thus defining the role for advertising companies. In a capitalist society nothing is more sacrosanct than the 'individual choice' of the consumer, thus making any move not to allow such techniques to be commercially developed much more difficult. There is an echo of this in the debate over the test-tube babies announced at the 1974 British Medical Association meeting by Professor Bevis. While traditional morality questions whether it is an ethically correct action, the doctors legitimize themselves by invoking the individual choice of the mothers themselves. However, at the level of individual choice the ability to determine the sex of the unborn child has more market potential than choosing to have a test-tube baby. There would be no difficulty in securing investment to launch a sex-determinant as it would obviously be very profitable.

Apart from the logistics of securing the production and adoption of the sex determinant, Etzioni permits himself to consider the societal effects. Clearly a sexual imbalance would occur, though not an enormous imbalance, and therefore homosexuality would increase. The shortage of women would also increase female prostitution and there would be certain changes in cultural life. Overall, in terms of the basic power and economic structures of society, Etzioni thinks the new sexual imbalance would have little effect. The society he portrays is in fact partially observable in those towns and areas in Western Europe where the single male migrant worker is employed, although here the effect is achieved through social techniques. In these societies the existing social order is, if anything, strengthened while conditions worsen for those in the lower strata.

(2) *Leaping to breed male with Postgate*
The biologist Postgate (1973) is a bolder sociological prophet.

Firestone's antithesis, he offers a male utopian conception of how sex selection would change male-female relations and deal with the population question. Like Firestone, Postgate's thesis depends on a technological fix. Unlike Firestone he, as a biologist, is part of that fix.

Postgate links the three eugenicist concerns: class, race, and sex. He argues that overpopulation is the most important problem facing humanity today, and that starvation and instability are dependent upon it. Birth control is rejected as he claims it works best in countries that least need it, ie. 'wealthy educated countries', but not in 'underdeveloped unenlightened ones'. Alternative forms of population control, such as war, disease, legalized infanticide and euthanasia are rejected as they are not selective, acceptable, quickly effective, or permanent enough.

Breeding male, however, meets these criteria as 'countless millions of people would leap at the opportunity to breed male' (particularly in the Third World) and 'no compulsion or even propaganda would be needed to encourage its use, only evidence of success by example'. The rate of population decline brought about by fewer females would depend on how quickly 'ordinary' men and women caught on to what was happening. When the world population stabilized at a much lower number of people, the real benefits of developing changes in industrial production could be reaped.

Some people, of course, might object to a 'male child pill' because of the social consequences of the 'transitional phase', which he describes as a 'matter of taste, rather than serious concern'. During this period women would be kept in purdah, no longer able to work or travel freely, given as rewards for the most outstanding males. Polyandry could be introduced and women come to be treated as queen ants. While no woman could begin to equal a queen ant in production, the term indicates an intensified technological process where women bear children throughout their fertile years: the analogy is factory farming — battery rather than free range hens. Thus the production of children would mirror existing industrial techniques; a realistic form once the absolute numbers of women are reduced. The logic of capitalism is to rationalize production and this is one way it could be accomplished. Rowbotham's (1973) suggestion that the logical thrust of 'pure capitalism' is towards 'baby farms and state controlled breeding' is another. While Postgate's Utopia will come to resemble (we quote) 'a giant boys public school or huge male prison', the model the physicist Shockley (1972) offers us is one of friendly fascism. (Postgate's view can perhaps be compared with National Socialism before the Night of the Long Knives, while Shockley's is after.)

(3) *Friendly fascism with Shockley*

Shockley, Nobel Laureate for his work on the transister and notorious for his views of the heritability of I.Q. genes, is also concerned with the population question. Although his plan embraces both social and biological engineering, it turns on a new technology and is therefore included here. He offers a population control plan that reinforces the monogamous family unit and strengthens the patriarchal system. There are five steps, beginning by convincing people that population limitation is desirable and necessary for survival. The Census Bureau then calculates the number of children each woman may have (2.2 if one-third of a per cent increase is permitted each year). The Public Health Dept then sterilizes every girl as she enters puberty by a subcutaneous injection of a contraceptive time capsule that provides a slow seepage of contraceptive hormones until it is removed. When the girl marries she is issued twenty-two deci-child certificates, and her doctor will remove the contraceptive capsule on payment of ten certificates. The capsule is replaced when the baby is born. After two babies, the couple may either sell their remaining two certificates (through the Stock Exchange), or try to buy eight more on the open market and have a third child. Those who do not have children have twenty-two to sell.

This technology, which in principle is not impossible, transfers control not merely from the woman to the man — as in the case of the condom or the cap — but transfers control directly to the state. Nor is it chance that Shockley's baby credit system would disfavour those with low incomes, which in the United States would felicitously coincide with the Blacks, a group he regards as eugenically inferior. Low-income people are more likely to sell their credits and, in this friendly model, the eugenicist goal of limiting inferior children is achieved by the workings of the market. In addition power is not distributed evenly within the family unit; consequently the situation of all women, but particularly those with low incomes, who want children when their husbands do not, would be markedly worsened.

(4) *Cloning geniuses — fact or fantasy*

Cloning is asexual reproduction of identical individuals. One technique in animals is to transplant the nucleus of any body cell into the denucleated infertile female egg cell. This technique has formed a central element in the proof that each body cell contains all the genetic information originally thought only to be found in the sex cells. Asexual reproduction is different from sexual reproduction not only in its process but also in that the outcomes are different.

Cloning produces, or rather potentially reproduces, large numbers of identical people. The work originally carried out on frogs is central to the theories of developmental biology. What we have recently seen is the transfer of this work to human genetics, ostensibly because knowledge of foetal growth would aid the clinical treatment of infertility.

The best known of this work on test-tube babies has been carried out in Britain by Edwards and his colleagues (1969, 1971) and is conducted within a particular set of beliefs about women and their biologically determined social role. Like Firestone, Edwards and Steptoe recognize the crucial significance of biological reproduction as determining the structure of the family. Their work is explicitly designed to enable women, otherwise barren, to fulfill their biological destiny. They set to one side the possibility of adoption. Thus their work, while using the language of helping women, is in fact deeply conservative in terms of preserving women's role. Their speculation that some women, who are better breeders, could carry the babies of other mothers, suggests a form of biological emancipation of a dominant class of women achieved only by the biological exploitation of another subordinate class. Updated and appropriately modernized by the scientific and technological revolution, it is at root uncommonly similar to wet nursing, whereby poor women nursed rich women's babies at the expense of their own children and bodies. Rent-a-tit gives way to rent-a-belly, and it is suggested that this is progress!

Apart from the particular implications for women, the general and sinister implications of cloning have not escaped a public educated by Aldous Huxley's *Brave New World* (1947) where natural reproduction had become obsolete and babies were bred in test tubes to be conditioned for their place in the division of labour by the best behaviourist techniques.

What is interesting in this situation is that whereas in the '30s the Marxist geneticists, such as J.B.S. Haldane or H. Müller, considered human cloning to be an interesting and eventually practical possibiltiy, today the orthodox Left liberal geneticists, such as J. Lederburg, M. Pollock, W. Hayes and M.H. Wilkins, seem to suggest that cloning is a science fiction, which, because it is unthinkable, will therefore not happen. It is left to the Right to argue that cloning is practicable. J.D. Watson (like Wilkins, one of the D.N.A. model builders and thus a leading biological evolutionary) argued recently in *The Atlantic* 'We must therefore assume that techniques for the *in vitro* manipulation of human eggs are likely to be in general practice, capable of routine performance in many

(offered in the spirit of Alice)

The publishers and authors are grateful to the French cartoonist, Willem, for permission to reproduce this cartoon.

major countries, within some ten to twenty years' (1971).

The possibilities of cloning for genius nourish the strong eugenicist current which has emerged over the last five years or so within the scientific community. Mainly focussed around the IQ question, the scientific legitimation for contemporary eugenicism is provided by the work of W. Shockley, A.R. Jensen, H.J. Eysenck, and R. Hernnstein. For the most part the response to this latest wave of eugenicism has raised questions concerning class and race, to which we would add the third dimension — sex.

If the discussion of cloning is carried out at a biological level, then because the woman has both the egg cells — to be denucleated — and the body cells from which the nucleus can be transferred to the egg cells, in principle a kind of virgin reproduction could take place. In this sense a world without men is biologically possible, and, further, so long as female egg cells are necessary, a world without women is not. (Although as each woman has several hundred egg cells it would be possible to make do with very few women.)

The main argument against the advocacy of cloning for the women's movement must be that it mystifies the actual character of science and technology under capitalism. When we examine the kinds of people who might contribute the crucial nuclei of their body cells discussed by the potential engineers themselves, we find that they are males and are characterized by cerebral and power attributes (e.g. Lenin — as in Muller's original scheme — or Einstein, a favourite candidate of both Left and Right scientists), whereas women are chosen for their sexual attraction. Thus the only two names of women we have been able to see listed by the genetic engineers themselves are Brigitte Bardot and Elizabeth Taylor.

Summary and prospects

What we have tried to do in this paper is to isolate what Mitchell describes as one of the four basic structures of women's position, namely reproduction. This analytic division represents a theoretical advance on orthodox Marxism, which tends to represent women's position as a monolithic entity and at the same time to invoke an invisible hand of socialism which ensures that when the class liberates itself so too will women. By focussing on the one structure of reproduction we have neglected the other three, and to that extent the paper is one-sided. The gain from this distortion is that we have been able to examine both the theories of the women's movement on this crucial problem and relate these to the potential implications of the new biological means of regulating reproduction.

We argue that Firestone, as one of the most influential of the radical feminists, has, in her misplaced advocacy of asexual modes of reproduction, ignored the actual character of science and technology under contemporary capitalism. Essentially her argument is that of the *deus ex machina*, whereby the god in a white laboratory coat resolves the biologically founded contradictions of women's situation. The male biological engineers are thus to create the feminist Utopia.

The Italian radical feminists, while acknowledging that reproduction is central, avoid the trap of Firestone's technological fix, instead arguing that women should only consort to conceive. It is left to Dalla Costa and James to argue that women must work to control the means of regulating reproduction, including the research and development of new technologies.

We then considered the means of regulating reproduction presently being considered by the biological engineers themselves. Whether the proposal is choosing the sex of the unborn child, almost immediately practicable under liberal capitalism, or whether the proposal involves 'leaping to breed male', or quasi-sterilization, or cloning, which would require a more corporate form of capitalism for successful implementation — there is little advantage to women.

Between the old technologies of regulating reproduction and the new is a major shift from the individually controlled technology to a potentially state controlled technology. Between using a condom or a pill and putting a contraceptive agent in the drinking water lies not merely a comparison of lesser or greater efficiency in birth control, but a whole series of complex issues concerning social relationships, the relationsip of women to their own bodies, and so forth.

Women's inferior social position, both in terms of status and power, will make it easier to deprive them of even their present gains in terms of controlling their reproductive function. Further, if the past holds a key for understanding the future, women are in for a very tough time indeed.[10] Rather than forcing reproduction upon her as did the Catholic Church, today's religion — science — seems to be moving in the opposite direction, limiting her right to reproduce, if not asking her to commit 'voluntary' femicide.

Technology is thus not something separate from humanity, but as Marx puts it, 'technology discloses man's mode of dealing with nature, the process of production by which he sustains his life, and thereby also lays bare the mode of formation of his social relations and of the mental conceptions that flow from them' (1887). If this view of technology is applied to birth control, potentially reproduction could be transformed by being for all women a voluntary act. Women could live in harmony with their biology. Nature would be humanized and the long struggle from nature to a truly human culture advanced. But while it becomes possible through science and technology to humanize nature, dehumanizing nature by turning reproduction into a mechanical process is a logical development within an increasingly managed society.

Notes

1 A common view in classical sociology was that women's social inferiority stems from the male's superior strength. See Ward (1914:349).

2 It is not without interest that Comte pointed out that the meaning of the concept 'family' is servants or slaves. In a not dissimilar vein Engels likens the relationship between husband and wife under capitalism as that of bourgeoise and worker.

3 Our own observations of communes would tend to support Abrams and McCulloch's dismal conclusions. However some communes, set up explicitly to help free the women and provide for the children, within the constraints imposed by the larger society, have achieved a certain modest success.

4 *Employed* Russian women spent 415 minutes per day on household chores as against 185 minute for *employed* men. The figures for the USA are women 315 minutes: men 182 minutes, and for British (London) 295 minutes: men 162 minutes. While the level of domestic technology affects the overall amount of household work to be done, the sexual distribution of housework, regardless of economic systems, seems to be that men do rather under 40% and women over 60%. (Cullen 1974).

5 We are grateful for discussions with several women interested in China, particularly Elizabeth Croll, for clarification of Chinese policy.

6 As the women's movement grows, Marxist groups find it increasingly necessary to develop both a line and activities that relate to women's liberation. At the 1974 Communist University in London the best attended section discussed 'Women's Liberation'. Earlier in the same year *New Left Review* published W. Secombe's *The Politics of Housework* (1974), and *Marxism Today* ran a long series of Marxism and the Family from the end of 1972 to Spring 1974.

7 Dalla Costa rejects both the solution advocated by one section of

the movement, that women should be paid for housework, and is opposed to the traditional marxist solution that women should 'enter the work situation'. For Dalla Costa housework *is* work.

8   Not only does the advent of scientific birth control increase the possibilities for women's freedom, but the actual technology itself is expressive of social relations between men and women. An example of the way in which the existing technologies are not neutral is exemplified in the difference between the condom and the cap or pill. The former is a male controlled technology and the latter two female controlled. The accounts in *Coal is Our Life* (Dennis *et al.* 1956) of the condoms being thrown on the fire because they diminish male satisfaction, shows that where the technology is male controlled, when there are conflicting interests — satisfaction versus pregnancy — it is the woman's interests which will be sacrificed. Thus the cap and the pill represent for women a gain in securing control over their bodies. We argue that future technologies, including those presently under discussion, are likely to be more repressive than liberatory.

9   Mary McCarthy's *The Group* (1970) in its portrayal of a small group of '30s college educated women, provides in the account of Dorothy's visit to the birth control-clinic, a sensitive account of the kind of gentle feminist solidarity which many of these pioneering clinics provided.

10 In present day society we can see trends in the mechanization of reproduction that conceivably may reflect the transitional phase towards full biological engineering. As Margaret Stacey pointed out in the discussion of this paper at Aberdeen, in one major Regional Health Authority, rather than allowing childbirth to take its natural course there is a deliberate policy of inducing all births in order that children are born at hours convenient for the doctors — long a practice in America.

References

Belden, J. 1949. *China Shakes the World*. Republished 1973. Harmondsworth: Penguin.

Cullen, I. 1971. A day in the life of … *New Society, 28* (601).

Dennis, N., Henriques, L.F., and Slaughter, C. 1956. *Coal is Our Life*. London: Eyre and Spottiswoode.

Dalla Costa, M. and James, S. 1972. *The Power of Women and the Subversion of the Community*. Bristol: Falling Wall Press.

222 *Hilary Rose and Jalna Hanmer*

Edwards, R.G. 1971. Aspects of Human Reproduction. In W. Fuller, *The Social Impact of Modern Biology*. London: Routledge & Kegan Paul.

Edwards, R.G., Banister, B.D., and Steptoe, P.C. 1969. Early Stages of Fertilization of Human Oocytes Matured in Vitro. *Nature 221* 632-35. 15 February.

Ehrenreich, B. and English, D. 1973. *Witches, Midwives and Nurses*. Glass Mountain Pamphlets. New York: The Feminist Press.

Ellul, A. 1965. *The Technological Society*. London: Cape.

Etzioni, A. 1971. Sex Control, Science and Society. In A. Skolnick and J. Skolnick (eds.), *Family in Transition*. Boston: Little and Brown.

Firestone, S. 1971. *The Dialectic of Sex: The Case for Feminist Revolution*. London: Jonathan Cape.

Grunchow, N. 1970. Discrimination: Women Charge Universities/Colleges with Bias. *Science 168* (3931): 559-61.

Habermas, J. 1971. *Towards a Rational Society*. London: Heinemann Educational Books.

Halperin, P., Kenrick, J., and Segal, B. 1973. *Fertility Economics and Ideology*. Women's Liberation and Socialism Conference. London, September 22-23. Mimeo.

Hawthorne, G. 1970. *The Sociology of Fertility*. London: Collier MacMillan.

Himes, N. 1936. *A Medical History of Contraception*. Baltimore: William & Wilkins.

Hinton, W. 1966. *Fanshen: A Documentary of a Revolution in a Chinese Village*. Republished 1972. Harmondsworth: Penguin.

H.M. Government (Haldane Report) 1918. *Machinery of Government Report*. London: HMSO.

— (Rothschild Report) 1972. *A Framework for Government Research and Development*. Cmnd. 1272. London: HMSO.

— (Ross Report). 1973. *Report of the Population Panel. Cmnd. 5258*. London: HMSO.

Huxley, A. 1947. *Brave New World*. London: Chatto & Windus.

Lewin, A.Y., and Duchan, L. 1971. Women in Academia. *Science 173* (4000): 892-95.

Lonzi, C. 1970. *Sputiamo su Hegel*. Milano: Scritti di Rivolta Feminile. Available in English (mimeo), London, 1972.

Mao Tse-Tung. 1927. Report on an Investigation of the Peasant Movement in Hunan. In *Selected Works*. Vol. 1.

McCarthy, M. 1970. *The Group*. Harmondsworth: Penguin.

Marcuse, H. 1964. *One Dimensional Man*. London: Routledge & Kegan Paul.

Marx, K. 1887. *Capital* Vol.1. London: Allen & Unwin (1938).

Michel, L. and Southwick, C. 1972. *In Defence of Feminism.* London Conference Report. Mimeo.

Mitchell, J. 1966. Women: The longest revolution. *New Left Review* (40):11-37. Nov/Dec.

— 1971. *Woman's Estate.* Harmondsworth: Penguin.

National Welfare Rights Organisation (editorial) 1974. Forced Sterilisation: threat to poor. *The Welfare Fighter 4* (1).

Ogburn, W.F. 1964. *On Culture and Social Change.* Chicago: University of Chicago.

Packard, V. 1968. *The Sexual Wilderness.* Harlow: Longmans.

Pickens, D.K. 1968. *Eugenics and the Progressives.* Nashville, Tennessee: Vanderbilt University Press.

Postgate, J. 1973. Bat's Chance in Hell. *New Scientist 58* (840): 12-16. April 5.

Rose, H. 1971. Pangloss and Jeremiah. *Nature* (229): 459-62.

Rose, H. and Rose, S. 1969. *Science and Society.* London: Allen Lane.

Roszack, T. 1970. *The Making of a Counter Culture.* London: Faber.

Rowbotham, S. 1973. *Women's Consciousness, Man's World.* Harmondsworth: Penguin.

Schmidt, A. 1971. *The Concept of Nature in Marx.* London: New Left Books.

Secombe, W. 1974. The Politics of Housework. *New Left Review.* No. 83:3-24. Jan/Feb.

Shockley, W. 1972. Dysgenics — A Social Problem. Reality Evaded by the Illusion of Infinite Plasticity of Human Intelligence. *Phi Delta Kappen I:* 291-295. March.

Skolnick, A. and Skolnick, J. 1971. *Family in Transition.* Boston: Little and Brown.

Suyin, H. 1974. Population Growth and Birth Planning. *China Now* (43): 8 July/August.

Taylor, L. (ed.) 1973. *An Optimal Population for Britain.* Oxford: Blackwells.

Titmuss, R.M., Abel-Smith, B., and Lynes, T. 1961. *Social Policies and Population Growth in Mauritius.* London: Methuen.

Watson, J.D. 1971. Moving Toward the Clonal Man. *The Atlantic 227* (5): 50-53. May.

Ward, L.F. 1914. *Pure Sociology: A Treatise on the Origins and Spontaneous Development of Society.* New York: Macmillan.

Zetkin, C. 1934. *Reminiscences of Lenin.* New York: International Publishers.

DELIA DAVIN

'Free-choice Marriage' in China: The Evolution of an Ideal

The efforts made by the Chinese communists to replace traditional arranged marriages with free-choice marriage, the difficulties which they have encountered, and the compromises which have been accepted may be better understood if the context in which the Chinese leaders first formed their attitudes to marriage is considered.

The 1920s

A concern with marriage reform has been a pronounced feature of all the radical, political, and social movements of twentieth century China. In the decade of intellectual ferment that followed the nationalist May Fourth Movement of 1919,[1] no traditional institution was more firmly rejected by young radicals than that of the old marriage system, and no social innovation was more fervently advocated than that of 'free-choice marriage' (*hunyin ziyou*).*

Ibsen was immensely popular with the young intellectuals of this period. China had already produced her own Nora: Qiu Jin (Ch'iu Chin), an astounding figure who walked out of her 'Doll's House' in 1903 when she was twenty-eight. Leaving her husband and two children for ever, she went alone to Japan to study. After a short though spectacular career as a revolutionary, she was executed as the leader of an anti-dynastic rising in 1908 (Rankin 1971). The voluminous literature of the May Fourth period contains many allusions to Qiu Jin and even more to Nora.

It is easy to understand the appeal of these heroines for that generation. The first two decades of the twentieth century had seen an enormous expansion of the modern educational system. By the 1920s, several hundreds of thousands of young people were studying in secondary schools, colleges, and universities.[2] Although the great majority of students were, of course, men, increasing numbers

---

*I have used the Hanyu Pinyin system of romanizing Chinese in this paper except where a name is already widely known in the West in another form.

of women obtained entry to schools. Traditionally women had received no book education or a very limited one. However this convention was sometimes flouted in elite families by fathers who chose to educate a favourite daughter, often the youngest or the only child, like a boy. Qiu Jin herself had been brought up according to this deviant pattern. She was allowed to wear boy's clothes, was well-versed in classical Chinese, and stayed unmarried until the late age of twenty-four. It seems probable that many of the first girls to attend Western schools were the favourites of their fathers. Others, like the Soong sisters, belonged to Christian families susceptible to Western influence (Hahn 1942).

The early feminists made women's education a major goal. As the number of schools increased more girls appeared who were prepared to struggle with or to break from their families in order to attend them. For both men and women, modern education often meant physical separation from their families as they went to school in the provincial or even the national capital. Even more certainly, it put an intellectual and emotional distance between them as the students acquired new ideas and new values. Each fresh humiliation suffered by China intensified the nationalism of students, and strengthened their conviction that her traditions were corrupt, and that only thorough change could bring national regeneration. Among the changes they demanded was a reform of the family system whose evils they perceived especially sharply from the conflicts of their own lives.

Frequently the first confrontation between the students and their families took place over the question of marriage. Power in the patriarchal family system of traditional China was conferred not only by sex but also by age, and young men were subject to the decisions of their seniors until quite a late age. Their marriages were arranged in the interests of the family rather than those of the couple, and it was not normal for the bride and groom to meet before their wedding day.

Attracted by what they had read of courtship and love matches in the West, students began to refuse such arrangements or to repudiate them where they had already been made, claiming the 'freedom to love' [lianai ziyou] and to make free-choice marriages. This assertion of their individuality over the family meant an absolute negation of their childhood values. Lost in a new and uncharted world, such young people were attracted and perhaps even comforted by the heroic individualism of models like Qiu Jin and Nora.

Few students could ignore the problem of marriage, for it was thrust upon them by their families. If they did not capitulate, the struggle often drove them to deep reflection on China's family system and the position of women within it. Many young students, both male and female, thus developed a sympathy for the women's struggle, and feminist goals were early integrated into general revolutionary programmes. Some of the earliest political writing by Mao Tsetung was on the 'woman question' (Witke 1967), and many others were led into politics by their involvement with the problem.

Once they had made a break with their families, young people had to evolve their own ways of ordering their lives. Since marriage had been entirely a family affair, the Chinese state had never required its registration. There were therefore no legal obstacles to experiment and, in the towns, independent young people began to live together in free unions, or to marry, and indeed to divorce, in new ways.

Deng Yingchao said of her marriage to Chou En-lai; 'We started our married life in 1925. We had no marriage ceremony at all, only inviting our friends. We promised to love, to respect, to help, to encourage, and to console each other, to have confidence and mutual understanding' (Cusack 1958:188).

This was a relationship that lasted, but many new partnerships were short-lived. The state no more insisted on a role in divorce than it did in marriage. One strange new city custom was that of advertising a divorce in the newspapers. The announcement then came to constitute the divorce. There were no rules, and though such divorces were often concluded by mutual agreement, they could also be unilateral.

In a situation where knowledge of birth control was still rudimentary, young avant-garde intellectuals were still a tiny and isolated minority, and as it was hard for a woman to support herself alone, women in such partnerships were obviously very vulnerable. When a man capitulated to family pressure and accepted as his wife the girl to whom he had been betrothed in infancy, he sometimes deserted a woman in the city, perhaps a fellow-student, with whom he had formerly shared his life and his ideals. The problem was a real one. If he repudiated his village wife, it would be a disgrace from which she would never recover and he might provoke a serious rupture with his family. It was difficult for a young man to accept that romantic love and the freedom to form his own relationships, which were part of the wonderful new world education had opened for him, where never to be his to enjoy.[3]

The continuing sufferings of women even in radical circles inclined many young intellectuals to support free-choice marriage — itself a revolutionary innovation — rather than free love, in the belief that even in the new society women would need the protection of formal marriage.

Many of the men and women who were later to become important policy makers in the Chinese Communist Party belonged to this intellectual world in the 1920s. They fought their family battles, they endured emotional crises and weathered personal storms. The ascetic strain detectable in European Marxism was to find fertile ground in some of them. Several communists at first resolved to remain single. Cai Chang, today one of the most important women's leaders recalled:

'I hated marriage because of the experience of my mother and oldest sister, and in the society around me I saw the unhappy family life of most married people. I wanted to study and not to marry. My brother and Mao Tsetung also hated marriage and declared they would never marry. Our mutual agreement on this subject is one reason why they were good friends with me. Soon afterwards we all three married very happily.' (Snow 1967:236).

Orthodox communists early rejected and often attacked free love, though some in fact practised it. Puritanism however was a powerful force in the movement. Xiang Jingyu sister-in-law to Cai Chang, a founder member of the Chinese Communist Party, and briefly one of its most important theorists until her execution by the Kuomintang in Hankow in 1928, identified three types among the women intellectuals of her day: 'the small family woman', the professional woman, and the romanticist. She criticized the first whose aim was to struggle free of the traditional Chinese family system, to choose her own partner in a monogamous match and to found a nuclear family of her own. Such women, typically the wives of wealthy scholars or politicians, once they had achieved their aim, immersed themselves in family cares, neither social questions nor women's problems reached them in their luxurious domesticity. The third type, the romanticist, she also condemned. Such women sought absolute freedom and absolute happiness for themselves. They neither worked nor studied. Always preoccupied with personal affairs, though critical of society, they did not fight to change it. Xiang Jingyu believed that even the second type of woman, the professional, might have shortcomings since in her desire for success, she would become conservative and conformist. Nevertheless she argued, such women who valued their independence and ability to work above all else, were committed to serving society and were thus the only female intellectuals who might become leaders of the revolution (Xiang 1923).

After 1927, the communist movement was suppressed and its battered remains went underground. For the next two decades the main organization of the Party was based in remote rural areas which they had now to defend and govern. The idealistic students of the 1920s became the administrators. The establishment of the People's Republic in 1949 brought vast new areas of the conservative countryside under the control of the Party. In the rest of this paper, I will examine the sort of marriage reform they attempted to bring about and the compromises which, in the countryside, they were forced to accept.

Traditional marriage

One of the declared objectives of the Communist Party was equality between men and women. The traditional Chinese family was perceived as the institution through which women were oppressed, but the struggle against it did not take the form of frontal assault. Instead traditional marriage forms which served to perpetuate the unchanging family were bitterly attacked. Such attacks were not, as we have seen, new in the towns. In the countryside, where even after the modernizing Kuomintang family code of 1931[4] the old social order continued, they were revolutionary and had far-reaching implications.

As we have seen, marriage was traditionally arranged by the parents rather than by the spouses. It was patrilocal, and its purpose was to provide the man's family with male heirs who alone could serve the ancestral cult, supplying the material needs of living ancestors and the spiritual needs of dead ones. An anthropologist has characterized the disadvantages to women of patriarchy thus: 'Firstly, the stepmotherly treatment generally allotted to daughters as potential deserters, and, secondly, that under which daughters-in-law usually labour in patriarchy. Then they join the husband's family like intruders and are often treated as such' (Ehrenfels 1954:41). This admirably summarizes the Chinese situation. The birth of a girl was never as welcome as that of a boy. She represented another mouth to feed, yet almost as soon as she was old enough to be of use, she would go to another family. Her family received a cash payment for her on her marriage, though some of this had to be spent on a trousseau. (The rest often went on the acquisition of a wife for her brother.) To the family she entered she was a stranger, a possible threat to group cohesion, and she represented an expense that would only be justified when (and if) she produced a male child. Her mother-in-law frequently regarded her with particular suspicion and indeed hostility. The mother-son relationship tended to be the main source of emotional satisfaction in a woman's life and she feared her daughter-in-law as a rival with a stronger hand. This situation was the source of appalling tensions in Chinese family life, exacerbated by the fact that sex roles were clearly defined, women worked together usually within the house or courtyard, and a bride would see more of her mother-in-law than of her husband.

The priority given to the interest of the family was expressed in other traditional rules about marriage. Chastity was expected of women, and their lives were as enclosed as was practicable both before and after marriage. Concubinage was permitted to those men who could afford it and indeed it was approved when the first wife failed to produce heirs. The remarriage of widows was officially frowned on. In fact it often took place, because only elite families could afford to keep a useless woman, but the family of the deceased arranged the marriage, took a cash payment from new in-laws, and kept the children of the first marriage.

The New Marriage Law

The Marriage Law of the People's Republic of China was not the first attempt by the Communist Party to legislate on marriage reform. Two important pieces of legislation were drawn up in the 1930s during the period of the Chinese Soviets and in the 1940s each liberated area had its own marriage regulations.[5] Though minor differences between the laws are of interest, the spirit behind them is the same. For the sake of brevity, I have here to confine my discussion to the Marriage Law of the People's Republic of China, whose application was nationwide and which is of contemporary interest. I concentrate on its implementation in the countryside because it was there that the most interesting problems arose. In the cities, of course, the situation was rather different, but I do not have the space to consider them here.

The fundamental principles of the marriage laws were that marriage should be based on the free choice of both partners, on monogamy, and on equal rights for both sexes. The freedom to divorce was held to be a necessary corollary to free-choice marriage, but just how great that freedom should be was often a matter of controversy. Not only did the conditions for divorce vary slightly from one law to another, implementation policy made it, as we will see, very much easier to obtain in some periods than in others. The marriage laws also prohibited bigamy, concubinage, child betrothal, interference with the remarriage of widows, and the exaction of money or gifts in connection with marriage. Minimum ages for marriage were set at twenty for men and eighteen for women. Medical conditions were laid down, and the state's interest in what had formerly been a family affair was further expressed in a clause which made the registration of marriage with the local government a condition for its validity.

In the 1950 law, equality of man and wife was asserted in a declaration of their freedom to choose their own occupations and social activities, their equal status in the home, their equal right to the possession and management of family property, and their joint duty of striving for the welfare of the family and the construction of the new society. The responsibility for rearing and educating children lay with the parents. Children born out of wedlock were given the same rights as other children.

Divorce by mutual consent was recognized, although like all forms of divorce it had to be registered with the local government. Ex-parte divorce could be granted by the county or municipal government, though only after mediation both at that level and at district level had failed. Men were not allowed to apply for divorce when their wives were pregnant or for a year after the birth. Ex-parte divorce was not permitted to the spouse of a member of the armed forces still in touch with his (her) family. Each party had the duty of rendering the other economic assistance should he (she) get into economic difficulties after divorce. The articles on custody made the interests of the children the guiding principle for decisions. The father was to be at least partly responsible for the maintenance if the mother was given custody, but there was no such regulation for the cases in which the father had custody.

The importance that the communists attached to the marriage law in their struggle to revolutionize society is indicated by the fact that its drafting, which took several months, took place while the Civil War was still raging. They knew from their experience in Jiangxi and in the liberated areas that the promulgation of such a law was only a beginning, and that it was extremely difficult to implement new social legislation. They attacked the problem by trying to change the whole way in which law functioned in China. Under the imperial administration the lowest representative of the Central Government was the magistrate at the county seat. Law and legal procedures impinged little on the lives of ordinary people although they were regarded with a vague dread. For thirty years after the 1911 revolution, under the Kuomintang and the warlord regimes, law and the courts remained something remote and incomprehensible to country people; and the legal system, when it functioned at all, was often very corrupt.

When the new marriage law was promulgated, it was not the responsibility of the court alone to get it implemented; the whole population was asked to live by it, publicize it, and to support anyone who tried personally to benefit by it. Though obviously members and cadres of the Women's Federation[6] were particularly deeply involved, cadres at all levels, officers of the Peasants' Associations, and of course members of the Party and the Youth League, were constantly urged to check up on the observance of the law. Disputes so difficult that they had to be settled by litigation were taken to the District People's Court, or to the local government if no such court existed. But many more cases were settled locally with patient reasoning and argument, or at times a firm ruling from responsible cadres. As many reports of injustices show, these cadres were sometimes governed more by their old prejudices than by law, but in general it was the authority of the marriage law that they invoked in their decisions and thus such decisions differed from locally-mediated settlements in pre-liberation China which had merely followed custom.

After the promulgation of the law, tremendous campaigns were launched to publicize and enforce it. With land reform it became a major theme of all the propaganda for social reform. The old system was condemned, and the new advocated in newspapers, magazines, special booklets and comic strips, stories, posters, and leaflets. To ensure that the new law reached the illiterate, thousands of drama troupes were organized to take plays and skits about it to the villages, the radio carried material on it, and on a local scale, literacy classes and newspaper-reading groups concentrated on it. Though much of this material was intended for use on a national scale, propaganda for local use which took account of special local conditions was also produced. For example, a picture book published in Canton in 1952 with contrasting illustrations of life before and after the marriage law, showed a woman farm labourer being sacked because she was pregnant, and a girl escaping from an unwelcome betrothal by entering a 'home for those who have decided to remain single' (S.C.W.F. 1952). The woman hired labourer was a familiar figure for Cantonese women and one with whom many could identify, but she would have seemed alien to the women of many other provinces. Completely peculiar to the extreme south, 'the home for those who have decided to remain single', was an institution abhorrent to Confucian values, yet well enough known in silk-producing areas of Canton, where it was possible for women to live together in small self-supporting communities because they could work in the silk industry. Such meticulous attention to detail is typical of marriage law tracts.

The most publicized examples of women oppressed by the old system to whom the new law brought relief were nationally known, but many towns and villages had their own stories which were written up in the local press or on the blackboards that served small communities as newspapers. Yet despite such activities the implementation of the marriage law remained unsatisfactory. Investigation revealed that many cadres intervened for the parents rather than their children when young people demanded freedom of choice in marrage, and for the husbands of women who unilaterally demanded divorce. In 1951 ten thousand women were said to have suffered death by suicide or homicide in Central and South China alone after family disputes about questions of marriage and divorce, and in 1955 it was officially estimated that seventy to eighty thousand women were dying annually because of such disputes (Yang 1959:108). The accuracy of such statistics is obviously open to question: the genuine concern of the government authorities at the frequency of violent deaths amongst women is not; the problem was not after all a very good propaganda point for the new law, and yet it was frequently discussed.

In 1950, Deng Yingchao had identified the shortage of able local cadres as a crucial difficulty in the administration of the marriage law (Deng 1950), and in the years that followed, the press carried regular admonishments of cadres who opposed the marriage law and exhortations to administer it better. The tone of these became more urgent as it became clear that cadres were often particularly culpable for the deaths of women who had claimed their rights under the new law only to meet opposition from those who were meant to be carrying it out.

This concern culminated in the campaign of 1953, the greatest of the implementation campaigns, in which the main target was cadres rather than feudal-minded parents, parents-in-law, and husbands. The campaign was inaugurated on February 1, 1953 by a directive signed by Chou En-lai.[7] The emphasis was laid more strongly than ever on the slow process of education as the main weapon, and indeed the Central Committee's directive on the campaign expressly directed that, except in the case of serious offenders, propaganda should be made the limit. It was firm that violent deaths of women had to be thoroughly investigated and the culprits properly punished.

Even more publicity and effort were devoted to the marriage law than it had first received in 1950. The public was deluged with information about it through every possible channel, and directives went out to Party and Government cadres at all levels to study the law again, to correct their own attitudes towards it and to improve its implementation in their own areas. Tens of thousands of people, many of them village cadres in the Women's Federation, travelled to their local county seats to do training courses of a few days' duration. They returned to their villages with a clearer knowledge of, and perhaps a firmer belief in, the marriage law, which enabled them to explain its principles better and to assist people to claim their rights. The campaign uncovered many cases where cadres had been apathetic about enforcing the law for fear that it might cause trouble, and others where they had actually been opposed to it, and had hindered its implementation wherever they had had the power to do so.

As in the original campaign at the time of the promulgation of the law, many cases of tragically unhappy arranged marriages being dissolved and followed by happy unions based on free choice were publicized. This time however there were also numerous stories told about cadres who had not supported young people and had even punished them when they tried to marry the partner of their choice. The campaign is said to have encouraged many unhappy people to seek divorce, and to have reformed cadres with feudal attitudes to marriage and divorce.

Among the standard complaints about the marriage law, sometimes voiced even by cadres, was that it was really a 'divorce law' and that free-choice marriage was bound to result in chaos. Though marriage law publicity indignantly rejected such allegations, in a sense they were confirmed by articles and news items. A striking feature of these is that very few describe a simple case of young unattached people meeting, falling in love, and deciding of their own free will to marry, whether or not they will have to face parental opposition. Those that do are atypical in that they are often set in the town. The themes of marriage propaganda are unhappy young people, and especially girls, struggling to free themselves from long-standing betrothals, rejecting the matches their parents make for them, or demanding divorce.

This will be easily understood if it is recalled that the minimum ages at which marriage was permitted under the marriage law, twenty for a man and eighteen for a woman, were about the same as the normal age at marriage in pre-liberation China.[8] Of course many would still have been single at this age, but few would have been completely free of the necessity of dissolving some sort of marriage arrangement made by their families for the future before becoming involved with someone of their own choice.

Many of the stories do illustrate free-choice marriage positively in that as soon as the girl is free of the man chosen by her parents, she marries somebody else, but very few are so bold as to represent the girl's primary motive in rejecting the arranged match as her love for another man. In those that do, the girl is normally only betrothed, and she still lives in her own home. The stories of child daughters-in-law and of wives who want a divorce are usually more circumspect. There are lengthy accounts of the unhappiness and ill-treatment suffered by these girls in their in-laws' homes, meant to explain what has driven them to divorce. Occasionally 'the other man' is mentioned and even described as having admirable qualities such as industry, thrift, and enthusiasm for the new order. But he is not allowed to appear to break up the existing marriage and the close relationship between him and the girl cannot be developed until after the divorce. It is impossible to prove, but it seems likely that the literature of the marriage law here betrays more caution about probable public reaction than concern for realism.

A story which is typical of those used to propagate the law was that of Liu Fahuai who lived in Bishan county, Sichuan (Szechuan) province.[9] Her father was a poor peasant who had betrothed her very early to a boy three years her junior to whom she was married at the age of sixteen. Her mother-in-law was cruel and she was very unhappy, but when she begged her mother to allow her to come home, the older woman was horrified. Four years later, in 1951, Liu Fahuai was elected village head in place of a cadre who had been transferred to work elsewhere. At the same time, a boy a year younger than she, who had been a childhood friend, became chairman of the Peasants' Association. In the same year, the Women's Federation in the village held a meeting to discuss a case of wife murder with reference to the marriage law. This meeting made Liu think about her own unhappy marriage and she resolved to ask for a divorce. However, when she spoke to the district head who was also a woman, she met with firm opposition. The senior woman pointed out that the old people of the village were already opposed to young women attending meetings and that such a scandal would undoubtedly lead to their being forbidden to do so. She also hinted that it might affect Liu's application to join the Youth League.

When she consulted the chairman of the District Peasants' Association, he took a very similar line. He argued that old marriages were very numerous and that if Liu asked for a divorce it would set an example that could lead to chaos. Poor Liu dropped the matter for a time, but when she joined the Youth League, its secretary took a more progressive line and urged her to persist. A cadre from the County People's Court came to hear some divorce cases at a public meeting so Liu took the chance to raise her case. She was granted a divorce and the cadres who had opposed her application criticized themselves so that the whole story became known throughout the village. The story illustrates well the weight of conservatism. Both the girl and the village must have been exceptional, or she would never have become village head. If such an important local figure, in a village which had shown itself to be progressive about women by accepting one as its head, met such obstacles in her fight for a divorce, things must have been still more difficult for ordinary women. Eventually Liu married her childhood friend, though we are told that a girlfriend acted as an 'introducer', a detail which shows how difficult it was to abolish the indirectness imposed by decorum in traditional marriage.

After the marriage law was first promulgated, some surveys of marriages made in the old liberated areas divided them into three types: those in which the couple married of their own volition, arranged marriages when the couple met and agreed to the match before the wedding, and marriages arranged by the parents without any consultation with the couple (L.C.C.P.G. 1950:37). The figures given indicate rather different trends, not surprisingly, since not only would conditions have varied anyway from one locality to another, but the areas surveyed had been liberated for different periods of time. Nor can we have any idea how uniformly the rather vague definitions of the survey were applied. Clearly it could not always have been easy to decide how to categorize a particular marriage. Nevertheless, it is interesting to note that the situation was considered good in areas where the majority of marriages fell into the second, 'semi-voluntary' category, a minority were completely voluntary, and a smaller minority were completely arranged.

It seems significant that in a booklet published in 1964, it was still thought necessary to urge young people to struggle for the right to choose their own spouse, although the same booklet stated that the old system of arranged marriage had already been destroyed (Zhou 1964: 6, 31). This apparent contradiction probably indicates that the author was thinking only of the system in which arranged marriage could be completely coercive, for he goes on to warn that some young people make unhappy marriages because they allowed themselves to be bullied into them through 'filial piety' and a fear of offending. Another booklet published in the same year, stated that marriage freedom did not imply that the marriage of children should not be the concern of their parents, and that on the contrary, parents could give advice, or make introductions (P.H.C.A. 1964). It even counselled young people to seek the advice of their parents since they were superior in age and experience, and to give weight to it, although advice could of course, be disregarded if it masked an attempt to interfere, or if it were ideologically incorrect.

These two booklets strengthen the impression given by much of the literature of the 1950s that the compromise 'semi-voluntary' marriages were common, in the countryside at least, and were accepted by the Party. Further evidence may be found in a description of village life as late as 1970 which shows that the initiative in arranging a marriage was always taken by the parents, although the young people normally met and approved each other before the wedding (Chen 1973:72-82).

The remarriage of widows under the New Marriage Law

It took much persuasion to establish the right of widows to remarry. Even in those areas where poor families had always arranged a second marriage for widows, problems now arose over the implementation of the new law. Whatever the custom in the old society, it was based on the idea that the widow belonged to her husband's family, bound by links that did not dissolve with his death and that she could not break of her own volition. This idea was as strong in communities where families had formerly disposed of widows for their own gain as it was where they had kept them for life as daughters-in-law, and the fact that a widow was free to get married when she wished to the man of her own choice, was equally unacceptable to both.

Under the new law, not only would her first husband's family cease to receive a price for her; until collectivization, she could take with her a share of the household property, including even land if the family had received any in land reform. Even more contro-family had received any in land reform. Even more controversial, she had the right to take her children with her if she wished to do so. Obviously all this would have caused deep conflict even where the old taboos on remarriage were no longer effective.

One case which received much publicity in 1950 was that of the Widow Chen, a Honan peasant woman who was murdered because she wished to remarry.[10] Those involved in the killing included even her own brothers, who felt that she was disgracing their family, and some of her husband's relatives who would no longer have been her heirs had she remarried. The ringleader was Peilian, the former boss of the village, who was jealous and angry because the widow's suitor, Yang, had been elected village head. Such was the strength of feudal feeling, that not only was Peilian able to make the whole village hostile to the couple, he even persuaded the district head to imprison Yang on some trumped-up corruption charges. This official took the view that since the widow was an 'immoral woman' (for she was considering remarriage), Yang, who was associating with her, was probably guilty of the charges. The true facts came out months after Yang's imprisonment and the widow's murder.

A case with a happier ending was that of the Widow Zhang.[11] This woman had been widowed before liberation and left with small children, so a cousin of her husband's came to live in the house and farm the land for her. In time they began to sleep together and she bore him two babies but killed them for fear of public opinion. In 1950, a woman cadre who was in the village to organize land reform heard this sad story and, realizing that the widow was again pregnant, began to fear that the tragedy would be compounded. She talked to many of the villagers separately about the case and then held a public meeting to discuss it. The older people, including even some village cadres, said that the couple were making the village lose face and that they should be punished or driven away. Some of the young people, especially the young women, said that they should have been allowed to marry long ago, and that the solution now was to let them marry and to keep the child, but it was many months before the majority was persuaded of this. It is an interesting case because it shows that the villagers were prepared to ignore the fact that a widow was living with a man. They felt forced to act only when the birth of a child forced the matter on their attention. However, they opposed a marriage which they felt would be immoral and would bring disgrace on them as a community.

Divorce

A report of 1950 stated: 'Amongst the masses and the village cadres there are those who accept the idea of free-choice marriage but not that of freedom to divorce for they regard divorce as disruptive to the family' (L.C.C.P.G. 1950:24). Yet in the China of 1950, the possibility of divorce was necessary to many young people before they could enjoy free-choice marriage. Even in the long-run it was a necessary safety value in a society where the marriage relationship was supposed to be based primarily on the wishes of the individuals directly concerned.

Divorce was, of course, unacceptable to the traditionalists and the fact that after liberation it was usually (i.e. in 60-90 per cent of cases

(L.C.C.P.G. 1950:37)) initiated by the woman did not make it less so. Male opposition to divorce increased after land reform because, if a family had obtained land, a woman leaving it through divorce had the right to take her share with her. One early report complained that in areas where land reform had not yet been carried out, women who got divorces were left without the means of support, while where it was already complete, men obstructed divorce because they did not want to lose land (You Tong 1958).

Considerable efforts were made to make divorce more acceptable to public opinion. Cases where the wife's misery was evident and easily justifiable, as when she had been treated with exceptional cruelty or married to a simpleton or an infant, were given great publicity. Cases where divorce was granted were not the only ones to be publicized. It was stressed that freedom to divorce did not mean divorce at will, and examples were given where divorce demanded on unreasonable grounds, such as the poverty of the husband or the unattractiveness of the wife had been refused (You Tong 1958:13). The court's power to mediate was extensive. For example, in one case the court investigator found that in the opinion of the neighbours the couple had originally got on well, and it was the bullying behaviour of the mother-in-law that had driven the wife to apply for a divorce. The investigator then sought out the mother-in-law, had a long talk with her and asked the couple to try again (Lo Yi-jun 1950).

Nevertheless, early reports from divorce courts give the impression that divorces were usually demanded on what were considered anti-feudal grounds, and were fairly easily granted. Later in the 1950s, divorce seems to have become more difficult to obtain, at least where only one partner really wanted it. Investigations became more searching and couples were sometimes flatly advised that an emotional basis for marriage did still exist between them and that they should try again.[12]

A pamphlet published in 1958 (You Tong 1958:13), reflects the growing ambivalence of official attitudes to divorce. It stated that it was unrealistic to suppose that divorce would ever disappear since it was a rational way to end a marriage which had become a source of unhappiness to all. This could happen even with a relationship that was originally healthy and based on love if the contradictions which normally arise in everyday life had not been satisfactorily solved. On the other hand, it certainly implied that divorce was an undesirable social phenomenon, quoting figures to refute the allegation of a rising divorce rate, and stating that a high proportion of contemporary divorces were products of the feudal marriage system.

In the detailed discussion of the reasons for divorce in China, the pamphlet said that since most divorces were brought by young women, some people wrongly believed that the commonest reason for divorce after co-operativization, especially after the transition to higher co-ops when women became economically independent, was financial discontent. Others believed that the prevalence of bourgeois thought was giving rise to divorce. The article challenges both these ideas, using figures from an investigation of divorces in various areas of ten provinces from June to December 1956, which revealed that about 50 per cent of the cases concerned marriages that had been arranged. The article claimed that in backward areas as many as 70 per cent of marriages were still arranged. It admitted a connection between divorce and the co-ops, only in as far as they had enabled women who really wished for a divorce to apply for it.

Even cases of young people who married by choice and then quickly demanded divorce were blamed on the old society, for as the article rather quaintly explained, when young people started to make their own decisions after thousands of years of feudalism, it was quite likely that they would not at first be very good at it.

The tenacity of tradition

The implementation of the marriage law has proved difficult and the attention devoted to it in the early years after its promulgation has not always been sustained. As we have seen, arranged marriages continue in the countryside though in a modified form. During the Cultural Revolution there was a spate of reports of feudal-style arranged marriages and of dowries still being asked (Ning Ming-ye 1966). In 1966 *Chinese Youth* carried an article praising three girls for persuading their parents not to take gifts, send them in sedan chairs to force them to stay home for six months when they were getting married (Zhang Zhe 1966). This implied that these were still common practices at least in some areas, yet they ran completely counter to the letter or at least to the spirit of the law. Such evidence of the tenacity of custom makes it clear that it would be wrong to claim absolute success for the Marriage Law of the 1950s. However, as far as we can judge from the available evidence, it did strike a death-blow at the old system. No new marriages, even when they were only a compromise between the old and the new, could wholly escape the influence of the law. The compulsory registration of marriage, when properly carried out, eliminated absolute coercion in marriage since the cadre in charge had the responsibility of checking that the union was voluntary. Of course strong moral pressure could only be weakened gradually by a changing climate of opinion; the economic pressure which could be mounted was gradually reduced by land reform, the participation of women in production, and finally by collectivization, which all helped to undermine the basis for an authoritarian family structure and made young people's independence a more practical possibility. At the same time the support of local cadres, and of organizations like the Women's Federation and the Youth League, increased as the popularity of the law grew and the cadres' own doubts about it waned. Finally, if, in spite of all this, young people were forced into marriage, the threat of a divorce on terms that were likely to be economically disadvantageous to the boy's family would moderate its members' behaviour towards the girl. Thus even new marriages initiated mainly by the parents might be based more on the interests of the boy and the girl than was formerly the case.

The persistence of semi-voluntary marriage is only difficult to understand if it is considered in isolation from the society in which it evolved.

The Party has been conscious of the danger of alienating its supporters by over-radical policies on marriage and the family, so reforms have been brought about with patience and caution. Though the family has undergone great changes, no attempt has been made to destroy it; on the contrary, it has frequently been stressed that in another form, the institution will survive into socialist and communist society. At present it forms the basic unit of both urban and rural society.

Both the marriage law and the propaganda written for it advocated the 'new democratic family'. The basic relationship in this ideal structure was to be that between husband and wife who were to work together at home to bring up their children to be good members of society while outside the home they were to contribute as much as possible to society. Other family relationships were considered subordinate to this central one.

Nevertheless the young wife's relationship with her mother-in-law remained extremely important to them both if, as was usual at least in the early years of a rural marriage, they both belonged to the same household. It is very interesting that the tensions between the two women are a frequent theme in fiction and that they actually seem to receive more attention than marital difficulties in articles and advice columns on marriage and family problems. This is indicative of the depth of emotional turmoil to which the change in women's relative positions gave rise. Discussions on the criteria for choosing a husband give some weight to the temperament of the mother-in-law.

The parents continue to play a role in their son's marriages because their relationship with the girls will be of real importance.

In traditional Chinese society, there had been very little opportunity for young people to acquire friends of the opposite sex and this situation changed slowly, at least in the countryside. It is true that women's lives were much less enclosed than before, and they attended meetings and literacy classes and worked outside their homes far more often than before. But many of these were women's meetings not attended by men. In any case, meetings, even when attended by both sexes, were not social occasions. When women worked on the land it was at first with members of their own families, and later, after the start of mutual aid, they were often in all-women teams. Of course, contact between the sexes did gradually increase, especially among young activists, but they normally met in groups, and for a specific purpose. Many villages in China are inhabited mainly or even completely by families bearing the same surname. In country areas surname exogamy is still the rule. The young people of such villages may then be forced to seek their spouses outside their own village and it is only within the village that they are likely to have had much contact with members of the other sex. The inhibitions of the old society remain strong and even a boy and girl who saw each other regularly in the course of political activity and were attracted to each other, might find it hard to speak to each other of love. It is common to read of young people being attracted to each other on sight, and asking a friend for an introduction, or, when they felt they knew no one eligible, asking a friend to suggest someone. If marriage resulted from such a meeting, it was considered to have been arranged by the young people themselves.

Since the family is still an economic unit, the timing of a marriage is very relevant to the whole family. When a girl leaves her family, it loses her labour power. (As the value of women's labour has increased, this may tend to increase the average age of marriage.) The family of the husband, on the other hand, gain labour power, at least in the short-run, but they must be prepared for the increase in the ratio of dependents to work point earners that the next few years will bring as the young couple have children. Though under strong official pressure extravagant expenditure on weddings has been reduced, a marriage still involves both families in certain expenses and ways of meeting them must be planned over a considerable time. In the Honan village of Upper Felicity in 1970, the Man family paid for their son's betrothal gifts and feast by selling one of their two pigs which they had fattened over many months (Chen 1973:82).

Weddings have thus to fit the cycle of the household economy and this economic factor reinforces the parents' claim to a say in their children's marriage.

There has been a change in the balance of power in the family in favour of women. Each member of the family receives work points as an individual. Though women's earning power in heavy farm work is often less than that of men, they do at least have some possibility of independence. The young may be better able to contribute to the family income, not only because they are strong, but also because they are better educated than the old. Basic literacy is important in collective farming, and so are the simple technical courses to which some young people get access.

Since they are able to contribute to the family income, young women are now better able to persuade their families to postpone their marriages until they feel ready for them. They can and do oppose matches which will obviously bring them unhappiness. When they marry, their earning power and an increased stress on affectionate, co-operative, and equal marriage relationships eases their entry into the new family. From being her daughter-in-law's supervisor, the mother-in-law is now often relegated to the position of helpmate. When the young women go out to work in the fields, the older women often care for their children and do the menial tasks which were once the lot of the younger women.

Nevertheless, certain aspects of the family system have proved very strong in the countryside for they are rooted in the social and economic realities of the Chinese village life and organization. The expression 'free-choice marriage' [*hunyin ziyou*] which so stirred the students of the 1920s is used of every marriage registered in China today, for the law recognizes no other type of union. Yet the nature of these unions is not that of the romantic student alliances of the 1920s. Revolutionary ideals cannot be unchanging, but have to submit to the realities of place and time.

Notes

1   The news that under the terms of the Versailles Peace Treaty Japan would receive the former German concessions in China gave rise to a storm of protest. Informed Chinese had previously expected that with the defeat of Germany these concessions would be restored to China who was after all one of the victorious allies. A student demonstration against pro-Japanese

tendencies in the Peking government in Peking on May 4, 1919 marked the beginning of an era characterized by demonstrations, strikes, social unrest, intense intellectual debate, and a literary renaissance now known as the May Fourth period.

2 If the students and graduates of primary schools are included, this number is even greater. Chow Tse-tung (1960:37) calculates that by the time of the May Fourth Movement some ten million may have received some form of new education. However, as he points out, this enormous number would only have represented about 3% of the population.

3 One of the few personal details that Bertrand Russell (1968:182) noted about his students during his year of teaching in Peking in 1921, was that most of them were troubled by the ethical question of whether to break off arranged betrothals.

4 The new family law (Van der Valk 1956) contained in the Kuomintang Civil Code of 1931 was an attempt to give China a law based, in keeping with an image as a modernizing state, on monogamy and a more equal position for women. Its effects were limited in the towns and negligible in the countryside.

5 After the suppression of the communist movement in the towns in 1927, its main centre of activity shifted to the countryside where it built up Soviet areas. The most important of these were in the south until 1934, when the party was forced under strong military pressure to evacuate its southern bases. The Long March carried the focus of the movement northwards, and from 1935 onwards its power was centred in the liberated areas of the north from which both the anti-Japanese and then the Civil War were fought. Texts of the various Marriage Laws of these areas are in Meijer (1972).

6 The Women's Federation is a mass organization for women. It is under close Party direction and part of its function is to mobilize women for general political campaigns. However it is also the special guardian of women's interests, and was often of great use to women who had been illegally refused rights such as divorce, or the ownership of property and income by male cadres slow to accept Party teaching on sexual equality.

7 This and other directives were assembled in C.T.I.M.L. (1953).

8 See Buck (1937:381) for age at marrage in pre-liberation China.

9 This story is taken from one of the many books published as part of the campaign to implement the Marriage Law (Anon 1953).

10 This case was widely reported in the Chinese Press. A detailed account of it was published in L.C.C.P.G. (1950).

11 There is an account of this case in P.C.A.C.D.W.F. (1949).

12 This case is reported in You Tong (1958:13).

References

Anon. 1953. *Emulate the Most Advanced People in Implementing Marriage Law*. Peking: People's Publishing House. In Chinese.

Buck, J.L. 1937. *Land Utilization in China*. Nanking: University of Nanking.

Chen, J. 1973. *A Year in Upper Felicity*. London: Harrap.

Chow Tse-tung 1960. *The May Fourth Movement*. Stanford, Calif.: Stanford University Press.

C.T.I.M.L. (Committee for the Thorough Implementation of the Marriage Law) (ed.) 1953. *Important Documents of the Campaign to Implement the Marriage Law Thoroughly*. Peking: People's Publishing House. In Chinese.

Cusack, D. 1958. *Chinese Women Speak*. Sydney: Angus and Robertson.

Deng, Yingchao. 1950. Comrade Deng Yingchao Reports on the Marriage Law. *People's Daily*, 26 May. In Chinese.

Ehrehfels, U.R. 1954. The Anthropological Background of Matrilineal Societies. In A. Appadorai (ed.), *The Status of Women in South Asia*. Bombay: Orient Longmans.

Hahn, E. 1942. *The Soong Sisters*. London: Robert Hale.

L.C.C.P.G. (Legislative Committee of the Central People's Gov.) (ed.) 1950. *Reference Materials on Marriage Problems*. Peking: People's Publishing House. In Chinese.

Lo Yi-jun 1950. *New Words on the Marriage Law*. Shanghai: no publishers. In Chinese.

Meijer, M.J. 1972. *Marriage Law and Policy in the Chinese People's Republic*. Hongkong: Hongkong University Press.

Ning Ming-ye. 1966. The Party Helps Me to Gain Self-Determination in Marriage. *Women of China*. February 1. In Chinese.

P.C.A.C.D.W.F. (Preparatory Committee of the All-China Democratic Women's Federation) (ed.) 1949. *The Movement in Which the Women of the Liberated Areas of China Are Standing Up*. No place of publication: New China Bookstore. In Chinese.

P.H.C.A. (People's High Court of Anhwei) 1964. *Questions and Answers on the Marriage Law*. Hofei: People's High Court of Anhwei. In Chinese.

Rankin, M.B. 1971. *Early Chinese Revolutionaries*. Cambridge, Mass.: Harvard University Press.

Russell, B. 1968. *The Autobiography of Bertrand Russell 1914-1944*. New York: Little and Brown.

S.C.W.F. (South China Women's Federation) (ed.) 1952.

Contrasting Pictures of Old and New Style Marriage. Canton: South China Publishing House. In Chinese.

Snow, H.F. 1967. *Women in Modern China.* The Hague: Mouton.

Van der Valk, M.H. 1956. *Conservatism in Modern Chinese Family Law.* Leiden: E.J. Brill.

Witke, R. 1967. Mao Tse-tung, Women and Suicide. In M.B. Young (ed.), *Women in China: Studies in Social Change and Feminism* (1973). Ann Arbor: Center for Chinese Studies, University of Michigan.

Xiang, Jingyu. 1923. Three Types Among Women Intellectuals in China. *Funu Zhoubao.* 28 October. In Chinese.

Yang, C.K. 1959. *The Chinese Family in the Communist Revolution* Cambridge, Mass.: M.I.T. Press.

You Tong and Others. 1958. *Selected Essays on Divorce Problems.* Peking: Legal Publishing House. In Chinese.

Zhang Zhe. 1966. When Getting Married. Do Not Have Betrothal Gifts. *Chinese Youth.* No. 2. In Chinese.

Zhou, Jiaqing. 1964. *Talks on the Marriage Law.* Peking: Youth Publishing House. In Chinese.

PHILIP ABRAMS AND ANDREW MCCULLOCH

Men, Women, and Communes

When we started the research on which this paper is based we had
been led to believe by the then existing literature on modern
communes, including the writings of active advocates and
practitioners of communal living, that the commune movement
involved a serious, open-ended attempt to achieve a radical
alternative to the nuclear family. [1] That is to say we expected to find
a number of deliberate efforts to re-structure the relationships of
men and women and of adults and children in such a way as to
perform at least the tasks of building and protecting the emotional
commitments of adults and of carrying out the initial socialization of
infants through patterns of association that avoided the more
painful costs to the individual commonly attributed to the structures
of conventional domesticity.

It is not our intention in this paper to describe the research in detail
or to present its main findings. That work is being done elsewhere. [2]
Our object here is to consider the meaning of a curious non-finding
of the research: our impression of the virtual irrelevance of
communes as a solution to the problem of sexual inequality.

Our research involved three main types of enquiry: the analysis of
a substantial body of published and unpublished writing on
communes; observation of a quasi-participant nature of a snowball
sample of communes — sixty-seven in all; and a postal questionnaire
sent to 700 members of the Commune Movement and supported by
interviews with key members of the Movement.

The task of reading the situations we were allowed to observe
proved particularly difficult and we are well aware that we shall not
have satisfied the methodological expectations of either positivist
empiricists or phenomenologists on this score. We visited communes
singly or in pairs and tried to merge in, talking to as many people as
possible in the easiest way we could, staying as long as we were
welcome or as our other commitments would allow. Our princial aim
was to observe and assess as carefully as possible the ways and
degrees in which different communal projects could be said to be
conducive, as structures, to the achievement of an 'alternative
society' and specifically of an 'alternative family'. We took the idea
of an alternative in this context to imply relationships that were

functionally equivalent to those of the family so far as adult emotional attachments and childrearing were concerned but which took a significantly different structural form and had significantly different effects in terms of the moral and emotional climate in which individuals dealt with one another.

From the outset it was our intention to deceive our informants as little as possible, but the research encounters were almost always such as to involve some distortion — springing mainly of course from the moral ambivalence of our interest in other people's intimate domestic circumstances. We always presented ourselves as sociologists and made it as clear as we could that our interest was academic — that we were not for example wishing to set up or join communes personally (although one of us has in fact done so since finishing the research). This refusal to assume the role of genuine participants may have reduced our data-gathering capacity somewhat — the stock attitudes reserved for sociologists in the commune movement, as in other alternative society groups, are of course attitudes of derision and distrust. On the other hand we may have gained some credit as ethical persons and the identity of sociologist was in any case virtually forced upon us by the very close overlap of the academic and commune circles in which we were moving. In the event of the role of naive seeker after truth turned out to be perhaps as successful an approach to the private lives of sophisticated hostile groups in one's own society as one could hope to find.

The second major limitation, imposed upon ourselves, given the nature of the enquiry, was that of unobtrusiveness. Our interest lay in the practised relationships of communes and we were therefore committed to contaminating the milieux in which we found ourselves as little as possible. This meant abandoning quite early on the use of all noticeable apparatus of observation, including interview schedules and tape recorders and certain kinds of question. We were left with little more than our ill-assorted talents as human beings. By the same token the work of analysing and evaluating our observations became largely a matter of mutual criticism of the adequacy and sensitivity of one another's reports and judgements.

A final preliminary point has to do with what a commune is. The creation of new social facts entails, to follow Durkheim, 'the transformation of morality by association'. Communes, however defined, are plainly a project in this area and we therefore adopted a largely descriptive definition which builds on this idea while seizing also what appear to us to be some of the more important specific features of communes as a type of such projects. In this respect a manifest, and as we shall show later analytically vital, property of communes is their combination of an insistence on ideological separateness from the surrounding society with structural openness to that society. For the rest, our working definition of communes simply draws together some of their more obvious, immediately observed, internal characteristics. We are talking about intentional groups of more than three adults with or without children, recruited from more than one nuclear family and strongly, albeit conditionally, committed to living together on the basis of a high degree of mutuality and equality in the allocation of costs, resources, and values, in the belief that new and important moral realities will thereby be achieved. Residence is territorially concentrated and within the place of residence members in principle share the work of the household and the responsibility for maintaining it. A degree of commensality is normal and many other activities are also organized and take place in common so that the value of the life of the group may be emphasized. The group is bound together by ideological, emotional, and economic commitments on the part of members. Two further specific features of contemporary British communes that may be added to this general definition are that communes are perceived by their members as involving among other things, a rejection of constraints seen as typifying the way of life of the isolated nuclear family; and that the processes of commitment through which the bonding of the group takes place revolve around the perception of the group as a medium of self-discovery and self-realization.

The antithesis between communes and an idea-typical (or stereo-typical) notion of the nuclear family is frequently cited as a principal element in the case for communal living.[3] Among people trying to start or join communes we found the positive qualities of communes are perceived with overwhelming frequency in contradistinction to the negative qualities of the nuclear family: 'To me a commune-type set-up seems to answer many of the problems of the conventional isolated family structure and to be a means of being independent of a society which is heading for collapse.' For some, this sense of the need to re-design family relationships was evidently paramount: 'We have no uniting ethic apart from a belief in communal life as a possibly happier alternative to the normal family unit', as two writers in *Communes* (1972 October. No. 40:16) put it. For others, such a reconstruction — to substitute openness, spontaneity and growth for domination, possession, and violence — was at least a prominent part of the larger imagery of an alternative society associated with communes. In a diffuse but surprisingly consistent way, advocates of communes shared the view of the 'straight' family developed by sociologists such as Bronfenbrenner (1961) and Green (1946), anthropologists such as Leach (1968), and psychologists such as Cooper (1971) and Laing (1961, 1971). Green's account of the processes of personality absorption finds constant echoes in the commonsense talk of members of the commune movement. The echoes of Edmund Leach's Reith Lecture are even stronger:

> 'Today the domestic household is isolated. The family looks inward upon itself; there is an intensification of emotional stress between husband and wife, parents and children. The strain is greater than most of us can bear. Far from being the basis of the good society, the family with all its tawdry secrets and narrow privacy is the source of all discontents.' (Leach 1968:44)

This familiar quotation is worth citing again because both its emotionalism and its tendency to psychological rather than sociological analysis turned out to be symptomatic of what is happening in communes and to be a clue to explaining the general inability of communes, in our view, to achieve a sufficient solution to the problems their members sense so keenly.

The formal critique of the conventional family that comes closest to expressing the pattern of sentiment we found in the commune movement is thus, not surprisingly, that offered in the work of Cooper and Laing. Conversely, those which are least realized in the rhetoric of the commune movement are those that treat the inner life of the family as an aspect of a larger political economy, whether in the manner of Parsons (1949) or of Engels (1962). This emphasis springs directly of course from the primary concern of the commune movement with the self. Cooper's search, after all, is above everything else a search for 'the spontaneous assertion of full personal autonomy'. It is in this context, for him, that the family destroys people, turning the possibility of mutual affirmation into the reality of systematic mutual invalidation. Cooper and Laing are not interested in any close way in why the ethos and economy of love, the love-nexus one might say, have been introduced so totally into the domestic relationships of capitalist societies. They would not necessarily disagree with such arguments as those of Parsons or Firestone (1971), which suggest a direct and causal connection between these inter-personal developments and critical structural features of capitalist economies. But their concern is emphatically with the micro-dramas resulting from the love-nexus, the binding of individuals into universes of bad-faith legitimated by the supposed debts of love, and not with the social explanation of the general patterns of inequality in the setting in which those dramas are staged and acted out.

Thus Cooper presents the family as legitimating the perpetration of four evasions of autonomy: (1) the manufacturing of self-other dependencies — the 'family' — to fill out the incompleteness of the individual, permitting the latter to live stiltedly through others rather than self-sufficiently; (2) the locking of the individual into the specified roles required by the 'family' as an alternative to 'laying down the conditions for the free assumption of identity'; (3) teaching the child to accept the social order as naturally given at the expense of its own integrity; and (4), specifically, equipping both mother and child with a 'need-for-love' which is then used not as the basis for a growth of spontaneity and tenderness but to justify represion, violence, and guilt.[4] Although the adult woman as wife and mother is at the centre of this system of personal invalidation, the analysis is not pursued at the level of the 'woman questin', ie. as a matter of the class and status position of women generally. Instead, like the idea of the 'family', it has a curiously self-contained, socially isolated quality. What is presented is the way in which the hopes of love are turned into the debts of love; motherliness generating childishness; romance generating a stale and ritual togetherness; spontaneity generating compulsion.

Some parts of our research indicated strongly that, in this sense of self-realization, building an alternative to the family was really what the commune movement was about. This was particularly true of the results of our questionnaire study of members in the Commune Movement. The appeal of communes was explained by those who answered the questionnaire broadly in terms of the stock discontents and broken promises of industrial society — 'materialism', 'rat race', 'heinz duo-cans', the 'technological society' — but specifically, and with striking emphasis, in terms of the particular discontents of family life. The most often recurring and most precisely expressed single aspect of the whole broad pattern of estrangement that we encountered was 'disillusionment with the nuclear family', the 'farce of the semi-detached existence'.

It was within and around revulsion from the family, in connection with the perception of the family as the specific cause and context of alienation, that platitudes and cliches about the rat race gave way to more directly felt and sharply expressed reasons for innovation. Insofar as a motive for communes, adequate on the level of meaning, emerged from the research, it lay in the perceived idiocy of normal domesticity: 'the realisation that the nuclear family and suburban living are too often isolated, narrow-minded, egotistical, lacking in concern for others.' However dimly the larger society might have been seen, the family as a setting for inhumanity was seen in plain relief: people spoke of their 'deep unhappiness with the nuclear family, from my own experience and observation of other families', and of the ways in which the family tends to 'restrict human potential, freeze relationships, stunt the exploratory and innovating side to our consciousness and cause manifold frustrations'. Some replies to our questionnaire spoke mainly of the material world of the family:

'Present methods of family living put great stress on even happily married couples with adequate finance; if you are unhappy or a single parent or faced with illness the stresses are often intolerable and result in breakdowns for adults and disturbed children and poverty'.

Others, and these were the majority, spoke very much in Cooper's terms, of its psychic world, of

'disliking the limitations of existing male-female roles — both for any particular couple and especially for the mother and child forced to learn only from each other and often not able to get any relief from each other ... Our first ideas were of trying to find a way of living that would begin in the right direction, towards un-hung-up, loving, fully-realised children.'

All this, together with other bits of superficial evidence — such as the names chosen by many communes, Shrubb Family, Miller Family Commune, Family Embryo, and the very large numbers of unattached mothers among these looking for or trying to start communes — tended to confirm our first impression of the meaning of the contemporary commune movement. In a way which, so far as one can tell, was not true in the past, the family has indeed now become one of the main problems communes are designed to solve. Insofar as there is a social demand for communes today, one of the things that distinguishes it from the long-standing tradition of interest in communal living documented by, for example, Armytage (1961), is its emphasis on the commune as an alternative family: 'communes offer an excellent, workable alternative to the monogamous single household'. The concern with property and work and with mystical communion and education that emerge so prominently as the central meaning of communes in earlier periods have been joined and to some degree pushed aside by a distinctly modern imperative, the desire not just for an escape from the family but for a new setting for familism, which, while performing essential family functions, will sustain for the individual those self-discovering and self-fulfilling relationships that our folklore leads us to expect of the family but that our experience teaches us the family can seldom support and often denies.

The family as a setting for intimate relationships is seen as a threat to the free development of the individual. It is not clear whether what is needed to combine intimacy with personal autonomy is no family at all or a different sort of family. Communes have assumed the latter. Their general position is a romantic-interactionist one — that the self is created through processes of social confirmation — but only insofar as those processes are genuinely open-ended and exploratory — not, in other words, governed by prescribed roles, especially by the prescribed roles of the family: husband, wife, father, mother, child. Whether or not a particular commune is aware of itself as an alternative family system, this commitment to open-ended interaction as a formula for both love and self-realization makes every commune immediately relevant as a possible model of new modes of domesticity.

As a result it came as no surprise to arrive at one of the communes we had decided to study closely and find two women busy putting a new roof on the barn while one of the men cooked dinner indoors. More generally what we found was an elaborate and varied array of arrangements designed to disperse conventional male-female divisions of labour. Some of these were formally defined, involving rotas of housework, the creation of limited companies as a means of pooling ownership and commitment, provision for overt collective decision-making, explicit policies of treating children as children of the commune rather than of particular parents. But most were informal, a matter of continuous and fairly elaborate relationship-work, an open-ended and pragmatic struggle to preserve the viability of relationships in which gender had simply ceased to be a conceivable basis of inequality. There was of course plenty of falling-off: 'Hey, look what *your* kid has done to *my* trousers ...', as it were. And there were plenty of communes that turned out to be little more than ego-trips for dominant males, or dominant females, obscured in part by rich and complicated ideologies of together-ness.

We found many different types of commune, many with core projects which played down or obliterated altogether the issue of a possible reconstruction of the family; groups for whom mystical or religious exploration, drugs or farming, politics or voluntary social services, or craft production of various kinds dominated the issue of personal relationships. Conversely we found groups for whom private sexual and parental life of a more or less experimental kind was an overwhelming concern. In general, and not surprisingly since we were dealing with intentional self-selecting groups for whom a crucial element of any particular group's reasons for being was a will to abolish sexual divisions, we found that communes could indeed do just that. And here, too, whether or not the nature of domestic relationships was felt to be an important part of the communal project, almost all of these communes were inescapably *relevant* to any consideration of the possibility of any reconstruction of domestic life.

The more important finding to which we were driven, and which is our main concern in this paper, was that although communes *could* do away with sexual divisions, there was no sense in which they *had* to do so. Communes, that is, do not provide a social structure in which a re-working of gender relationships along more egalitarian lines is in any way unavoidable, a component of the structure. The most they provide is a precarious area of freedom in which people who are sufficiently determined to re-work gender relationships can, under certain conditions, do so. Those conditions in turn are closely linked to the relationships developed between any given commune and the outside world. And looked at in this way it will be seen that communes are not really all that different from ordinary families. The important difference seems to be that unscrambling a 'commune' (an introjected set of relations based on recent, conditional choice and a strong sense of equality including sexual equality) is a little easier than unscrambling a 'family'.

Familism without the family: Communes as anti-structure

Communes are made by teachers, psychologists, and students, by unattached mothers, potters, silversmiths, and architects; by, as one commune member put it, 'the sons and daughters of the middle class'. Recruited from the rump of the free craft occupations and the fringes of the minor professions, they can be characterized more precisely than that. They are, in Poulantzas's sense, (1973), a phenomenon of the petty-bourgeoisie.[5] In a repertoire of petty-bourgeois protest — anarchism, free-thinking, nudism, civil-liberties, and the whole gamut of 'spiritual-healing' projects — communes are the specific response to an ambivalent discontent with the specific experience of the petty-bourgeois family. In almost all its forms, therefore, the commune movement is an attempt to maximize values while minimizing structure.[6] This is not entailed in living communally of course. It is what happens given the sorts of people who are making the most serious efforts to live communally in this country just now.

The values in question are themselves both distinctively petty-bourgeois and peculiarly problematic. What is sought is *both* freedom (self-realization) and security (togetherness); both a sense of autonomy and a sense of attachment. Merely to admit that one finds these values difficult to reconcile is arguably to admit that one is oneself difficult to live with. But if one then goes on to repudiate the possibility of drawing on externalized, 'structural' arrangements as a source of reconciliation, the whole burden of solving the problem is thrown on the daily ad hoc practice of relationships. Among other things this makes the life of a commune highly unpredictable. Again and again communes we had judged stable and successful a few weeks earlier turned out on a second visit to be in crisis or to have broken up completely. The story was almost always the same: 'the emotions involved were very strong and eventually the whole thing collapsed.' Here is an example.

> 'Our nucleus is now seven or eight adults and three or four kids, our ages about two to forty. Usually there are also transient members and visiting friends. The adults share chores without sex distinction and all pay the same weekly sum, finding the cash however they can (writing, painting, occasional jobs). We accept people according to how they behave, not according to age, politics or hair length. Because we are open about each other there is a constant liveliness, and we don't accumulate emotional hang-ups. Visitors usually find a stay healing. We have no formal aims or policy. We don't consider ourselves part of any movement, including the commune one. We think that the way to heal this society is by healing ourselves. By trying to live full and interesting lives we automatically work some change on the people we meet. Life is pretty good here, and we've hardly begun.' (Commune Movement 1970:18)

So one group described themselves in the autumn of 1970. By the autumn of 1971 their project was dead; the commune had vanished. The pages of *Communes*, like our own research files, are replete with such records. Police harassment and financial insecurity compound the difficulties of many groups, but the common problem is that, in the absence of structure, it is impossible to separate the fleeting difficulty from the life and death issue: the question of why there is never any toilet paper in the loo turns out to be a matter involving the basic lack of commitment of some members to the group. More often than not, when we were able to unravel the reasons for the breakdown of a commune, what we found was a familiar domestic crisis, a crisis of emotional possessiveness with all its usual reduction of people to commodities. Having put £3,000 of her savings into getting the commune going, Anne was simply not willing to share 'her' Paul with Margaret; Paul's insistence that his simultaneous relationship with both women was part and parcel of the commune's commitment to self-expression deflected Anne's rage, denying her the normal legitimate grievances, but did nothing to pacify it. The other members of the commune were dragged into a tide of complaint and recrimination which eventually so soured the atmosphere that the group broke up.

Experiences such as this are a common feature of the world of communes. But in commenting on such experiences members of the commune movement reveal again their extraordinary ambivalence about any sort of social structure. The recognition of any ground rules for the relationships in question would have pointed to a solution of the crisis short of disintegration. The more sanctioned such rules were the more they would have done so; but only at the price of binding members into something rather like the 'family', and of restricting self expression, above all the expression of love. So the favoured interpretations of such difficulties turn either on statements about personal qualities ('Anne was too hung-up'), or on the possibility of achieving values without structures through sheer hard relationship-work ('we should have given Anne more help'). We would stress again that under certain conditions, with the right combination of people this can be done.

The group of 'followers of D.H. Lawrence' discovered by Armytage (1961) in Cornwall in the 1940s still exist and have grown into something like a small intentional village based on a mixture of farming, craft production, and some slight involvement in professional careers 'outside'. They have worked their way through a variety of crises towards a chosen way of life based on craft skills, Jung and Catholic religion practised in their own chapel, beautifully decorated with their own work. At various times in their thirty-year history they have deliberately torn up the sets of rules they had evolved as the basis for their life in order to confront a new problem freely. Then, they have slowly, under the guise of developing new beliefs, evolved new rules, new social relations. Significant endowments of capital (a gift of £10,000 to buy the farm) and of skills that could be pursued without involvement in socially organized work have allowed this group to repudiate the dominant social relation of the outside world — wage-labour. Once that has been done and a suitably closed environment created there is little difficulty about reconstructing other relations. When husband and wife are both poets or potters and can afford to work only at what they find fulfilling, the sexual divisions built into normal marriages are at least much less compelling. Here, and in a few other exceptional communes, something like a society of free craftsmen (and craftswomen) has been created. The question is, is this any sort of model for a larger reconstruction of social relations? Here the issue of just how far the repudiation of social relations is to go becomes crucial.

The ideology of petty bourgeois protest seeks to detach the bourgeois ideal of complete personal freedom from the unfree realities of bourgeois society. It seeks in a variety of fantastic ways to withdraw the individual from the social. The commitment of the Commune Movement is immediately of this kind: 'Everyone shall be free to do whatever he wishes provided only that he doesn't transgress the freedom of another.'[7] The initial publication of the Movement 'A Federal Society Based on the Free Commune', the Commune Manifesto as it were, not only proclaims this contradiction as its ideal, but sets it firmly in an almost ideally petty bourgeois account of the bourgeois world:

> 'We are beset with troubles which we have neglected for far too long and which could be brought to an end in an ideal community. We feel we want to do something of real value but there is nothing we can do; hands without power-tools on the end of them have become almost redundant and whatever we would like to be active in we find the ground already covered by a whole army of experts with supporting administrative and executive teams. We can read the paper but cannot write to it effectively; we can listen to the wireless but cannot speak to it; we can read a thousand books but cannot write one unless we have special ability. We feel utterly inferior and impotent in the face of this social monolith.' (Commune Movement 1970:4)

There is a true distress here, but it is expressed flailingly, without location in any specific sense of what has gone wrong. Capitalism is indicated, but only vaguely; industrialism in the form of large-scale organized work is a more sharply felt evil — specifically as it obliterates the individual:

> 'We have, sadly, reached that stage of evolution, where few individuals are valued in themselves in such a way that they cannot be readily replaced. It is too expensive to be unique. In the time it takes a craftsman to create an object which is a thing of beauty as

well as utility, a machine will produce a thousand, stamped out
with unerring precision and monotony and fed on the vast
conveyor belts which are the lifeblood of this regimented society
to the stereotyped minds that lie like doomed prisoners in the
gloomy shades of bodies tied to an endless round of work, sleep
and play.' (Commune Movement 1970:3)

'Stereotyped minds' is a revealing phrase and is taken up elsewhere
in reference to mediocrity, to 'civilisation in the mass' as 'basically a
dictatorship', to mass ridicule and the 'smooth stagnation of the
secure and glorious muddle of the present' The prospect of the
proletariat is as horrific as the prospect of capital. Not of course that
the language of class is used. The analysis is at the level of the
individual; masses of individuals but merely individuals:

'What has life to offer for these millions of beings who provide
the main part of the productive labour upon which the monolith
rests? The average man with only average intelligence and average
parents gets little encouragement or incentive to strive for higher
things. He enters school in a soulless industrial town and
consciously or otherwise competes fiercely for what education is
available only to discover that his average abilities afford him only
average opportunities and therefore approximately half of
average pay. He is doomed to a life of poverty or endless overtime
or both sapping his energies both physically and culturally. He has
a wife and usually two children to support, and can offer them
nothing better than to keep their heads above water in the same
endless rut; he can offer them no capital sum; he will not win the
football pools and he could offer them nothing in any way spectacular in their genetic makeup. He can only admit to his children
that in the mad rat-race they have been born to be losers. His
relaxation is conditioned by his lack of drive, lack of education.
He turns to drink ... he smokes ... he sacrifices what remains of his
life in mute supplication to the idiot's lantern until his thoughts
are those of the tinsel God and his millions of degenerate addicts
and lastly, in his mad frenzy, he drives his HP car in insatiable
fury to the horizon — any horizon — to escape the drab monotony
that was his death sentence at the moment of his birth.'
(Commune Movement 1970:4)

The task then is not to confront but to escape ('indeed why should
we not escape?') but not to escape alone. Members of the commune
movement depart in this from the pure-craft, surrealist, or art-for-
art's sake versions of the petty bourgeois rejections of the social.
Theirs is, as it were, the flight of the *average* petty bourgeois.

Lacking a secure art or other 'ideal' proficiency in the technical
cultivation of which the realities of the world can be denied, they
discover themselves simply as individuals — 'nobody but our small
family really values us' — with nothing but themselves to gain or
lose. And it is as selves that they protest: 'Isolation is probably our
greatest burden ... our greatest asset is each other: let's get together.'
Theirs is a movement to create not beautiful art but beautiful people.
And since people are created through being valued by others it
becomes, in its asocial way, a social movement.

This is the paradox: the social stifles the self; but the self can only
realize itself in a society. The only known society is a monstrous
offence; a new society must be created but the only account of it that
can be given is that it should be not society — that is not the society
that is known. The most that can be said is that it will be an opposite,
'we must create a sub-culture in which we, the deviationists, are the
normals'. Love, freedom, equality, self-expression, or for the less
ambitious, companionship, mutual help, convenience, are to be
won, but all with a startling lack of awareness of the way in which
any of these values must, to be realized, be embedded in specific
social relations (as distinct from gatherings of like-minded
individuals). Members of the commune movement commonly
recognize two kinds of problem which they must overcome if their
ideals are to be made good: 'emotional and mental problems' and
'problems of sheer practicability'. The former is the way in which,
given the denial of specific social relations, the relationships within
communes are experienced. The latter involve mainly the
relationships between communes and the outside world. What
emerges from our study of communes is that notwithstanding the
essentially fantastic nature of communalism as a project, a fair
number of communes have in fact found ways of solving these
problems, at least to their own satisfaction. What happens of course
is that social structure is smuggled back in — often in the form of a
religion. The question which then arises is, if one has made one's
own chains is one a slave or free?

We must look at these problems and their solutions more
carefully. But first it is worth insisting again that the creation of
communes as a denial of social relations is, within limits, really
possible. Thus, systematic sexual divisions can be abolished
voluntarily within communes because they are a derived type of
division. Once the involvement of personal relationships in a
wage-labour economy has been broken, sexual inequality at the level
of personal relationships is neither plausible nor necessary.
Communes can, for long periods of time, insist quite convincingly

that even the most inescapable variations between individuals — man, woman, adult, infant — are insignificant for them as bases of differential treatment. When they become significant, when a woman finds she is after all being treated 'like a woman', the failure will be explained either as a result of an 'emotional and mental problem', or as a consequence of some unavoidable practical difficulty. We must see what this means.

Beyond the notion of getting together and overcoming emotional, mental, and practical difficulties, the ideology of communes offers no coherent or detailed account at the level of social structure of how the self-denying properties of the larger world are to be transcended. All we can do therefore is to consider what happens in practice when the attempt to get together is made.[8]

Practical difficulties

Some problems are solved by a process of self-selection that occurs at the outset. Grammar school and university (started if not finished) provide the educational experience of the overwhelming majority of members of the commune movement. Their chosen fields of work are those in which a direct relation between producer and product, rooted in personal technique, persists; poetry at best, architecture acceptably, teaching at worst. The profession most consistently represented amongst commune members is that of primary or secondary school teacher. The shift envisaged by most is towards still more directly expressive modes of work, uncontaminated by the needs of capitalism. Coming from this sort of background with such intentions it is both desirable and to a degree possible to attenuate significantly at least the perceived involvement of most communes with the economy around them.

The financial basis of many communes is something few members of the commune movement are keen to study closely. A surprising number are launched on the basis of inherited capital or large gifts; in some cases the frankly middle-class character of members' occupations has induced a 'friendly bank manager' to produce substantial loans. Whatever common ownership or income-sharing arrangements may be made once a commune exists, a disconcerting proportion of the more stable communes we have discovered come into being on the basis of successful private transactions within a capitalist market. The effective terms of reference for communal experiments were more than hinted at in some passages of the manifesto of 1970: 'Setting up a community in a rural environment can be quite cheap ... we think £30,000 is an average figure to keep in mind for a good beginning' (Commune Movement 1970:12). In today's property market that presumably means £60,000 — which is not everyone's idea of being quite cheap. Mobilizing this kind of sum is of course something more than a problem of mere practicability. Those who can do it, however, may well be able to treat personal social relations as alterable at will.

The nature of the remaining relationship between communes and the economy around them is embarrassing, quite apart from questions about where the initial capital came from. There is a transparency about the image of economic life in communes which cannot bear much scrutiny. In the absence of an ability to insist on and demonstrate a mastery of genuinely esoteric skills, the image of craft work is curiously unconvincing:

> '——— Commune has the usual Commune aims. We want to make pots, posters, clothes, carpets, bags, beads, etc., grow our own food, become a family, an arts lab, a health food restaurant, folk club and country retreat. We are a happy bunch of artists, farmers, etc. who love the simple life, peace, quiet, meditating.' (Commune Movement 1970:20)

Making candles may be unalienated labour at a purely phenomenal level for the first few weeks. But it is hard to shield oneself from the real relationships with the larger economy which this quality of craft-work implies for very long. Talk of the intrinsic value of the craft product becomes hopelessly mixed up with the most blatant forms of commodity fetish when what one is really doing is making a living making bric-a-brac for tourists. Members of the commune movement come frequently to recognize, often with a brutal honesty, the contradiction at the root of their typical escape from the market. But what is left is only either subsistence farming — which calls for an organized and systematic division of labour, ie. structured social relations, of which only those communes that have accepted the discipline of a religion or managed to recruit trained farmers seem capable — or a return, perhaps part-time, to professional work, or odd-jobs, on other people's terms outside. In either case the limitations placed on communes as an anti-structure project become rather evident. There are exceptions of course. The farm and health-food shop type of product can be made to work — given sufficient initial capital and so long as the health-food fad lasts among the mediocre mass.

So far as their material conditions of existence are concerned, then, communes have been able to achieve only a restricted and partial freedom. Within that area of freedom, however, so long as the pots and belts sell, the illusion of a suspension of economic relationships can be sufficiently maintained. In this sense it is necessary to qualify Rowbotham's argument about the conditions governing the liberation of women.

> 'The woman at home', she writes, 'is thus a victim of the reflected alienation of the man's work situation and also an alienation of her own. Only significant structural changes can radically affect this. The production relations of the man would have to change, the woman would have to be paid directly by the community and the social division of labour would have to be transformed.' (Rowbotham 1972:11)

What this underestimates is the capacity of our society to sustain pockets of life within which alienation is wilfully redefined as freedom — within which, although the economic connection is not really broken, it is sufficiently attenuated for people to behave in their personal life *as though* significant structural change had occurred. Even with the high degree of official control of land, buildings, and accommodation which exists in this country, communes, and particularly the Commune Movement, are slowly finding ways in which at least fairly small scale common ownership and common residence projects can be set up and in which both men and women can withdraw from the labour market, if not from the commodity market, far enough to live as equals if they choose. Given appropriate recruitment, the alienation of the man's work situation can be seriously eased or at least made less obtrusive. Similarly, the entailed typing of domestic relations can be significantly relaxed so that the woman at least does not have to experience the 'alienation of her own'. Of course this may involve a good deal of fudging of economic realities, but the point again is that with goodwill it can be done. An account from one of the few communes which we are agreed in thinking has proved itself a success, shows how:

> 'The cash was put up by five people. Three of them had inheritances, and for the other two it was savings from hard work and economical living. One lump of capital is in the form of a loan over ten years. The whole thing is set up as a limited company, since basically this is a ready-made democratic structure in which all participants in the community can be shareholders. We were seeking to avoid the ownership principle, but because we have not got all the details of the shareholders agreement yet sorted out, the people who put in the money are still technically the owners.

'The trouble is that it isn't that easy to have a place non-owned unless the capital holders who bought the place actually divest themselves of their money and give it to the company. But they still may need that money to use again, especially those persons who put in all their savings and have nothing much coming in as income. So we have chosen to accept the risk that the place might get sold up if certain people are not satisfied, or cannot carry out their plans due to circumstances beyond their control. But it took a long time for many of us to understand the complications and implications of this.' (Eno 1972a:4)

Having watched this particular group live their way through this particular problem is to be more than half convinced that at least some of the practical problems of communes can be solved *in practice*: 'we create our own problems that other people wouldn't dream of having; still, that's our fun in life, and that's how we like to be.'

But at this point another kind of practical difficulty presents itself. At the level of domestic relations very few men or women are actually qualified to live as equals; they lack the technical skills to effect the structural changes that would have to take place *within* the domestic group. The point is made constantly in accounts of communes that have broken up. The experience of communes that survive for any length of time is normally one of continual selection and reselection of individuals until a viable mix of talents — for cooking and cleaning as much as for teaching or loving — is found. This is a persistent theme of articles in *Communes*; it was for example particularly stressed by one of the secretaries of the Commune Movement summing up her first year in office:

'If you are interested in joining or starting a community sometime, I would suggest that in the meantime you get yourself as skilled as possible in things like electricals, plumbing, gardening, animal keeping, driving, sewing, cooking, cleaning, building and carpentry.' (Eno: 1972b:20)

If domestic tasks are not to be attached to types of people it is not enough to free domestic relationships from the external-internal division of labour and the sweeping dominance of outside work relations: in addition, domestic skills and a belief in their intrinsic validity (for the self) must be dispersed. The crucial difficulty in this respect, and not just for communes, appears to be that of dispersing mothering. But at this point 'practical' difficulties begin to blur into 'emotional' and 'mental' difficulties.

Thus insofar as a systematic reconstruction of domestic relations is blocked by the practical problems, communes tend to solve these problems by partially re-entering the 'plastic society' or drawing on its resources just enough to maintain economic viability without enforcing a conventional allocation of domestic roles. This delicate balance can be struck at the occupational margins of an industrial economy, but only at the cost of a degree of involvement with 'supermarket culture' to which many members of the commune movement cannot take kindly. Communal groups are in this respect little different from newly married couples from the same sorts of social circles as those from which communes are largely recruited. Enjoying maximum disposable income and minimum responsibilities they can very considerably arrange their lives to suit themselves. But as most women in such situations know perfectly well, their relative freedom and equality have been bought, briefly, at the cost of not being 'really women' — not having children, that is. In winning their freedom they proclaim their unfreedom. The freedom of communes to re-cast domestic relations is equally conditional upon the rejection of other kinds of relations — a rejection which is in the last resort spurious (the owner of the commune always might sell-up if he is sufficiently thwarted; sooner or later factory production will produce better candles, cheaper), and not realistically available to most people.

Emotional and mental difficulties

The same incapacity of communes to master the issue of personal domestic relationships in principle (as distinct from settling it satisfactorily for particular carefully selected groups *ad hoc*) is revealed in their distinctive ways of dealing with 'emotional and mental' problems. The largest single source of such problems is probably also the largest and most socially challenging source of the demand for communes — young mothers unattached to men. These women have simple but irreducible demands to make of communes: for companionship, for social recongition of the value of their labour as mothers — or as non-mothers in the form of substitute mothering so that they can work at other things — and for an opportunity for new intimate adult relationships. It might well seem that if communes have a recipe better than that of the nuclear family for an unalienated, meaningful life for the individual, it would be revealed especially in their ability to accommodate the unattached mother in these respects. In a sense her demands do not amount to very much — mainly to the idea that there should be a sufficient opening up of domestic relationships for the obliteration of her life in that of her child to be prevented.

As a principle this is a notion widely supported in the commune movement. In the actual life of communes, however, it is experienced as a problem — one much discussed in the pages of *Communes* and in most of the communes we visited. The problem is presented in a language of giving and taking, a language remarkably similar to that one might expect from the nuclear family. Communes, it is argued, are not cheap hotels but fragile social experiments; the question to be asked is what a potential newcomer could contribute to that experiment in return for what she (or he) would undoubtedly impose on it in the form of new strains:

> 'Another frequent request is for communes that are willing to take drug-addicts, so-called social deviants, young mothers and babies and so on. Now I know ideally that probably communes would suit many of these people, but please bear with us that life in a commune is not easy anyway and much as we would like to take people who have difficult problems, unless they can help the commune as well, it is not likely to be a success. Perhaps some day when the community scene is much more together, and more common, we can all share the burdens and help people less able than ourselves. I'm sure that most communal places would like to help but they often have a lot of problems already.' (Eno 1972b:20).

So writes the secretary of the Commune Movement in what is of course effectively the emotional equivalent of the demand for access to £60,000. The practised sentiment — 'we're terribly sorry, but you can't join us' — contrasts starkly with the ideal statements about communes made to us by so many members of the movement for whom the case for communes turned on their ability to 'extend the strong and protect the weak'. The general ideological stance of the commune movement stresses open relationships both within communes and between communes and the outside world. In principle doors are open to visitors, observers, every sort of would-be member. In practice, with one or two exceptions, such as the Anarchist Commune in Sheffield, all actual communes move towards some degree of closure in the interests of the cohesion of the existing group: 'we are choosy about new members after lots of bad experiences with "beautiful people" who expect a community to be a family (mums and dads, brothers and sisters, just to look after them)', or 'others assume too much about our willingness to give; we see many needs in others but do not propose to sacrifice ourselves to all of them, only certain sorts on some conditions'. After a few months of experiencing the costs of openness, communes can become pretty tough-minded and explicit about their real terms of entry:

> 'One important rule should I think be pinned to the entrance of every commune, NO ROMANTICS WANTED.'
>
> 'Communal living is more stressful than single or paired set-ups. It tends to divide well paired people. To smooth over frictions *à la* love-and-peace brigade is to reduce viability frequently below survival level. To apply criteria of practical effectiveness and to be firmly realistic is too heavy for many a communal aspirant.'
>
> 'Our experiences have led us to become very selective in who we accept on a visiting or trial basis, as some go to a commune seeking the mother that will feed, shelter and love them, but they are unable to help the commune in any way.'

It is of course perfectly 'realistic' to side-step problems by excluding them from one's sphere of responsibility, but in this case it does rather diminish the plausibility of the claim that communes constitute a setting *within which* such problems can be solved. No doubt the life of ordinary families could also be made much freer and more fulfilling if excessively dependent members could be excluded at will.

Yet essentially the same procedure is adopted by most communes in handling mental and emotional problems that arise within a group once it has been constituted as are applied to the vetting of newcomers. If the difficulty becomes acute the group splits. The conditional nature of membership is in fact an all-important condition for the fullness, equality, and autonomy of members' relations with one another. As one writer in *Communes* (1973 April. No. 43:16) put it after arguing that communes had, contrary to the opinions of some other members of the movement, to have rules, 'or the chickens would not be fed', these are rules of a rather special sort: 'Of course no punishment or fines follow if rules are not kept. The individual concerned would leave.' That is indeed just what tends to happen. When the struggle for consensus becomes too wearing it is normally solved, not by one party accepting the domination of another, as perhaps in the family, but by one or other party going away:

> 'I eventually left to live with Hilary ... after feeling that I couldn't continue to live in a house in which I wasn't an équal psychological shareholder. I was going off Barry's trip. I had begun to resent

... the general ideal of being "one of his household".'
    'So this guy plonks himself in the commune and after a while
bad vibes start to infuse the building. Maybe some of the group
like him, and some don't. Little arguments take place behind
closed doors. Eventually either he goes or the commune splits and
he stays with the new group.'
    ' 'So what are communal objectives and priorities and what
happens when it has been agreed by everyone to do something and
then half the people change their minds? It seems that with the
split into two groups no balance or compromise was possible, so
one group left, taking four adults and five children.' (Crowther
1972:11; Eno 1972a:3)

It would seem that in one respect communes really are an
alternative to the family; members retain their right to decamp. The
active prospect of dissolution is the condition for equality. To an
outsider it might well seem that communes are coping with the
problems of family life by deliberately not coping. This is in fact
unfair. A lot of strenuous work is put into making relationships
within communes succeed — most successfully it sems to us by
diverting members' attention away from the problem of
relationships as such and towards either practical matters (getting
the garden organized) or transcendent matters (understanding God's
will). But the seriousness with which the voluntaristic or intentional
element in the commune movement is invoked to give individual
members the right to decide whether or not they will stand for 'bad
vibes', for the costs of domestic relationships, cannot but make
communes in the last resort a fantasy solution to the problems of
domestic life — *someone* is going to get stuck with the addicts,
deviants, and mothers with babies.
    The position towards which most communes tend to move in
facing the issue of emotional problems is not very different from the
unashamedly hard-line taken by Postlip Housing Association on
practical problems:

'We are looking for a stable young couple to come and live in one
of our cottages. They will need enough income to be able to find
about £25 a month for rent and for Association dues; and they will
also have to find or borrow £500 ... We know that this, sadly, lets a
lot of people out straight away and we're sorry about it; we can
help with advice and encouragement, but they will have to come
up regularly with dirty pound notes, or it will all fall down. The
hard fact is that you do need some money if you want to live the
way you want; if you want to live our way, it's essential.'
(*Communes* 1972, no. 38, June:15).

The emotional equivalent of this is of course to build communes around the strong, around just those people who in any case would find the problems of domestic relationships least problematic.

Interpretation: Communes as fantasy

'The communal type of relationship is, according to the usual interpretation of its subjective meaning, the most radical anti-thesis of conflict. This should not, however, be allowed to obscure the fact that *coercion* of all sorts is a very common thing in even the most intimate of such communal relationships.' (Weber 1947: 137)

We have chosen to regard the commune movement as a species of petty bourgeois protest. There are quite compelling reasons for members of that class to take to protest of this kind in contemporary Britain. It is not so much that the traditional predicament of the petty bourgeoisie has changed — although of course the steady decline in status and income differentials between middle and working-class occupations and especially the withdrawal of esteem from many traditional craft-like occupations, has greatly increased the transparency of that predicament. The notion of the special standing of these occupations becomes manifestly more illusory in the face of the inability of modern capitalism to maintain their special rewards. Nor has the traditional ideology of this class been significantly modified. For example, their critique of the economy of which they are victims still fails to move beyond the idea of capitalism as a way of life; the issue of emancipation remains essentially an issue of the emancipation of the individual — that is, emancipation *from* social relations rather than *through* social relations. There is a minor innovation here, associated, it would seem, with the popularization of certain kinds of anthropological and psychological work in which the creation of personal autonomy is seen as a task accomplished in the setting of intimate personal relationships. But even here the point of concern turns out, when put to the test, to be the individual not the relationships.

Within this fairly stable structural and ideological setting certain new things have happened, however. To begin with the tumultuous experiences of a previous decade, from the fall of Eden to the rise of Nixon, have served to exhaust and discredit, or perhaps more importantly to block-off, previously conventional channels of political protest for the petty bourgeoisie. After a few years of apparent freedom, politics have as it were been recaptured by

Capital and Labour, now locked again in a series of relations from which the petty bourgeoisie are excluded. The eating-up of CND by the Labour Party was clearly an especially poignant symbolic moment for many of the older people we met in the course of the research.

At the same time the diminishing functional relevance of the nuclear family as a component of capitalism has permitted the champions of individualism to wage a relatively successful war against traditional domestic structures ('The chain of capitalism breaks at the weakest link', perhaps?). The withdrawal from politics was thus followed by a quick reconstitution of the problem of individual liberty as a problem of the family. And in this campaign, as we hope to have shown, limited victories were possible; unlike the state the family turned out to be unsupported by other powers. The world of the family looked as though it might be the one world which the petty bourgeois, deeply committed to individualism and thus impelled to eschew large-scale solidaristic action, could after all conquer. At the very least he could effect a real escape from *its* constraints however helpless he might be in the face of the larger movements of history.

In Poulantzas's account (1973) the petty bourgeois class is composed of two sharply distinguished economic groups who nevertheless constitute an ideological and political unity. There is a traditional group engaged in small production, trading, and craft work, and experiencing a steady decline in both numbers and status; and a modern group thrown up by the inner technological revolutions of capitalism and found particularly now in the communication industries, the educational system, and cultural institutions (the 'ideological apparatuses' in Poulantzas' terms) a group experiencing the peculiarly uncomfortable predicament of being both constantly faced with obsolescence, status-withdrawal, and loss of income, and constantly replaced by new equivalents of itself. What we observe in the commune movement is a double flight of the petty bourgeoisie: first, from occupations in the 'modern' sector of the class to more or less serious attempts to live in the 'traditional' sector; second, from the supposedly 'modern' nuclear family formation to the supposedly 'traditional' extended family formation (or in some cases explicitly, the tribe). Would it be inappropriate to call the symbolism of such a movement reactionary? Or would it be fanciful to see in the insistence of the commune movement on the tyranny of things over people, in their efforts to rescue people from the world of things, the crisis of a social group whose most cherished values have been outraged by the discovery that their own life work is for others merely a commodity?

But our point is that the rescue operation only *appears* to succeed. It is in fact undermined by the very individualism that leads to the selection of communes as a solution in the first place. We hope to have demonstrated this in an illustrative way already. Now we should like to approach the same conclusion by way of an explicit discussion of the experience of women in communes in the context of some of the arguments to have emerged from the Women's Liberation Movement. By far the most useful concept thrown up in recent discussions of the position of women is, in our view, the notion of 'social secondariness' suggested by Rowbotham (1972). The value of this idea is that it recognizes the degree to which the inequality of which women are victims is mediated by, among other things, personal relationships rather than springing directly from economic or political oppression. It directs attention to the practice of social relationships between men and women; to the constructed facticity of the woman's world. It raises the Durkheimian issue of the extent to which we create our own constraints — and could therefore hope by our own action to free ourselves: 'the peculiar characteristic of social constraint is that it is due not to the rigidity of certain molecular arrangements but to the prestige with which certain representations are invested' (Durkheim 1938: Preface).

Freeman (1972) has suggested a number of ways in which the secondariness of women is mediated; the 'core concepts of sexist thought' in her terms. First, 'men do the important work in the world and the work done by men is what is important'; second, 'women are here for the pleasure and assistance of men'; and third, 'women's identities are defined by their relationship to men and their social value by that of the men they are related to'. In each of these respects a woman sees the world through one end of a male telescope and is herself seen, suitably diminished, through the other end of it. In each of these respects, however, one might think that the situation of women would be drastically altered in communes. To begin with the home becomes, in principle, the primary scene of value and action for men and women alike. 'What is important' is deliberately not what is done outside but what is done in and for the home. Again, among the social relations that communes seek to repudiate, those involving explicit recognition of structured differences between men and women are prominent. Their intention would be to re-write Freeman's second proposition as '*people* are here for the pleasure and assistance of each other'. Although few communes are consciously concerned with women's liberation as an issue, their unconcern is meant to have egalitarian implications. Similarly, their commitment to the openness of relationships, to the freedom of men and women to make and break relationships on their own terms, is tied directly to a rejection of the idea of any partner to a relationship being 'defined' by the relationship.

Now whatever the differences between the theory and practice of communes might be, communes clearly do involve something more than a mere transplanting of the conjugal family into a collective setting. To the extent that the conjugal family is a cornerstone of the exploitation of women, communes should therefore offer at least a serious potential for change — even allowing for the fact that the location and status of conjugal and quasi-conjugal units within communes is one of the main sources of communes' emotional problems. If, that is, the secondariness of women is felt to be embedded in the conjugal family, communes might be expected to provide settings in which women could innovate in social relationships — at least to the point of lifting the veil of secondariness and sharing on equal terms the alienation of men. And yet quite plainly this does not normally happen. Any attempt by women in communes to assert themselves as women is more likely to lead to the departure of the man than to anything else. What does happen is that men in communes concede a certain enlargement of the significance of domestic relationships for them, but in a context still strongly dominated by effective — albeit potential — inequalities of freedom and economic competence 'outside'. Thus what commonly occurs is that women in communes broadly go along with everything that femininity, motherhood, and the like ordinarily connote, and seek to alleviate the burdens of their role through essentially passive co-operative female action; for instance, a rota of mothers feed the children. In many communes one sees what is tantamount to a conspiracy to enlarge the value and meaningfulness of conventional women's roles on the basis of more or less elaborate symbolic concessions to participation by men — and the guarantee that 'women's work' will be in the end performed by women. The understanding that this is the real state of affairs — not perhaps hard to grasp when one hears commune men talking casually of the need to 'find more chicks' — probably inhibits many women from snatching up even the few crumbs of freedom that the communal situation does offer. The root of the problem seems to be the very uneven way in which the elementary structures of the nuclear family are dismantled in communes. Of the three links that comprise the basic family unit — wife-husband, father-child, mother-child — the first two are often seriously opened-up in communes, but the third is hardly touched. Motherhood remains an all-demanding and totally female role. The notion that communal relationships are intentional and sustained only on the condition that both parties find the necessary relationship-work gratifying, breaks down in the face of child-rearing.

There seem to be two main reasons for the general failure of women to seize even the limited opportunities for liberation that are available in communes. First, the aim of communes to create situations in which people can be 'more themselves' is in practice susceptible to exploitation, mainly, but not exclusively, by men to their own advantage. Given that the terms of reference of male-female relationships have not changed all that much, many kinds of 'emotional problems' can be made systematically less burdensome by the values of communes. In effect, the male can exploit the female with a lighter conscience in a situation in which she poses as his equal without the strength of real equality to defend herself, and in which he can maintain in the face of emotional havoc that 'she wants it that way'. Femininity was, after all, some protection against this sort of treatment. Ironically the initial effect of abandoning it as a mode of personal relationships seems to be to make the weaker sex still weaker. For all the extra housework contributed by men in communes, and it is not always all that much, the woman, especially the woman with a child, is not appreciably freed from dependence by the communal commitment to equality in male-female relationships. Her secondariness can be too easily recreated by some man.

The second reason has to do directly with the enormous pressure that continues to be applied from without for children to have 'normal parents' and to know who they are. This pressure is of course especially strong if the children are at school. Because the man is able to assert his freedom within the commune these pressures tend again to be met by the mother succumbing to the demand that a social role be filled. She meets outside society half way by accepting the traditional status, which in turn gives the child the fixed point essential for its well-being and self-respect in the world at large. Here again the element of fantasy in the communal withdrawal from social relations becomes transparent. The basic problem is of course not very different from that which Mitchell and others have attributed to the ordinary family:

'The belief that the family provides an impregnable enclave of intimacy and security in an atomized and chaotic cosmos assumes the absurd — that the family can be isolated from the community and that its internal relationships will not reproduce in their own

terms the external relationships which dominate the society.'
(Mitchell 1971)

The odd thing about communes in this context is that while many of
their members would wholeheartedly agree with this comment as
applied to the family, they largely fail to see that there is no reason
why it should not apply equally to communes.

Communes, then, represent a reconstitution of familism on the
basis of a marginal relaxation of the facticity in which the ordinary
family is engulfed. What happens when the constraints of legally
enforced monogamy and the wage-work — house-work division of
roles are removed, is not the creation of an alternative system of
personal relationships, but rather a making plain of the deeper
obstacles to equality through which men and women in this society
struggle to relate. Voluntarism and a commitment to self-realization, far from being a way of transcending these obstacles, turn out
to be a way of realizing them more acutely. The commonest worry of
women in communes, so far as we could tell, was still 'what shall I do
if he leaves me?'. The commune provided some insulation against
the worst and most painful denouements of such predicaments; it
did not provide a setting in which women could count on not having
to experience such predicaments.

Afterword

Other people's studies of communes have been largely optimistic:
ours is plainly sceptical if not frankly glum. We suspect, however,
that this difference is not so much a consequence of any difference in
methods or assumptions between us and other writers, but simply
that we have been interested in an aspect of communal relationships
that previous studies have largely ignored. One can be interested in
communes as a laboratory for investigating the basic principles of
social solidarity (Kanter 1972), or as an expression of the issue of
identity created by our existing social organization of generations
(Speck 1972), or from many other points of view. Only if one looks
at them as 'alternative families' is one likely to reach the conclusion
to which we have been forced.

The original version of this paper was completed before the
publication of Andrew Rigby's excellent study of British communes,
Alternative Realities (Rigby 1974). We have to some extent trodden
in his footsteps so far as the field research is concerned, visiting
many of the same communes and being told much the same things by
much the same people. However, our interpretations appear to
differ widely. Where Rigby tends to be humanistic and hopeful

about communes and sees them as having a serious revolutionary potential, our view is significantly more sceptical; we would tend to see them as alternative *unrealities*. It is particularly noteworthy in this respect that Rigby does not deal directly or in any substance with the issue of gender relationships in communes. Moreover what he *does* say about such relationships is at odds with his general interpretation of communes and very much in line, implicitly, with ours. Thus, most of his chapter 'Communes and the Nuclear Family' is devoted to a discussion of what we have termed the 'practical difficulties' of communes, but in a very brief passage on 'sexual relationships' he observes that 'there can be little doubt that this can be, and is, an important area of conflict'. He goes on to quote the experience of one American woman: 'The talk of love is profuse but the quality of relationships is otherwise. The hip man like his straight counterpart is nothing more, nothing less, than a predator'. (Rigby 1974:285) What one makes of communes perhaps depends on what one is looking at. Gender relations were of passing interest to Rigby and of central concern to us. So far as such relationships are concerned, communes in contemporary Britain cannot easily detach themselves from the constraints of a larger moral economy. For·that reason these relationships themselves remain a field of coercion.

Notes

1   We use the expression 'commune movement' to refer indifferently to all those living in or actively sympathetic to communes whether or not they are members of the Commune Movement. The latter is a formal organization of fluctuating membership and with the aim, to which all communes do not subscribe, of transforming Britain into a society of federated communes.
2   The research was supported by the Social Science Research Council and carried out by the present authors and two colleagues over a period of two years from November 1971. Our colleagues Sheila Abrams and Pat Gore agree with the argument presented here. They have not been cited as co-authors because they are currently engaged in writing up other aspects of the research. The project as a whole will be reported in our joint study, *Communes, Sociology and Society* to be published by Cambridge University Press. Unless otherwise indicated all quotations, are from our own research materials — question-

naires, interviews, recorded conversations, or diaries of visits to communes.

4   The account of Cooper's position comes mainly from Cooper (1971). The use of the term 'family' is taken from R.D. Laing (1971) to refer to the family as an internalized coercive fantasy an 'introjected set of relations'. In general, Laing's treatment of these matters is both subtler and more sociological than Cooper's; but Cooper seems to be the more resonant author for the commune movement.

5   This argument is developed in the next section; meanwhile we adopt the term petty-bourgeois as, simply, the best available analytical category. Readers must try to convince themselves that the normal derogatory connotations are *not* intended (cf. Poulantzas 1973). In any event the term must be broadly construed. At one commune we visited we found ourselves sharing a meal with graduates of Eton, Marlborough, and Benenden and discussing the hazards of going to school with royalty.

6   'The value of our place is the lack of formal structure' (Commune Movement 1970:22). At both a personal and an organizational level there are many connections between the commune movement and anarchism.

7   This is the formally stated object of the Commune Movement; it appears as such on the inside cover of every issue of *Communes*.

8   We must recognize again the enormous variety of practice and experience encountered in actual communes, however. Our account is probably not true in detail of any one commune. Nevertheless, we are satisfied that as a model abstracted from our observations it accurately states the relational logic of almost all communes.

References

Armytage, W.H. 1961. *Heavens Below*. London: Routledge & Kegan Paul.

Bronfenbrenner, U. 1961. The Changing American Child. *Journal of Social Issues 17* (1).

Commune Movement. 1970. *Directory of Communes*. London: BIT

Crowther, G. 1972. The Elms. *Communes* No. 40, October.

Durkheim, E. 1938 (2nd ed.) *The Rules of Sociological Method*. Glencoe: The Free Press.

Engels, F. 1962. *The Origins of the Family, Private Property and the*

State. Moscow: Foreign Languages Publishing House.

Eno, S. 1972a Spring Waits for No Man. *Communes* No 41, December.

— 1972b. Signposts on the Roads to Communes. *Communes* No 41, December.

— 1972a. The Commune Movement. *Peace News* No 1855. January 28.

Firestone, S. 1971. *The Dialectic of Sex: The Case for Feminist Revolution.* London: Cape.

Freeman, J. 1972. The Women's Liberation Movement. In H.P. Dreitzel (ed.) *Marriage, Family and the Struggle of the Sexes.* New York: Macmillan Co.

Green, A. 1946. The Middle Class Male Child and Neurosis. *American Sociological Review XI,* February: 31-41.

Hill, M. 1970a. Patterns of Living and Loving. *The Freethinker. January.*

— 1970b. Patterns of Living and Loving *Communes* No 38, June.

Kanter, R.M. 1972. *Commitment and Community.* Harvard; Harvard U.P.

Laing, R.D. 1961. *The Self and Others.* London: Tavistock Publications.

— 1971. *The Politics of the Family.* London: Tavistock Publications.

Leach, E.R. 1968. *A Runaway World?* London: BBC Publications.

Mitchell, J. 1971. *Women's Estate.* Harmondsworth: Penguin Books.

Parsons, T. 1949. The Social Structure of the Family. In R. Anshen (ed.), *The Family.* New York: Harper & Row.

Poulantzas, N. 1973. Marxism and Social Classes. *New Left Review* No 78.

Rigby, A. 1974. *Alternative Realites.* London: Routledge & Kegan Paul, 1974.

Rowbotham, S. 1972. Women's Liberation and the New Politics. In M. Wandor (ed.), *The Body Politic.* London: Stage One.

Speck, R.V. 1972. *The New Families.* London: Tavistock Publications.

Weber, M. 1947. *The Theory of Social and Economic Organisation.* London: Oxford University Press.

Communes: Journal of the Commune Movement
   1972a Postlip Housing Association. No. 38 June.
   1972b Wanted People. No. 40, October.
   1973. Getting Together, No. 43, April.

Name Index

Subject Index